HOGS!

— A HISTORY —

GEORGE SCHROEDER

A FIRESIDE BOOK

Published by Simon & Schuster

New York   London   Toronto   Sydney

FIRESIDE
Rockefeller Center
1230 Avenue of the Americas
New York, NY 10020

FIRESIDE and colophon are registered trademarks
of Simon & Schuster, Inc.

For information regarding special discounts for bulk purchases,
please contact Simon & Schuster Special Sales:
1-800-456-6798 or business@simonandschuster.com

Designed by Ruth Lee-Mui

Manufactured in the United States of America

1   3   5   7   9   10   8   6   4   2

Library of Congress Control Number: 2005050605

ISBN-13: 978-0-7432-8052-5
ISBN-10: 0-7432-8052-0

Photographs provided by the University of Arkansas,
the *Arkansas Democrat-Gazette,* and Mr. James D. Smith

For Dad,
who rescued my Hog hat

ACKNOWLEDGMENTS

My wife, Shannon, has always been my most enthusiastic supporter. Throughout this process, her constant encouragement sustained me. She, as ever, completes me. Meanwhile, Elizabeth and George William just loved me, even if they didn't quite understand why Daddy kept heading out of town.

Bob Mecoy, my agent, was the project's catalyst in so many ways. He believed in and promoted an unproven commodity, then served as the perfect sounding board at each new twist and turn. Brett Valley, my editor, was saddled with two major handicaps: a new author and a demanding time schedule. He was unfailingly patient while juggling both; his sharp eye for detail made the finished product much better than the original manuscript.

Good friends Bob Holt and Scott Cain, Arkansas beat writers for the *Arkansas Democrat-Gazette*—and two of the finest reporters on any beat, anywhere—provided keen insight and critical feedback. Bob, in particular, read each chapter and offered valuable advice and correction. Perhaps as important, they were always up for lunch at Elenita's.

Kevin Trainor, the University of Arkansas' sports information director, opened his office to me, providing assistance in myriad ways. Rick Schaeffer, Kevin's predecessor, provided trustworthy guidance on a vital task. Stephen B. Thornton and Meredith Adams dug through archives at the *Arkansas Democrat-Gazette* and the University of Arkansas, respectively, searching for photographs. Their discoveries, as well as the photos of James Smith, were worth far more than any written words.

I am indebted, as well, to Jim Bailey and the late Orville Henry, sportswriters I grew up reading. Their book, *The Razorbacks: A Story of Arkansas Football,* remains the exhaustive source. Larry Foley and Jim Borden's exceptional DVD, *22 Straight,* which chronicles the Hogs' 1964 and 1965 seasons, was an invaluable resource. In addition, their previous gathering of many photographs from that golden era greatly reduced the photo research task for this book.

The *Arkansas Democrat-Gazette*'s executive editor, Griffin Smith jr., along with sports editor Wally Hall and photography editor Barry Arthur, offered support and aid, as well. The *Arkansas Democrat-Gazette* and its predecessors, the *Arkansas Democrat* and the *Arkansas Gazette,* have long recorded the Hogs' history as it happened. Facts gleaned from the newspapers' pages provided the essential framework for this book.

I am also grateful to another newspaper. My employers at *The Oklahoman,* especially sports editor Mike Sherman, understood and allowed me to pursue an exciting opportunity, even when it meant some time away during a busy season. My beat partner and friend, Carter Strickland, who pushes me professionally, cheerfully picked up much of the slack.

For certain, this book would not have been possible without the cooperation and support of the Razorbacks themselves. Frank Broyles, the architect of so much of Arkansas' football history, graciously relived his half-century with the Hogs, spending several hours with me in twenty-minute increments. A multitude of other former players and coaches shared their experiences in dozens of delightful interviews. Their proud membership in a special fraternity was obvious; their willingness to reminisce, in person or by phone, was crucial in painting the rich picture that is Arkansas football.

All this help, assistance, and inspiration aside, any mistakes herein are all mine. Any credit and praise for getting it right is due to the aforementioned—and most important, to One other: My Lord and Savior, in Whom all things hold together, certainly held me together during an exhausting, yet exhilarating process.

CONTENTS

CONTENTS

1

Calling the Hogs

I N THE END, he could not resist the call. A private jet sat on the tarmac, waiting to whisk him away. A rabid, statewide fan base waited expectantly for the man who would lead its program back to prominence. Fabulous tradition. Fantastic money. All were his for the taking.

▲ PREVIOUS PAGE
Running through
the A before games is
a cherished Arkansas
tradition.

There was only one problem. Houston Nutt already had all this. And something more. And so, even though mighty Nebraska beckoned, dangling enough tangibles and intangibles to entice any football coach, the jet lifted off without Nutt. He remained behind. At home.

Though Arkansas fans waited anxiously in those wintry days in January 2004 while their head football coach pondered Nebraska's enticing offer, perhaps they shouldn't have. In the end, he remained Arkansas' own for the same reasons they lived and died with his team's fortunes. Like the fans, Nutt could not escape the call of the Hogs.

"No one else," he says, "has that *Woo, pig, sooie!*"

For generations, Arkansans have heard it, and been inexorably drawn. In 1909, Hugo Bezdek said his Cardinals—the original team name, denoting the deep red uniform—played "like a wild bunch of Razorback hogs," like the animals that then roamed freely through rural Arkansas.

The student body, enthralled by Bezdek's description, soon voted to adopt the Razorback as the mascot. And the rest is history.

That's the officially accepted version, anyway. Turns out, Arkansas' teams were referred to as Razorbacks in several newspaper accounts before Bezdek's famous statement. Whatever the origin, the name stuck. And, for

generations, Arkansans have proudly identified with a wild hog.

The most identifiable tradition began in the 1920s. As the team sputtered one day, several farmers in the stands began yelling as if they were calling home their pigs, hoping to encourage the players. Soon, the hog call found its final form, which remains the Razorbacks' unmistakable battle cry:

Woooooooo, pig, sooie!
Woooooooo, pig, sooie!
Woooooooo, pig, sooie!
Razorbacks!

Anywhere, any time a group of Arkansans is together, it's liable to break out. In airports. In restaurants. Even in bathrooms, says former Arkansas quarterback Quinn Grovey. Which means wherever Arkansans go, so to speak, the Hog call goes with them.

A quick tale of misplaced emotion. Ronnie Caveness, a standout linebacker from the 1964 national championship team, traveled to New York to be hon-

ored on *The Tonight Show* as part of *Look* magazine's All-American team. Johnny Carson hosted the show. As cameras rolled, he engaged each player in a few seconds of small talk, often punctuated by a mild Carson one-liner. As Caveness was introduced, a yell came from way back in the studio audience.

"Woooooo, pig, sooie!"

Whatever quip Carson had planned for Caveness, he didn't get to it. Startled, he just looked at Caveness. "He looked up at me," Caveness recalls with a chuckle. "I didn't know what to say. But I mean, some guy up there just let it rip. Johnny didn't say anything. It stopped him. You go all the way to New York City and they introduce you on television and some guy, I mean, he let that 'Woo, pig, sooie!' rip."

And there was no doubt about the fan's allegiance. The Hog call is among the most recognizable traditions in college sports.

"No matter where you go, they may not know what the name of it is— 'that hog call, that pig sooie call'—but they know about it," Grovey says. "When those Hog fans get to callin', they don't care. They're not ashamed. They just do it. They'll have people look 'em up one side and down the other. They don't care."

Care? If the Hog call startles some, if it's looked down upon by others, it's sounded in defiance by Arkansans. All too well, they understand the national image of their state as unsophisticated, lagging behind—an unfair perception, really, but pervasive. They revel in the delightful unsophistication of the Hog call.

Want to understand its power? Listen as fifty thousand fans—or these days, upward of seventy thousand—call in unison. Forty-two thousand was once enough to move the earth, Ask Bill McClard. The former Razorbacks kicker swears it happened just prior to kickoff of the Big Shootout in 1969— perhaps the biggest game in Arkansas history, and easily its most devastating loss.

Seems McClard set the football on the tee for the opening kickoff, then backed away. Just then, the crowd at Razorback Stadium in Fayetteville finished calling the hogs. "RAZORBACKS!" sounded with a roar.

The football shuddered, then fell to the artificial turf.

McClard insists there wasn't even a breath of wind. He says the referee would back his claim. "I wouldn't have believed that if I hadn't seen it," he says the official told him.

Okay, so it's not likely the fans' collective roar caused the ball to topple. Perhaps it's enough that McClard is sticking to his story.

Other players stick to this: The hog call meant plenty to them. It made their hair rise. Gave them goose bumps. Set their blood to boiling.

"You didn't know who those fans were," Caveness says. "You didn't know 'em on a first-name basis. But you knew they were pulling for you. And when they would call those Hogs, it was like, *c'mon!*"

They've called their Hogs in big wins and bad losses. During championship seasons and crushing disappointments. They've used it to cheer on legendary players such as Clyde "Smackover" Scott, Lance Alworth, and, more recently, Matt Jones.

The 25 Little Pigs of 1954. The national powerhouse teams of the 1960s. Southwest Conference champions. Southeastern Conference contenders. Frank Broyles' brilliance. Lou Holtz's magic, including that wonderful night in the Orange Bowl. Kenny Hatfield's flexbone and back-to-back Cotton Bowl trips. Danny Ford's 1995 surprise, the lone bright spot in the early years of the Hogs' foray into the Southeastern Conference. And now, Houston Nutt's revival of the program.

Through it all, they've called the Hogs. Children are quickly taught life's essentials: Hogs Smell Good. Beat Texas. And, of course, Woo, pig, sooie!

"It's just unreal," says Buddy Bob Benson, who had a starring role in the most important play in perhaps the most important game in the program's history, a 6–0 upset of Ole Miss in 1954. "People just live and die with the Hogs. That's all they can dream and talk about. People just go crazy for them. You'd think they were personal friends with each one of them."

Razorback football is a tie that binds a diverse population, the force

Arkansans have intertwining passions: calling the Hogs and hating Texas.

The Hog hat is perhaps the most recognizable accessory in college sports.

If the Hog call is the signature of Arkansas fans, the Hog hat has been their most visible symbol. The red, plastic headgear has long been possibly the most familiar identifier of Razorback mania, and perhaps the most famous fan accessory in college athletics. Fans wear the Hog hats to games, where television cameras are sure to seek them out.

The Hog hat took shape in 1969 in the mind of an enterprising Arkansas student. Uncle Heavy's Original Hog Hats soon grew into a full-fledged phenomenon. More than five hundred thousand were produced in the next thirty-four years. Even though outsiders may laugh, the Hog hats are sought-after tourist souvenirs and an essential accessory for true fans—some of whom, if the legend is correct, hide flasks of alcohol in the hat's long snout.

Over the years, poor imitations have arrived: Cheeseheads, Gators, even Longhorns. But nothing approaches the Hog hat. For the longest time, Arkansas fans had the market cornered on fun headgear. In 2003, however, Uncle Heavy's ceased production after allowing its licensing agreement with the university to lapse. A modern version, which looks more like the running Hog logo on the football helmets, has taken its place, but the classic Hog hat—now a collector's item—remains the Razorback fans' most visible symbol.

THAT PRIZED PLASTIC PIG

that unites Arkansans from the Mississippi River Delta to the Ozark Mountains, from the piney woods of South Arkansas to the Arkansas River Valley. Why, even yellow-dog Democrats, so called because they'd pull the lever if the Democrats ran a canine, and new-South Republicans can wholeheartedly agree on the Razorbacks.

Take Frank Broyles, Arkansas' athletic director and former coach—the most influential sports figure in the state's history, and among the top few figures in any category. Bring Broyles, as happened in February 2005, to the Arkansas legislature to politick for a bill that would require nursing home workers to take special training for care of patients suffering from Alzheimer's, then watch bitter political enemies unite. Yes, the politicians greeted Broyles by calling the Hogs.

It was this unity that long ago drew Broyles, a Decatur, Georgia, native who starred at nearby Georgia Tech. As a young Georgia Tech assistant coach in 1952, Broyles took to heart an exasperated muttering from legendary coach Bobby Dodd. The Yellow Jackets were in the midst of their 1950s greatness, unbeaten and rarely challenged. As they prepared for the annual game with archrival Georgia, Dodd suddenly spoke out: "Boy, wouldn't we have it made if there was no [University of] Georgia?"

"I never forgot that," says Broyles more than half a century later.

Broyles found such a place. In

Frank Broyles, a native Georgian, long ago recognized Arkansas' unique status.

Arkansas, there is no Georgia. Meaning, there is no other program to divide fans' loyalty.

"There's no Auburn and Alabama, no Oklahoma and Oklahoma State," says Broyles, noting the fierce rivalries that inhabit nearby states. "Wherever you go in the state, you have support. When I'm playing in a golf tournament in Pine Bluff and the evening meal is starting and I'm not even on the program, the first thing they do is stand up and call the Hogs.

"That's just the way it is."

And that's just the way it has been, for as long as Arkansans can remember.

In the beginning, it was a club sport, a recreational activity. In 1894, a group of students formed the school's first team. Hugo Bezdek became the first full-time paid coach in 1908. In his second season, Arkansas finished 7-0, with wins over LSU and Oklahoma. Steve Creekmore, a quarterback from Van Buren, led the way that year and again in 1910, when the Razorbacks (finally named the Razorbacks) went 7-1. Modest successes and failures followed as the evolution of college football continued. Players such as Wear Schoonover, Glen Rose, and George Cole thrilled fans, who began to follow this college team from the hills.

But it wasn't until 1936 that Arkansas won its first undisputed Southwest Conference title (the Hogs forfeited the 1933 title for using an ineligible player). And it wasn't until the mid-1950s that Razorback football became a statewide passion.

The most crucial development might have come in 1946.

First-year coach and athletic director John Barnhill lured homegrown players such as Clyde "Smackover" Scott, who later became an All-American and earned a silver medal in the 110-meter high hurdles in the 1948 Olympics, and Leon "Muscles" Campbell to Arkansas, and coached them to the Hogs' first Cotton Bowl appearance. That and a 7–0 upset of fifth-ranked Rice, then in its athletic heyday, provided the impetus for Barnhill and a group of influential businessmen to push through legislation to build a stadium in Little Rock, the state capital.

Arkansas had been dividing games between the campus in Fayetteville and Little Rock High School's ten-thousand-seat stadium. The Rice game drew more than sixteen thousand fans, who wedged themselves into temporary bleachers and various other nooks and crannies at the high-school facility.

In its original configuration, War Memorial Stadium held more than twice that (its current capacity is almost fifty-four thousand). Since its opening in 1948, it has served as the Hogs' home away from home; its construction had plenty to do with the Hogs' amicable takeover of the entire state.

The University of Arkansas' campus

▶ FACING PAGE
The 1909 Razorbacks were coached by Hugo Bezdek, whom many credit for the team's nickname.

UNIVERSITY OF ARKANSAS
1909

Donald W. Reynolds
Razorback Stadium was
renovated and expanded
in 2001, giving the Hogs
an on-campus showplace
to rival any.

Playing games at
Little Rock's War Memorial
Stadium helped build
a statewide following
for Arkansas football.

in Fayetteville is situated in the Ozark Mountains in the far northwest corner of the state, 190 miles from centrally located Little Rock. Until the latter part of the 1990s, Fayetteville was accessible only by dangerous mountain roads. Playing games in Little Rock allowed fans from east and south Arkansas to travel shorter distances to watch their team.

In 2001, the unveiling of expanded, seventy-two-thousand-seat Razorback Stadium in Fayetteville—renamed Donald W. Reynolds Razorback Stadium in honor of the major donor—changed the dynamics of Arkansas' home choice. With almost eighteen thousand more seats than War Memorial Stadium, Razorback Stadium is among the finest facilities in college football. The expansion necessitated moving some games from Little Rock back to campus.

Through 2015, at least, Arkansas continues to play at least two games a year in Little Rock. Though it's likely the Hogs will one day play all their home games on campus, no one disputes the role Little Rock has played in enabling the Hogs to capture the state's imagination.

Eugene "Bud" Canada, a former state senator from Hot Springs who was a four-year starter for Arkansas during the 1940s, once wrote in the *Arkansas Democrat-Gazette* of Little Rock of the new stadium's impact:

"The stadium . . . became a symbol of big-time college football for the University of Arkansas Razorbacks. All of a sudden, the Razorbacks belonged to the entire state. We no longer played at [Little Rock High's] Quigley Field and the other small arenas; we were walking out in front of thousands of screaming fans who had driven from the four corners of the state.

"It was so exciting to walk onto that field in Little Rock. War Memorial Stadium helped unite the state behind the Razorbacks, and we became Arkansas' team."

The program's coming-out party really didn't happen until six years later. In 1954, second-year coach Bowden Wyatt assembled a gritty bunch of un-

Bowden Wyatt coached Arkansas for just two years, but his 25 Little Pigs of 1954 laid the foundation for much of the Razorbacks' subsequent success.

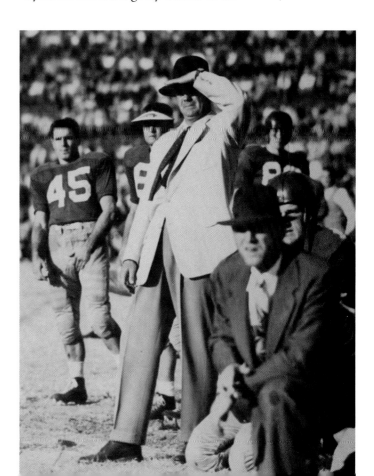

dersized, but fierce, players, from whom nothing much was expected. Known as the 25 Little Pigs in newspaper accounts—because that's about how many players contributed—the squad rolled to a Southwest Conference championship and a Cotton Bowl appearance against Georgia Tech. And an unlikely October victory paved the way for success far beyond that season.

A 20–7 win at Texas set up the biggest game in program history at that time, an improbable showdown with fifth-ranked Ole Miss in Little Rock. At 4-0, Arkansas was ranked seventh, and was established a seven-point underdog to the bigger, stronger Rebels, who were considered national championship contenders. Anticipation in Arkansas raged at unprecedented levels.

In the days before the game, newspaper classifieds in the *Arkansas Gazette** offered unusual trades for tickets: One would-be spectator was willing to part with a garden tractor, another with twenty-five pounds of coffee. A local clothing store offered two fifty-yard-line seats with the purchase of a suit.

Temperatures climbed into the upper seventies on game day. And an overflow crowd of at least thirty-eight thousand—the stadium's first sellout and, at the time, the largest crowd to witness a sporting event in the state—took the Hogs by surprise. Fans without tickets climbed atop trees and buses to peer over fences. Others massed along the sidelines and just beyond the end zones.

"There were people everywhere," says Buddy Bob Benson, a reserve tailback who was a pivotal part of the most important play in the program's most important game. "It was so crowded. You look around and boy, wall-to-wall people."

The Razorbacks responded with a dramatic win earned in the final minutes. The game was scoreless until late in the fourth quarter, when Benson and blocking back Preston Carpenter hooked up on a 66-yard touchdown pass, later to become known as the Powder River play. And when the final gun sounded—6–0, Arkansas—those fans swarmed the field, lifted Carpenter onto their shoulders, and celebrated long into the evening.

Even after they finally left the stadium, carloads of fans cruised up and down city streets, honking horns, yelling and calling the Hogs.

"It was pretty wild stuff," says Carpenter, who later had a long professional football career.

---

*This is not an error. For many years, the *Arkansas Gazette* competed with the *Arkansas Democrat.* In 1991, the *Gazette* closed its doors and the *Arkansas Democrat-Gazette* emerged. This book contains references to both newspapers and to all three names. Like every other Arkansas institution, the newspapers can't say enough about the Razorbacks.

A six-game winning streak, dating back to the last game of the 1953 season, was Arkansas' longest in seventeen seasons. And the Hogs won twice more, moving to 7-0, before faltering twice. Still, they notched their third Southwest Conference title and advanced to their second Cotton Bowl.

Wyatt didn't stick around long enough to revel in the success. Days after Arkansas' 14–6 Cotton Bowl loss to Georgia Tech—and after appreciative fans had given him a new white Cadillac—Wyatt bolted for Tennessee, his alma mater. But Broyles, for one, credits Wyatt and the 25 Little Pigs with laying the foundation for greatness. Even now, he calls the upset of Ole Miss "the most meaningful win since World War Two."

"That turned the tide for respect, which turned the tide for fan support and recruiting," Broyles says. "It just flipped it over. We became, in our minds, a contender rather than a pretender. It showed that it was possible. It showed that our team, under good coaching and with players responding to the coaching, had a chance to win."

A sportswriter from the *Houston Post,* one of many from regional and national media outlets that covered the Ole Miss game, wrote of the Hogs: "They never stopped gnawing and clawing. If Arkansas is undermanned, it should happen to more football teams." The description illustrated how the 25 Little Pigs exemplified a dearly held

Arkansas belief: Their boys might not be as talented as other teams, but they darn sure played harder. And now, fans knew, the Hogs could win.

From that date, sellouts at War Memorial Stadium became routine affairs. Thousands more Arkansans gathered in homes and businesses to listen—and very occasionally, to watch—as their Razorbacks battled for state pride.

When Broyles arrived at Arkansas in December 1957, replacing Jack Mitchell, who had replaced Wyatt, he wasted little time building upon the 1954 team's success. After a slow start, Broyles built the program into a perennial conference and consistent national contender. In nineteen seasons, as Broyles led Arkansas to seven conference crowns, to the 1964 national championship, and to the brink of two (perhaps three) more, fans' love affair with their beloved Razorbacks grew to an incredible intensity.

"It's our identity," says Dick Hatfield, a Little Rock attorney who grew up in Helena, Arkansas, on the banks of the Mississippi River, and played for the 1964 national championship squad. "It's a source of pride where [others] say, 'These poor, dumb Arkies aren't even wearing shoes.' It's a source of pride."

Like so many others, Houston Nutt first felt the call of the Hogs as a child. He grew up nearly in the shadow of Little Rock's War Memorial Stadium.

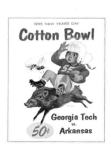

The 25 Little Pigs won the Southwest Conference and played in the Cotton Bowl, sending fans into euphoria.

With his father and brothers, he sat in the end zone and cheered on heroes such as Freddie Marshall and Ronnie Caveness and Jim Lindsey—those national champions of 1964. Bill Burnett and Bill Montgomery and Chuck Dicus and Cliff Powell. And plenty more.

"An awesome feeling," Nutt remembers. "It gives me goose bumps just thinking about it. And then the first time I heard the Hog call was just—it was just phenomenal."

Later, as a ball boy on the War Memorial Stadium sidelines, Nutt got even closer looks at the Hogs. When, after a standout career as a quarterback at Little Rock's Central High School, Nutt turned down Alabama's Bear Bryant to go to Arkansas, there was one reason.

It wasn't easy. Bryant had coached Joe Namath and Kenny Stabler. Nutt was a drop-back passer who dreamed of similar glory. There was a family connection, as well. Like the Nutt family, Bryant hailed from Fordyce, Arkansas, a rural football hotbed.

"I thought Alabama was where I needed to go," Nutt says. "But there's one thing that always comes back, and that's home. Where you're born and raised. Your first football game. Your first Razorback game. All those things are tugging at your heart."

Nutt signed with Arkansas—becoming, though he didn't know it at the time, Frank Broyles' last recruit. A detour to Oklahoma State notwithstanding—Nutt transferred after Broyles retired and Lou Holtz arrived, bringing with him a new offense and his own quarterback—Nutt remained a Razorback at heart.

And he answered when the Hogs called him home in December 1997 after two straight 4-7 seasons. The program had tanked. Fans' enthusiasm had waned; they had serious doubts about whether the Hogs could compete after a switch to the Southeastern Conference.

How badly did Nutt want the job? He told the search committee he would work for free the first year. With charisma unseen since Broyles, Nutt immediately embarked on a whirlwind tour of the state, drumming up support, then led the 1998 Hogs to an 8-0 start. Six bowl trips in his first six seasons—which finally ended in 2004, when Arkansas finished 5-6—matched the school's longest bowl streak.

"He's just what Arkansas needed," says Caveness, the former linebacker. "We had some rough times. But there's no question when Houston Nutt came in, he basically turned our program around."

Why, then, would anyone be surprised when Nutt couldn't resist the call to remain home in that winter of 2004?

Nebraska, another program without an in-state rival, offered plenty of

◀ FACING PAGE
Arkansas won the national championship in 1964.

the same things as Arkansas. From an outsider's perspective, the Cornhuskers, who won two national championships in the 1990s, had more potential. Yet, despite a likely offer of $1.8 million— some sources said his total package might have reached $2 million, around $500,000 more than his pay at Arkansas, even after an increase—Nutt chose to remain a Razorback.

At a news conference to announce he was staying, Nutt became emotional and fought tears, surely eliciting some from the fans glued to their television sets for the live, statewide broadcast.

"The bottom line was this. . . . I couldn't take my family and myself and get on that plane," Nutt said. "My heart was here, period. Arkansas is a special place and I love it, love that helmet."

◀ FACING PAGE
Houston Nutt answered the Hogs' call, and has led the program back to winning.

2

The "Best Job in America"

He dialed long distance one night with a half-joking request.

"Dad, keep that insurance job open for me," Frank Broyles said. "I might be home a lot quicker than I thought."

A nine-game losing streak will cause a man to consider

▲ PREVIOUS PAGE

Frank Broyles' Arkansas tenure began with six straight losses, not hinting at his future success.

other career options. It was autumn, 1958. Frank Broyles, not quite thirty-four, was in his first season as Arkansas' head coach. As the losses piled up, he idly wondered if it might also be his last; the honeymoon was most definitely over.

The Razorbacks had lost their first six games under Broyles. His personal streak, dating to the previous season at Missouri, included three more losses. For the first time in his life, he wondered if he was cut out for coaching.

A half-century has since passed, of course, and Broyles remains in Fayetteville. In nineteen seasons as head coach, Broyles turned Arkansas into a national football powerhouse. Seven times, his Razorbacks won or shared the Southwest Conference championship. In 1964, the Hogs won the national championship; they just missed out in 1965 and 1969 and weren't far off in 1962, either. Broyles took Arkansas to ten bowl games. His record—144-58-5—includes winning streaks of twenty-two and fifteen games.

Much of Broyles' legacy has been written since his retirement after the 1976 season. In more than thirty years as athletic director, Broyles has overseen the development of Arkansas' entire program into a consistent national power. Basketball, cross country, and track and field have added national championships to Broyles' football title; other sports teams have become consistent winners, as well.

With a Southern gentleman's "goodwill," as former Razorback wingback and current University of Arkansas trustee Jim Lindsey puts it, Broyles built a statewide network of Razorback booster clubs, and a powerful network of donors. Broyles cultivated relationships with wealthy businessmen such as the Walton family (located in nearby Bentonville, they were building an empire with their Wal-Mart stores) and others. Those connections led to astronomically successful fund-raising efforts, with more than $220 million procured to build Arkansas' athletic facilities into a collection that rivals that of any other university; by early 2005, the Razorbacks' oldest athletic facility was eleven-year-old Bud Walton Arena, which is considered one of the nation's finest basketball venues.

In 1999, the *Arkansas Democrat-Gazette* named Broyles the state's most influential sports personality of the twentieth century. The newspaper might not have gone far enough; Broyles was clearly one of the state's most influential personalities, period.

In the autumn of 1958, the young redhead couldn't envision anything of the sort. It was the first serious athletic adversity faced by Broyles, who had been a standout in almost everything he had played or coached to that point. His confidence was severely shaken.

Born December 26, 1924, in Decatur, Georgia, Broyles was the youngest of five children. Naturally drawn to athletics, it was soon apparent he had talent. He felt baseball was his best sport, and it was certainly his first love. Broyles was also better at basketball than football.

He starred in all three sports at Decatur's Boys High School. At six-foot-two and 185 pounds, he was larger than the average high-schooler and showed plenty of athletic prowess.

Broyles, who said college was always in his future, turned down a chance to sign with the New York Yankees after graduating from high school. He chose Georgia Tech over Georgia, the school many of his friends and family favored; Duke; and Clemson.

And in a career interrupted for one year by World War II, he earned ten letters in football, basketball, and baseball. It was as a single-wing tailback—a position akin to quarterback in today's game—that Broyles excelled, though he also played fullback and wingback.

Years later, speaking at a banquet, Bobby Dodd, the legend who coached Broyles at Georgia Tech, poked some fun at Broyles' lack of speed. As reported by the *Arkansas Gazette,* Dodd said, "He's the slowest man I have ever seen on a football field. I believe he's the only man to be penalized for delaying the game while carrying the ball."

The joke was one of several that sprang from a long punt return for a touchdown against Tulane during Broyles' senior season of 1946. Broyles zigged, zagged, circled, doubled back, and finally scored. As he wearily reached the end zone, he fell, prompting plenty of laughter from his teammates.

And the return was called back because of a clipping penalty.

Despite his lack of speed, Broyles could play. A three-time All-Southeastern Conference selection, he was named the conference's player of the year in 1944. To cap that season, he threw for 276 yards in an Orange Bowl loss to Tulsa. The record stood for twenty-one years, until Alabama's Steve Sloan threw for 296 in a win over Nebraska (January 1, 1966, was a tough day for Broyles: The Razorbacks ended a twenty-two-game winning streak and lost what would have been their second straight national championship in a Cotton Bowl loss to LSU).

Some of Broyles' spunk must have come from his mother. She wanted to watch Frank play in the Orange Bowl, but didn't have transportation. So she put a classified advertisement in the newspaper: "I'm Frank Broyles' mother and I want a ride to Miami to see the game." She found a ride.

Maybe it wasn't such a bad week, after all. Broyles asked Barbara Day to marry him—they had been dating since high school, when Day was a student at Decatur's Girls High, which was adjacent to but separate from Boys High.

The couple was married in 1945, had six children, and wasn't separated until late 2004, when Barbara Broyles passed away at seventy-nine, after fifty-nine years of marriage.

In December 1942, just before his eighteenth birthday, Broyles joined the Navy Reserves, which left him in school until spring 1945. By the time Broyles was commissioned, the war was almost over. After Japan surrendered, Broyles spent a couple of months in the Pacific, then returned home. He was discharged in February 1946, when he was already back at Georgia Tech. Granted extra eligibility because of the war, he played one more football and basketball season.

After the 1946 football season, Broyles was drafted by George Halas' Chicago Bears. A chronic shoulder injury limited him; he understood his chances in the professional ranks were slim. And he'd felt a growing desire to coach.

When Tech assistant Bob Woodruff got Baylor's head-coaching job, he asked the twenty-one-year-old Broyles to accompany him as backfield coach.

It was while in Waco, Texas, from 1947 to 1949 that Broyles first noticed

Arkansas' potential. He could see the Razorbacks, who were then coached by John Barnhill, had the support of the entire state, without competition. Texas, meanwhile, was divided into fan factions of Texas, Texas A&M, TCU, SMU, Rice, Baylor, and more.

Broyles followed Woodruff to Florida for one season, then rejoined Dodd at Georgia Tech, where he was a part of six straight bowl teams. He kept an eye on the Arkansas job. When Arkansas and Georgia Tech met in the 1955 Cotton Bowl (won by Georgia Tech), rumors were flying that Hogs coach Bowden Wyatt might be headed for Tennessee (his alma mater). Broyles asked Barnhill, by then the Hogs' athletic director, to consider him for the job.

Barnhill, whose policy was to hire only head coaches, instead hired former Oklahoma quarterback Jack Mitchell. But when, after the 1957 season, Mitchell left for the supposed greener pastures of Kansas, Barnhill called Broyles.

After waiting long enough that he worried time was passing him by, Broyles had finally landed a head-coaching job. In 1957, he had succeeded Don Faurot at Missouri; with the endorsements of Faurot and Dodd, he beat out forty other applicants. That season, Broyles led the Tigers to a 5-1-1 record before dropping the last three games.

The situation wasn't perfect. Faurot had seen fit to saddle the new coach with a severe disadvantage. Called the Missouri Plan, it was an idealistic philosophy that restricted the football program to recruiting players from Missouri, with few exceptions.

There was one other thing: Broyles remained intrigued by Arkansas. After Mitchell's departure, Broyles waited and hoped to hear from Barnhill. However, news reports had Minnesota's Murray Warmath as the likely successor. Other rumored candidates included Iowa State's Jim Myers and Mississippi State's Wade Walker. Wilson

Matthews, who had built a national powerhouse at Little Rock's Central High School, was pushed by a vocal group of central Arkansans.

Paul "Bear" Bryant, a Fordyce native who had seriously considered the Arkansas job in 1953, only to stay at Kentucky, might have been approached again but for one thing: He was in the process of leaving Texas A&M—where he'd built a winner with the famed "Junction Boys"—for Alabama. Bryant took the Alabama job a few days before Arkansas' new coach was announced.

The consensus was Warmath was Barnhill's man, though Barnhill wasn't

Broyles began his Arkansas tenure by installing a new offense, which fizzled.

saying. Several days passed before Broyles' phone rang. Barnhill was on the other end.

"What took you so long?" Broyles asked.

Barnhill asked if Broyles wanted the job, and got a quick affirmative.

"Do I want the job? You know I want the job, 'Barnie,'" Broyles said.

Barnhill asked Broyles to wait a few days, until he was able to "get the ducks on the pond." He told Broyles to call on Tuesday.

"Are they on the pond?" Broyles asked.

"Yes, come on down. You're hired."

Frank Broyles was announced as Arkansas' coach on December 7, 1957.

He had agreed to a five-year contract worth $15,000 annually. Orville Henry, the *Arkansas Gazette*'s longtime sports editor and chief chronicler of Arkansas football for six decades, wrote of Warmath and Broyles: "Either would have been a good choice. Broyles is perfect."

"Frank is the only man from the outside who could come in and pull us all together toward what we're after," Barnhill told the *Gazette* the day Broyles' hiring was announced. "We've lost no ground in the last three years and we're in good shape. Within a month I believe we'll be a lot better than we were."

Still, there was one lingering concern for many Arkansans: How long would the new coach be a Razorback? Though at thirty-three, Broyles had finally landed what he called the best job in America, for the longest time, no one was certain those were his true feelings. Yes, he said all the right things, as in a news conference two days after his hiring:

"When coach Barnhill talked to me, one of the first things I told him was, 'I am here to stay. I came to Arkansas because: One, I have always known Arkansas people. Two, Arkansas offered as much as any other school in the country. If hard work can do the job then I'll give you the kind of football program you want at Arkansas.'"

Bowden Wyatt's two-year stint, which ended when he took the new Cadillac given him by appreciative fans and headed for the Tennessee hills, had been followed by Jack Mitchell's departure for Kansas after three years. Those events had left Hog fans feeling jilted—and wary of trusting another carpetbagger.

During the coaching search, several letters to the editor published in the *Gazette* indicated as much. Others showed a healthy sense of humor about the affair. F. Barnes Hampton, of DeWitt, wrote: "Football or no—win or lose—I'm all for going with a native of Arkansas and he must also be a U of A graduate. And his wife must be a native of Arkansas and a U of A graduate. If this can't be—then I'll be bitter and not go to another U of A game until next fall."

All of this seems strange nearly fifty years later. These days, Frank Broyles is so closely identified with the Razorbacks that he and the athletic program are essentially synonymous. For years, he has officed in a building that bears his name (the Broyles Athletic Center is adjacent to the north end zone of Reynolds Razorback Stadium).

In 1955, however, all anyone really knew of Broyles was that he was a Georgia Tech man. Back home, he was considered the heir apparent to Dodd. Shortly after Broyles' arrival at Arkansas, Hogs basketball coach Glen Rose introduced the new football coach at a Fayetteville High School athletic banquet.

"Clearly, we don't expect him to stay very long," Rose told the crowd, playing for an easy laugh, which he got. "Like the rest of them, he'll go back to Georgia Tech."

Broyles understood the sentiment, and he didn't like it. During the early portion of his career, several schools came calling, but he had no intention of leaving Arkansas.

In 1959, the supposed news broke in Florida that Broyles was set to become Florida's coach. Except he wasn't. With two games left in the season, he was trying to win a conference championship.

"I was so mad, I couldn't see straight," Broyles says. "So I made it clear to the press and everybody that if Arkansas wanted me to stay, I was gonna stay. And that's been proven true for forty-eight years."

Several years later, when Dodd was nearing retirement, Broyles and then Arkansas publicity man Bob Cheyne collaborated on a statement. Broyles kept it in his wallet. One day in 1967, a newspaperman called with news of Dodd's resignation and a question as to Broyles' future. The coach read the prepared release saying he was committed to Arkansas, and wasn't leaving.

Georgia Tech called again five years later, offering a package worth more than $2 million for six years. Broyles turned down his alma mater again. Almost a half-century after the day he was hired, Broyles remains at Arkansas. He can't envision anything else.

As October became November in 1958, however, Broyles couldn't envision much of anything. He'd arrived at Arkansas with high hopes. And the fans had responded, buying a record number of tickets well before the season opener against Baylor in Little Rock.

Though some prognosticators warned the depth chart (especially on the line) indicated a down year, expectations were high. There was the new coaching staff, and a new offense—the Iowa-Delaware winged-T, installed in the spring after Broyles became fascinated with its possibilities—and several fine skill players to run the attack.

And there was Broyles' optimism, as well. Shortly before the season began, he told the team of his respect for the 1954 Arkansas team (Bowden Wyatt's 25 Little Pigs), which Georgia Tech played in the Cotton Bowl.

"It was a dedicated team," Broyles told the Razorbacks. "And football is a dedicated game. If we are as dedicated to the things we believe in and pay the price, we can be just as fine a football team."

To the *Gazette,* he explained, "Breaks may decide the early games and the team that gets the momentum will continue to get the breaks. The team that suddenly feels that it's lucky will turn out to be lucky and make the best of everything to take it."

Broyles considered a fast start— meaning a win over Baylor in Little Rock—to be essential. Instead, on September 20, 1958, the Broyles era opened with a thud. On a damp, foggy night, a capacity crowd of thirty-six thousand crowded into War Memorial Stadium. The number might have been low; several hundred fans stampeded their way past ticket-takers.

They watched Baylor win 12–0. And it wasn't nearly that close. The *Gazette's* Henry described the debacle: "For four brutal periods it was as if a giant were squelching some Lilliputian whose feet were moving like mad—and taking him nowhere at all."

The Hogs' new, high-powered offense sputtered for 60 yards and 3 first downs and never sniffed the goal line. In the second half, Arkansas actually *lost* 7 yards. Making it worse, the Baylor unit wasn't exactly a juggernaut. The Bears had been picked to finish last in the Southwest Conference; it was their first SWC win in two seasons.

The problem was obvious to all, including Broyles: "Our offense," he said.

The winged-T "was a disaster," remembers Barry Switzer, who was a junior center. "We were trying to do things we couldn't do. We just needed to line up and use our quickness and speed and run at people."

The next day, as Broyles traveled with assistant coach Dixie White back to Little Rock for his weekly television

Broyles' debut in 1957 was accompanied by plenty of excitement, personified by this cheerleader leading the Hog call.

show, the coaches discussed their offensive options.

"We may have to change some of our offense," Broyles told a reporter after the show, before White and he hopped back into the car. By the time they returned to Fayetteville, an eight-hour round trip, they had junked most of the winged-T and decided to return to Broyles' roots, Georgia Tech's belly series from the split-T, which was better suited to Arkansas' small, inexperienced line.

The change didn't bring immediate results. The losses mounted, and so did the anxiety. Broyles lost almost twenty-five pounds during the season.

"It was a shock to Frank," says Merv Johnson, who was a senior captain on Broyles' Missouri team and was a graduate assistant at Arkansas in 1958. "He had been such a successful assistant coach."

Even as Broyles was pondering the world of insurance, the tide was turning. Arkansas lost to sixth-ranked Ole Miss by 14–12 in Little Rock; significant improvement, but another loss. The Hogs were 0-6 and needed more than a moral victory.

Then came November 1, and a trip to College Station, Texas, to play Texas A&M.

On the game's first play, Arkansas' Wayne "Thumper" Harris recovered a fumble at the A&M 19. Five plays later, from the 9, the coaches signaled in an off-tackle play to the right side. Quarterback Jim Monroe went left, without blockers. And scored easily.

"Nobody was there," Broyles recalls. "He walked in. We scored on a busted play."

On the sidelines, Broyles turned to White.

"This is fate," he told White. "We're gonna win this one."

And maybe it was fate. Texas A&M led 8–7 at halftime. Arkansas' Joe Paul Alberty grabbed the second-half kickoff and raced left—as his blocking wall formed on the right. Seventy-seven yards later, Alberty was finally dragged down at the Aggies' 16-yard line, setting up the go-ahead score. Broyles again turned to White.

"You see?" he said. "We can't lose."

Final score: Arkansas 21, Texas A&M 8. Happy Hogs carried Broyles off the field. In the locker room, players mingled with fans (no one was sure how they'd gotten inside, but no one cared) in a raucous celebration. They called the hogs. Some just yelled.

"It feels great to win," said halfback Jim Mooty, a future All-American, after the game. "Man, I mean it feels great." And Broyles expressed similar sentiments, saying he was "the happiest I've ever been."

Three more victories followed to finish the season.

"If you're only gonna win four, the

last four are the ones to win," says Johnson, who was later a longtime Arkansas assistant coach.

Arkansas won the next three Southwest Conference championships. Broyles built the program into one of the nation's best in the 1960s. And yet, asked to identify his biggest win, he points back to 1958.

"My first win," Broyles remembers, "was bigger than all of them."

He learned a lot from the losing streak. "It was the first negative part of my career as a player or a coach," he remembers. "On a personal side, it made me a lot more understanding, a lot more forgiving. I was cocky. But [the losing streak] brought me down and taught me."

After the 1958 season, Barnhill gave

Broyles a vote of confidence backed with action: a contract extension and raise. For good measure, he purchased for Broyles a $150,000 life insurance policy and a station wagon (to be used by Barbara Broyles in ferrying their four boys).

It didn't take long for Broyles to prove Barnhill right. And he was helped considerably by a bright young coaching staff, something that was to become a staple of Broyles' entire career.

Through the years, twenty-nine Broyles assistants or players later became head coaches (many in direct moves from Arkansas). Among the notables: Barry Switzer (Oklahoma, three national championships; Dallas Cowboys, one Super Bowl championship); Johnny Majors (Iowa State, Pittsburgh, and Ten-

GEORGE SCHROEDER

Over the years, Frank Broyles' coaching tree has grown to legendary status. Part of his legacy is the assistants who became great head coaches. And yet, the Broyles assistant most influential in helping build and maintain the program never left for another job. Many former Hogs insist Wilson Matthews should be given equal prominence with Hayden Fry, Joe Gibbs, Johnny Majors, and the like—Arkansas assistants who went on to become successful head coaches.

"Coach Matthews probably could have gone somewhere and been one of the great head coaches," says Terry Don Phillips, the former player and associate athletic director who's now Clemson's athletic director.

Instead, until his death in 2002, Matthews remained by Broyles' side at the school he loved. After leaving the field, Matthews served as an administrative aide; he helped Broyles formulate Arkansas' priority-seating program, which generated the revenue to transform the athletic program into an all-sports powerhouse.

When John Barnhill was considering a replacement for Jack Mitchell in 1957, there was plenty of support from some quarters for Matthews, who had built a national powerhouse at Little Rock Central High School. Instead, Barnhill hired Broyles, who hired Matthews as an assistant just days later.

Matthews quickly became his most trusted lieutenant. To the players, he served the role of enforcer of Broyles' will. He was the middleman who allowed Broyles to remain above the fray. And many times before games, Matthews was the final, best motivator.

"Coach Matthews could get [Broyles'] point across better than he could get it across," says Bill Burnett, a standout tailback in the late 1960s and early 1970s. "Coach Matthews could accomplish what Coach Broyles wanted to accomplish better than he could. We had high, high respect for Coach Matthews."

Fear, too. Matthews was an intimidating figure to players. Phillips, a defensive lineman from 1966 to 1969, recalls a story related to him by a former teammate. This guy had played briefly, then left the team. Years later, he called Phillips and requested some basketball tickets. While in Fayetteville, he visited the football offices, briefly stepping outside to smoke. Just then, he heard a familiar voice. Matthews was leaving the building.

The former Hog hid the cigarette behind his leg. And burned a hole in a new pair of pants.

"I only spent about seven months up there dealing with Coach Matthews," the man later wrote Phillips in a letter. "I'd hate to think what would have happened to me if I'd spent four years."

Phillips laughs as he tells the story. Yet, he fully understands the former teammate's reaction. Players say Matthews was tough. But years later, they understood they loved him.

"I'll tell you this. You didn't want to be on Coach Matthews' bad side," Phillips says. "But I would be shocked if you'd find anybody who'd have a negative word to say about him. You often wonder, had he chose to run his own show, what would he have done? But he loved Arkansas. He loved Fayetteville. And so he stayed."

Hired in the first days after Frank Broyles' arrival, Wilson Matthews never left. He may have been the Hogs' most important assistant coach.

nessee, one national championship); Jimmy Johnson (Oklahoma State and Miami, one national championship; Dallas Cowboys, two Super Bowl championships; Miami Dolphins); Joe Gibbs (Washington Redskins; three Super Bowl championships).

Broyles' coaching tree also includes Hayden Fry, who built a legend at Iowa (and spun off some pretty successful coaches in his own right, such as Kansas State's Bill Snyder and Oklahoma's Bob Stoops). Other notables: former Arkansas coach Ken Hatfield (now at Rice), former Tennessee coach and athletic director Doug Dickey, former Texas coach Freddy Akers . . .

The list could go on for pages.

"You sit down and just start listing the coaches he put out, it's hard to believe all the great coaches that came to the University of Arkansas," says Clemson athletic director Terry Don Phillips, who played for Broyles from 1966 to 1969 and later served as Arkansas' associate athletic director. "It's tremendous. He probably put out more marquee coaches than anybody else in their history. And how he got 'em to come to Fayetteville, I have no idea. Because you didn't have an interstate. You really had to want to get to Fayetteville to get to Fayetteville."

Suffice it to say Broyles lured many bright young minds to Fayetteville. He sent them off better prepared to run their own programs and, while they were at Arkansas, they helped produce winners.

"We were better-coached than everybody we played," says Dick Hatfield, a member of the 1964 national championship squad.

Broyles' coaching style was familiar to many who follow modern college football. However, back when he started, a CEO-style approach was somewhat of a rarity. He delegated authority to his assistants and spent most practices watching from a perch above the field. Still, it's wrong to think Broyles was uninvolved.

Merv Johnson and other former assistants remember Broyles' eagerness to try new wrinkles and innovations. Unlike the failed 1958 experiment with the winged-T, most of the changes worked out well. And Broyles was vitally involved in game planning.

"He was much more hands-on as far as the Xs and Os than probably any [other] head coach I've worked for," says Johnson, who later coached at Notre Dame and Oklahoma. "He wanted to be in all the meetings. And we met long and late. I think he enjoyed kicking football Xs and Os around and investigating new ideas.

"He wore about everybody out. Longest hours that I can ever remember."

"Coach Broyles had a better grip on the game than any head coach," says Harold Horton, who played for Broyles in the early 1960s, then coached under him. "I'm talking offense, defense, kicking game. He had a better grip."

During practices, Broyles might have been distant, but he wasn't detached. Bill Burnett, who starred at tailback from 1968 to 1970, remembers an encounter with Broyles one day after a practice in which he had fumbled. They passed in the hall.

"Buh-nett," Broyles said in that deep, Georgia drawl, "you *got* to hold on to the bah-ll, son. If you're gonna play at AH-kan-saw, you got to hold on to the bah-ll."

"I think that was probably about as much as I got out of him in the four or five years I was there," Burnett says, laughing. And Burnett, remember, developed into a starter, then a star.

Players remember Broyles would watch during the early portions of the week as assistants installed the game plan. Come Thursday? "He took over," says former All-American linebacker Ronnie Caveness. "You could just see he was listening. He had his finger on the pulse of the team. He was a great motivator in his own way."

There was more to Arkansas' success than good coaching. Part of the foundation for championships was laid before Broyles coached a game at Arkansas. He'd brought in some fifty recruits in 1958. And that class—which included a youngster by the name of Lance Alworth—formed the core of the Razorbacks' quick turnaround.

Broyles got Alworth out of Brookhaven, Mississippi, only because of Ole Miss Coach Johnny Vaught's hard-and-fast rule against married players; Alworth had married his high-school sweetheart.

Broyles credits landing Alworth for helping open the door to out-of-state recruiting.

"He was the first big recruit," Broyles says. "When he came, it raised eyebrows all over the South. And he proved the wisdom [of the decision]. He played on three championship

Lance Alworth's arrival at Arkansas was a key that helped unlock out-of-state recruiting for Broyles' fledgling program.

teams. And he helped us build even a firmer foundation, a wider base, more fan base, additional financial base.

"He certainly spread our recruiting base—particularly in Texas."

It was immediately apparent Alworth was special. Even as the 1958 Hogs struggled, word of his ability on the freshman team filtered out.

"He was a superstar," remembers Switzer, who was two years older. "The first day I saw him, I knew he was different than the rest of us. It blew me away when I saw him out there the first day."

Alworth, of course, would become known as "Bambi" for his deerlike grace and agility. With the San Diego Chargers of the American Football League, he forged a career that resulted in his induction into the Pro Football Hall of Fame. First, he was an integral part of Arkansas' quick rise to the top of the Southwest Conference.

Alworth wasn't the only gem, though. Broyles' first recruiting class also included a youngster from Little Rock's Central High School by the name of Billy Moore. A standout at quarterback and defensive back, as a senior Moore was an All-American.

Already on campus was an undersized linebacker from El Dorado named Wayne Harris. But everyone would come to know him as "Thumper." His hard-hitting style would lead the fierce Hogs' defenses from 1958 to 1960.

In 1959, the Hogs broke through. A 3–0 win over defending SWC champion TCU was the turning point. Reserve halfback Freddy Akers, a Blytheville boy who later succeeded Darrell Royal as Texas' coach, kicked a field goal for the game's only points.

The Hogs lost to Texas 13–12 and to Ole Miss 28–0, but won their final four regular-season games. They finished 8-2 overall, 5-1 in the SWC, tied for the league title with Texas and TCU.

That earned a trip to the Gator Bowl in Jacksonville, Florida, where Arkansas was matched with Georgia Tech. Student bested teacher; Broyles' young Hogs rallied to hand Dodd's Yellow Jackets a 14–7 loss.

"Our little boys hit 'em pretty good, didn't they?" Broyles asked some old friends from Atlanta.

It was Dodd's first bowl loss in nine tries. It was Arkansas' first win in a major bowl.

"I think we were a little jittery facing a team with Tech's history," said quarterback Jim Monroe after the game.

Jim Mooty, an All-American at halfback, rushed for 99 yards on 18 carries, including the 19-yard romp that provided the winning touchdown. Young Alworth, destined to replace Mooty the next season, added 40 more yards.

The same day, Senator John F. Kennedy announced his bid for the

Democratic presidential nomination. In Arkansas, the news was of those wondrous Porkers. When the Hogs returned home, landing in Fort Smith, they were swarmed by several thousand fans, who were eager to celebrate the big victory.

Broyles' request of a year earlier to his father was long forgotten. Arkansas' fan support prompted O. T. Broyles, the insurance agent, to say: "If Frank ever leaves Arkansas, he's an ingrate."

If 1959 was good, 1960 was better. It was that fall that Broyles first realized what the Texas rivalry really meant to Arkansas.

The Hogs traveled to Austin, Texas, still smarting from a 28–14 loss to Baylor the week before. The Longhorns were favored by 12 points. And sure enough, Arkansas trailed by 14 points in the second quarter and by 23–14 in the fourth. But led by quarterback George McKinney, who threw three touchdown passes, the Razorbacks rallied for a dramatic victory.

With just more than ten minutes left, McKinney connected with Jarrell Williams for 19 yards, pulling Arkansas within 23–21. And with 3:15 remaining, the Hogs regained possession with one last chance. Alworth's hard running netted 17 yards on four plays, including a fourth-and-2 conversion at the 19.

McKinney gained 5 yards, then called timeout. And, with fifteen seconds left, sophomore Mickey Cissell kicked the winning field goal from 30 yards out. The football fluttered toward the goal posts and cleared the cross bar by less than a foot, but it was enough for the 24–23 win.

"I thought I'd make it," said Cissell of his first college field goal. "I had it in mind to be sure and not kick too hard—kick easy. I wanted it easy so I would be sure not to slice. Finally I got scared it was too soft."

When Broyles reached the locker room, the players were teary-eyed, singing a song they'd just been taught by assistant coach Wilson Matthews. To the tune of the "Old Gray Mare," they wailed: "We don't give a damn about the whole state of Texas, the whole state of Texas, the whole state of Texas. We

Their teams were fierce rivals, battling most years for Southwest Conference supremacy, but Broyles and Texas coach Darrell Royal forged a close friendship.

don't give a damn about the whole state of Texas. We're from Ar-kin-saw!"

"It's the loudest I've ever heard anybody sing," Broyles remembers.

Late that night, the team planes arrived at Drake Field in Fayetteville, where several thousand students awaited. They carried the players on their shoulders to the buses.

"I realized that night," Broyles says, "how important it was for us to win against Texas."

It was something he would have reinforced time and again.

The next week, Ole Miss nipped Arkansas 10–7 in Little Rock on a controversial ending. With the game tied at 7 and time running out, the Rebels' Allen Green lined up for a 39-yard field goal. He hit it as time expired. But referee Tommy Bell had whistled the play dead before it started.

Bell gave Green another chance. This one, witnesses insisted, missed left. But Bell raised his arms, indicating the kick was good.

Several thousand Arkansas fans in the south end zone, where the ball landed, remained in their seats chanting, "Wide, wide, wide," and pointing in the direction they believed the football had gone awry. Fights broke out on the field between Ole Miss and Arkansas fans. The bitter feelings essentially meant the end of the traditional intrasectional series for the next two decades.

However, the Hogs won their next four games and won the league outright, earning a trip to the Cotton Bowl (where Duke stopped the party, winning 7–6).

In 1961, the Hogs again tied for the SWC championship. This time, they headed to the Sugar Bowl. And ran into a buzz saw. Bear Bryant's first national championship squad stopped Arkansas 10–3, which wasn't so bad: The Tide allowed just 25 total points in eleven wins that season.

In 1962, Arkansas didn't win the title—Texas did, of course—but the Razorbacks later felt they had just missed winning the national championship. A heart-breaking, last-minute loss at Texas denied them both.

Led by Moore, an All-American that year (and Arkansas' only All-American quarterback), the Hogs rolled in almost every other game that year. As the final seconds ticked away in Austin, the Hogs led 3–0. In the third quarter, they had almost put it away; but as fullback Danny Brabham plunged toward the goal line, he was hit by linebackers Pat Culpepper and Leon Treadwell. The ball popped loose. Many Hogs always believed he had reached the end zone first. But the officials didn't see it that way and Texas recovered to remain alive.

Dick Hatfield played center that day. "I remember going down and then looking up and seeing that ball pop out," Hatfield said.

Texas took full advantage of the reprieve. Late in the fourth quarter, the Longhorns took possession at their 15.

With thirty-six seconds left, Tommy Ford scored from the 4, giving Texas a 7–3 win.

Arkansas finished 9-2 with a 17–13 loss to Ole Miss in the Sugar Bowl. And that loss might not have occurred except for a knee injury suffered by Moore in the final regular-season game. But because in those days the Associated Press and United Press International awarded the national championship before the bowls, the near-miss at Texas cost the Razorbacks a conference and national

championship. USC was named champion at 9-1; but for the loss, Arkansas would have been the only undefeated team after the regular season.

Still, as Broyles' sixth season approached, it was apparent he had built the program into a powerhouse. "We had momentum," Broyles recalls. As summer turned into fall in 1963, prognosticators expected the Hogs to contend for conference and perhaps national crowns.

They were a year ahead of themselves.

Ronnie Caveness (no. 55) was a leader on fierce Razorback defenses.

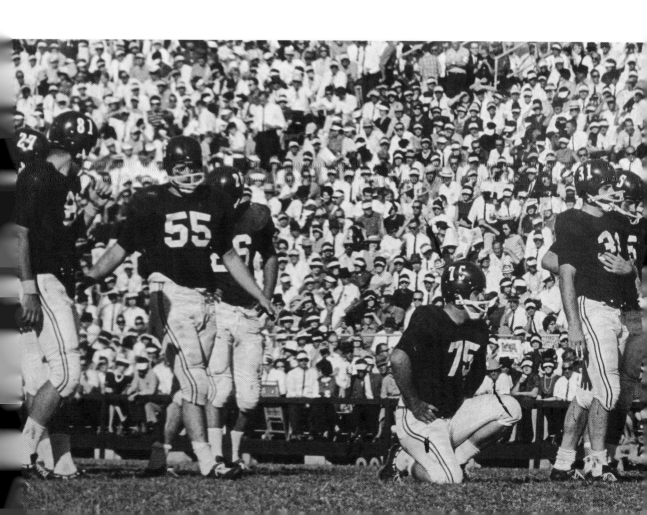

ARKANSAS 1964 NATIONAL CHAMPIONS 11-0

ARKANSAS

3

Winning 'em All

ARKANSAS' finest achievement came complete with an exciting new look, but only after a significant setback. The 1964 and 1965 seasons produced the greatest sustained run in school history, a period that ranks among the best in any school's history: twenty-two straight victo-

▲ Arkansas' 1964 national championship made the entire state proud.

▶ RIGHT
The Arkansas helmet, one of the most familiar in sports, is essentially unchanged since 1964, when the running hog was placed on the sides.

ries and a national championship in 1964.

"It was a special time in the history of the Razorbacks," says Ronnie Caveness, an All-American linebacker in 1964.

"It gave the state a unity and a pride," says Ken Hatfield, a senior defensive back that season. "It had always been there, but I think the national championship did as much to solidify that nationwide in [other] people's eyes. . . . This was the one thing that every person in Arkansas could be a part of."

As the 1964 season began, not many would have predicted such success. No one understood how changed the Razorbacks would be from the previous year, when despite preseason predictions of greatness, they'd finished 5-5. All anyone knew for sure was the Hogs looked different.

The Razorbacks' helmets had been painted cardinal rather than white only

a few years earlier. The shells' sides had featured individual player numbers, painted in white. For 1964, the numbers were replaced by a fierce, running hog. The design hasn't changed significantly since; it has long been one of college football's most recognizable helmets.

"It was a big departure from anything they'd ever done," says Hatfield. "They were trying to show this was a new era, a new beginning, a new everything."

And, yes, Hatfield says, "they were trying to eliminate any reference to the nineteen-sixty-three season."

To understand 1964 and 1965, you must relive 1963. After just missing a national title in 1962, Arkansas was the choice of sportswriters to win the Southwest Conference in 1963.

Instead, the Razorbacks and their fans endured a disappointing season, considering the expectations. Their five losses were by a combined 23 points. One day in a meeting, offensive assistant Doug Dickey—later Tennessee's head coach and athletic director—told the Razorbacks: "Y'all are playing just good enough to look good losing."

And a group of players didn't like it one bit. A loss to SMU dropped the disconsolate Hogs to 4-5. During the flight home, several juniors approached Broyles, who was sitting, dejected, in the front of the cabin. Next year's seniors were distraught over the thought of another season of disappointment. Though one game remained, they wanted to immediately begin preparation for 1964.

"We've had a horrible season," they said. "We know we can do a lot better."

The players, including quarterback Freddie Marshall and end Jerry Lamb, told Broyles they wanted to scrimmage during practices before the Texas Tech game. It was a radical departure from the coach's philosophy, which was to keep workouts light to prevent injuries. Also, they asked Broyles not to exempt the rising seniors from spring practice, a traditional policy Broyles had used to reward the upperclassmen.

Another significant conversation took place at about that time. Part of Arkansas' troubles had resulted because coaches couldn't settle on a quarterback. Marshall, Billy Gray, and Jon Brittenum took turns. Each had strengths. And weaknesses. None played well for long.

"It was kind of a pitching rotation," Marshall remembers. "You went in and if you walked a couple of batters, then you came out and they put somebody else in. It wasn't a real good situation."

After a three-quarterback rotation proved unsuccessful in 1963, Frank Broyles named Freddie Marshall (no. 19) the starter for 1964, following this game against SMU. Marshall might not have been the most talented quarterback, but he possessed *it*, according to Broyles, referring to winning intangibles.

Eventually, Broyles and his coaches realized as much. Before the Hogs played SMU, Marshall visited Broyles to inform him of his plans. The junior from Memphis had enough credits to graduate the next spring, and he intended to do just that.

"I've been here three or four years," Marshall told Broyles. "I'm gonna do whatever I can to help the team the next two games, but I'm not coming back next year. I can finish my academic work, and I feel like I should have been playing this year.

"I think if I'd been playing, we'd have won more games. But I'm not the coach, you are. So I'm not gonna quit with a couple games left, but don't count on me coming back next year."

Broyles listened, but made no decision. The next week against SMU, Marshall relieved in the third quarter and played well. Afterward, Broyles informed Marshall and then the team that Marshall would be the starter for the season finale against Texas Tech, and for the 1964 season, as well.

"There was no question but what he had *it,*" says Broyles, referring to the undefined intangible possessed by certain winning quarterbacks. "I had jumped around with the quarterbacks. That didn't help him and it didn't help the team. I never made a firm commitment as to who it should be. And I wasn't gonna go through that again.

"I had seen in Freddie the toughness and the qualities that I wanted. It was an error on my part that I didn't start him and play him all of sixty-three. I wasn't gonna make that mistake again. He would be the quarterback and we would go from there."

Beginning that Monday, the Hogs battled in full pads and with full contact. "We're certainly not in a good mood," Broyles said two days before the game. "And maybe that's the way it's supposed to be. We know we have some things to do."

And on Saturday, Arkansas won, 27–20. There wasn't much celebration, for several reasons. The previous day, President John F. Kennedy had been assassinated in Dallas. The somber mood that gripped the nation also enveloped the Arkansas campus; officials debated what to do, but since Texas Tech had already arrived, the decision was made to play.

It was the only Southwest Conference game played that day. And as flags flew at half-mast, a few protestors stood around outside the stadium. And on the field?

"It felt very weird. Completely," Ken Hatfield says. "And yet at the same time, I'm trying to figure out what in the world we'd be doing if we weren't playing? Everyone was already there."

And although the crowd arrived late and was unusually subdued, predictions of less than fifteen-thousand were wrong. Perhaps three-thousand ticket-holders stayed home. The rest watched as the Razorbacks salvaged a .500 record, and immediately set their sights on next year.

The fourteen seniors-to-be participated in spring practice, and formed a tight-knit leadership group that was essential to the development of a champion.

The offseason conditioning program, run by assistant coach Wilson Matthews and dubbed the Fourth Quarter, was fiercer than ever before. And when the players scattered for the summer, the seniors wrote letters to underclassmen encouraging them—no, commanding them—to report to preseason practices in shape.

It worked.

"There was an urgency in our attitude," remembers Caveness. "It was, 'Let's get better!' "

There were two other significant changes. Arkansas had been hurt in 1963 when rulesmakers, who had been gradually moving toward the full-substitution game played today, pulled back toward one-platoon football. Arkansas had been using three squads—a first-team offense, a first-team defense, and a talented second-team bunch—and training to play one-way football.

After the 1963 season, the rules were loosened just a bit. Full substitution would be allowed when the clock stopped, as after a timeout, an incom-

plete pass, or a play out of bounds. In other instances, Broyles and his staff decided, they would take a 5-yard penalty in order to substitute. The Hogs returned to training players for offense or defense, not both. Texas and many other schools continued training two-way players.

Also, the Hogs installed a new offense, moving from the old split-T to John McKay's USC version of the I-formation. Broyles added a wingback to the package, and it fit well the Hogs' strengths: running ability, speed, and the occasional pass.

"We kind of hit our stride with it midyear," says Merv Johnson, who was then an offensive assistant.

Character was the hallmark of the 1964 team. Though they had some standouts—Caveness was an All-American at linebacker in 1964, and Loyd Phillips would win the Outland Trophy for best lineman in 1966—the Hogs weren't star-studded. They were made up mostly of try-hard kids.

"They were a bunch of guys like Jerry Jones," says Johnson. "Kind of an average athlete, but a try-hard, relentless, never-quit kind of guy. We had a lot of guys that were really average athletes that made up for it with their attitude."

They were quintessential Razorbacks. In 1964, Jones, who later gained fame as the Dallas Cowboys' owner, was a 190-pound halfback converted to guard. On the other side of the ball,

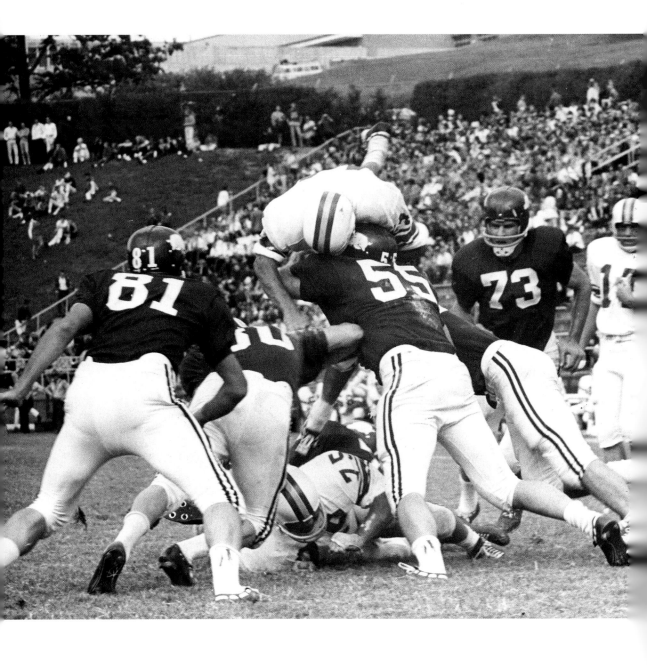

Jimmy Johnson, later a successful college and NFL coach, was an overachieving nose guard. Arkansas' 1964 squad was undersized, but quick. More important, they were scrappy and fiercely determined.

"We dedicated ourselves," says Freddie Marshall. "We realized in the sixty-three season that we weren't living up to our capability. And we were embarrassed."

Still, even after the season began, there wasn't much to indicate greatness. Arkansas won its first four games, but didn't look especially good doing so. The Razorbacks escaped Oklahoma State 14–10 with a third-quarter drive in Little Rock (Marshall reinjured a chronic shoulder), then rallied from a 14–0 deficit to beat Tulsa 31–22 as Caveness returned an interception for a touchdown and set up another score with a fumble recovery.

A 29–6 win over TCU the next week was closer than the score. Arkansas led 14–6 in the fourth quarter. It took Gray's second interception (he had returned to the secondary after spelling Marshall against Oklahoma State and Tulsa) to turn back the Horned Frogs' threat to tie. And Harry Jones' zigzagging, 24-yard interception return for a touchdown sealed the victory.

The next week, Arkansas failed to score four times after getting to the Baylor 10-yard line, or closer. But Marshall ran (132 yards) and passed (85 yards) the Hogs to a 17–6 win, pushing the Hogs to 4-0.

Like all national championship teams, the Hogs made big plays. They also took advantage of breaks.

"We were luckier than henhouse rats," says Jim Lindsey, a wingback who went on to play seven years for the Minnesota Vikings and is now a prominent realtor and a member of Arkansas' board of trustees. "We had good fortune at every turn. The henhouse rat gets to suck all the eggs. He's got the best break in the world.

"But somewhere in all that good fortune [the team] was steeled by determination and a ferocity that couldn't quite be measured unless you were there in the huddle."

As always, Texas presented the most daunting obstacle. For the third time in six years, both teams were unbeaten heading into what was becoming the most important showdown for the Southwest Conference crown.

Texas was the defending national champion. The Longhorns had won fifteen straight and were ranked number one after a 28–7 dismantling of Oklahoma. Though Arkansas had moved up to number eight in the Associated Press poll, number ten in the United Press International (coaches) poll, the consensus was Texas would win, and easily. While Arkansas' four wins had come with narrow escapes, the Longhorns had rolled to their wins.

"Nobody expected much from us," says Ken Hatfield. "They'd been a lot more impressive."

A *Dallas Morning News* sportswriter posed the question, "Who can beat Texas?" He then answered with a widely held opinion: "Nobody, that's who. Arkansas, this week's sacrifice upon football's orange altar, will have to play far better than it has to avoid outright embarrassment."

In the days before the game, civil rights leader Martin Luther King, Jr., was named a recipient of the Nobel Peace Prize. Nikita Khrushchev was ousted from power in the Soviet Union. China detonated its first atomic bomb. And it was a remarkable week in sports, as well.

New York Yankees' sluggers Roger Maris and Mickey Mantle hit back-to-back home runs to force a seventh game in the World Series against St. Louis, setting up a showdown between dominating right-hander Bob Gibson and rookie sinkerballer Mel Stottlemyre (the Cardinals won the deciding game; a day later, the Yankees fired manager Yogi Berra while the Cardinals accepted the resignation of manager Johnny Keane).

The Milwaukee Braves announced that they would move the franchise to the minor-league city of Atlanta. At the Olympics in Tokyo, Bob Hayes broke 10 seconds in the 100-meter dash semifinal; the 9.9 second time wasn't a world record because Hayes ran with a tailwind.

In Arkansas, at least, there was only one real topic of conversation. Perhaps five thousand Arkansas fans traveled to Austin for the game, which was played on a hot, humid evening. Countless others listened to the radio broadcast over a statewide network; more stations carried the game that night than ever before.

And the Hogs understood the fans' passion.

"We felt like we were Arkansas' boys," says Dick Hatfield, Ken's older brother, who was a lineman on that team. "We were playing for the state."

The two Hatfield boys—graduates of Helena's Central High School—did their state proud that night.

Ken had the more spectacular play. The senior had led the nation in punt returns in 1963 and was on his way to doing it again. In the days before the game, Texas assistant Russell Coffee, whose assignment was to scout the Hogs, told the *Dallas Morning News* that Hatfield's punt returns were "the most dangerous thing they've got. . . . Boy, is he wicked!"

In the second quarter, Texas' Ernie Koy unleashed a long punt—too long for his coverage. Ken Hatfield took it at Arkansas' 19. He started forward, then bounced left, kicking his way out of a tackle, and headed for the sidelines. Lindsey's block helped spring him. And when Hatfield turned the corner, he was flanked by Razorbacks—cheering spectators on the visitors' sideline and, more important, determined blockers on the other side.

Eighty-one yards later, Hatfield raced into the end zone. Arkansas led 7–0. The score was worth much more than a touchdown.

"It turned the whole game around," Broyles says.

"It was huge for us," Lindsey concurs.

Back home, they agreed. Since the game wasn't televised, folks huddled near their radios. Around seven thousand people were watching a small-college game in Conway between Arkansas State Teachers College (later to become the University of Central Arkansas) and Arkansas Tech. While the Tech band performed at halftime, a sudden roar arose from the crowd. Their transistor radios had told them Hatfield had just scored. As the band played—as well as during the second half—they kept hanging on every word of Arkansas publicity man Bud Cheyne.

After Texas tied it early in the fourth quarter, Arkansas answered with a twelve-play, 75-yard drive. Except for Dick Hatfield, the possession would have ended without a first down. He wasn't the athlete his younger brother was but, that year, he was the Hogs' deep snapper on punts and field goals. Earlier in the game, he had noticed the

Longhorns were slow to change units when Arkansas punted.

When the Hogs faltered a yard short of a first down at their own 34, Dick Hatfield encouraged his teammates to work quickly; the punt caught too many Texas players on the field, drawing a 5-yard penalty and a first down. The ploy worked in part because the ball was placed on the hash mark closest to Arkansas' bench.

"We went out and got out there quick," Dick Hatfield says. "They had a long way to go to get off the field. I snapped it quick."

Eight plays later, Marshall dropped back and found Bobby Crockett open; the pass hit the receiver from Dermott in stride for a 34-yard touchdown with 6:43 left in the game. Earlier in the drive, Crockett had made a diving grab for 11 yards on third-and-8. The call on the touchdown was the same out route, to the other side. But when Texas' defensive back played tight coverage, quarterback and receiver adjusted, changing to a deep route.

"A great, heads-up play by Bobby," Marshall says.

Texas rallied, moving 70 yards for a touchdown late in the fourth quarter. With 1:27 left, Koy plunged in from the 1, pulling Texas within 14–13.

Longhorns coach Darrell Royal might have settled for a tie in some situations. But not while carrying the number-one ranking and a 15-game

winning streak. The Longhorns had to go for two points.

The resulting situation eerily resembled the way Texas had beaten Arkansas in 1962. Tommy Ford had plunged into the same end zone with thirty-seven seconds left to give the Longhorns a 7–3 win.

During a timeout before the winning play in 1962, Royal first sent in a reserve tailback—indicating, to Broyles, a pass was coming. The Hogs signaled a pass defense, but Royal changed his mind and sent Ford back into the ballgame. Arkansas' coaches tried to get, but couldn't, their players' attention to change the defensive strategy. Ford plunged into the end zone with the winning score.

As it turned out, the loss denied Arkansas the national championship. And Broyles believed at the time he might "never again . . . have the opportunity to accomplish so much for Arkansas in one night."

Yet, two years later, here were the Hogs, with the opportunity. And here were the Longhorns, searching for victory in the same end zone. From the sidelines, offensive tackle Jerry Welch understood the similarities, even though it was a two-point try, not a touchdown. "Lord," he said, "Don't let it happen again."

Royal called timeout to ponder his options. He was uncertain whether to run or pass. Broyles waited and watched, determined not to be outfoxed.

He told his defensive assistants not to signal the defensive call until the Longhorns broke the huddle. First Hix Green, a receiving threat, then Ernie Koy, a powerful runner, moved into Texas' timeout huddle. Then, finally, Green came back in.

The signal from assistant Wilson Matthews came in late. Texas had broken the offensive huddle; Arkansas linebacker Ronnie Caveness was about to call timeout. As Texas' offensive line settled over the football, Hogs scram-

bled this way and that to get into position.

The defensive call was eagle-fire. Arkansas had worked on the strategy during two-a-days, but not much since. The ends were deployed wider than normal; both they and the linebackers were told to rush hard. The idea was to pressure the quarterback. The defense was vulnerable to a pass over the middle.

At the snap, Arkansas sent ends Bobby Roper and Jim Finch crashing toward the pocket. Quarterback Marv Kristynik faked a handoff left to the fullback, then dropped back, intending to roll out to the right. But when Kristynik turned and looked to his right, Finch was in his face.

Kristynik got the pass off just in time, but the hurried pass was low. Green reached back and got a hand on it near the goal line, but never had a realistic shot at a catch.

"Marvin couldn't get it off like he wanted," Green told reporters later. "He had to hurry it. It got to me on the bounce. I couldn't get to it."

It's a play Royal remembers with regret.

"We didn't have room to throw the ball," Royal says. "We had the receiver wide-open, but their defensive end made a great play and came right on through our pulling guard and put the heat on our quarterback.

"That lost that one."

As more than sixty thousand Texas fans watched in stunned silence, perhaps five thousand Arkansas fans perched high in a corner of Memorial Stadium called the Hogs as the final seconds melted away: Arkansas 14, Texas 13. Marshall heaved his helmet high into the air. Players and fans met at midfield for a raucous celebration; some fans took souvenirs, grabbing up clumps of grass from the spot where Kristynik's pass fell to earth.

Texas had dominated the statistics, outgaining Arkansas nearly two to one. However, on two big-play touchdowns and the defensive stop, the Razorbacks were winners.

Moments later, an unexpected visitor invaded Arkansas' locker room. Royal followed Broyles off the field and asked if he could address the Hogs. By then, the coaches were well on their way to developing a lifelong friendship that transcended the rivalry, but Royal had never addressed another team after a game before. And he never did it after that day, either.

Royal congratulated the Hogs on a "heck of a win," and told them they had beaten a great Texas team, not an ordinary one. He wished them luck the rest of the way and said they had what it took to win the conference and national championship.

But Royal also warned the Hogs: "If you stump your toe, remember, we're right behind you."

After beating the Longhorns, there

wasn't much chance of toe-stumping, because the Hogs returned home a changed bunch.

As the team planes lifted off from Austin, several players noted a landmark with satisfaction. The University of Texas' tower, traditionally bathed in orange light after victories, was dark.

As in 1960, the Hogs were met at Fayetteville's Drake Field by several thousand students. The team planes circled the airport three times, waiting for the fans to clear the runways. Upon landing, the fans swarmed the propeller-driven DC-3s, forcing pilots to cut the engines far from the terminal to prevent injury. As they waited on the runway, Dick Hatfield and Randy Stewart looked out the window.

"Some guy was on the wing looking in," Dick Hatfield recalls. "Some dude had crawled up on the darn wing and was looking at us."

There were fans everywhere. Cars were parked along U.S. 71 from Drake Field all the way back into Fayetteville proper. Downtown, Hog calls sounded late into the night, or early into the morning. And it wasn't just northwest Arkansas; streets in Little Rock were jammed with revelers, who honked horns and called the Hogs into the wee hours.

"Just a fabulous night," Dick Hatfield says. "That was some night."

Some life-changing night, apparently. The Razorbacks point to that victory as the one that transformed them into champions.

"When we got back and looked in the mirror, none of us were the same," says Jerry Jones.

Jim Finch told his father: "Y'all go to every ballgame and bet on us, because we ain't gonna lose. They may not even score."

Well, exactly. The Hogs shut out their last five regular-season opponents. They won by 17–0 over Wichita State, 17–0 over Texas A&M, 21–0 over Rice, 44–0 over SMU, and 17–0 over Texas Tech. Not surprisingly, considering that mark, Arkansas led the nation in scoring defense, allowing opponents an average of 5.7 points per game. The Hogs allowed only 1,805 total yards.

"Defense was really the key," Marshall says. "Our offense didn't make any mistakes, but we could have kicked a field goal and won the last five games three to nothing."

The shutouts—and the Cotton Bowl, and the national title shot—were in serious doubt on an afternoon in Lubbock, Texas. When the Razorbacks arrived for the final regular-season game, Texas Tech had lost only to Texas in the conference; a win over the Hogs would push the Red Raiders into a three-way tie with Arkansas and Texas, sending Texas Tech to the Cotton Bowl.

And it appeared for a while it might happen, that the Razorbacks' shutout streak and, more important,

their winning streak, might end. Handing the football to junior tailback Donnie Anderson, the Red Raiders moved up and down the field in the first half.

"It seemed like they'd start on their twenty, and the next thing you knew, they'd be on our twenty," Caveness says.

Near their own goal line, the Razorbacks stiffened, forcing the Red Raiders to try a field goal. And from right end, Bobby Roper charged, dived, and blocked the kick.

Moments later, Tech drove close again. Stalled again. Tried a field goal again. And Roper blocked it again, preserving the scoreless tie.

"He'd never blocked a kick before," Broyles says. "And he blocks two of the cotton-picking things. Out of nowhere. To me, that just illustrates what those players could reach out and do because of their character. I don't think he'd ever come close to blocking a kick before, and he blocks to protect the championship.

"But that was what players did all year. Those players on that team would just explode above their ability. If they were good, they became outstanding. If they were outstanding, they became great. And that's the way they played."

"It just seemed like at each point in the season, somebody would make a play," Caveness remembers. "And it seemed like it would turn it around, get the momentum."

There was an off-the-field example that day in Lubbock. Mired in a score-

less tie at halftime, Arkansas' seniors asked the coaches to leave the locker room. Jerry Lamb got up to speak. He was known as a quiet, unemotional type. Not on this day.

Lamb began talking and he became emotional. As his eyes swept the room, they landed on Caveness (like Lamb, a graduate of Houston's Smiley High School). Lamb began speaking directly to his childhood buddy.

" 'Cuz," Lamb said to Caveness, "We can't go out like this. We can't leave this game on the field. We can't go out any way but a winner."

The speech ended with Lamb and Caveness hugging and crying. Many of their teammates were wiping away sudden tears, as well.

A different team emerged from the locker room.

"That emotional expression between them was so powerful, they swept our team to another level," Lindsey remembers. "We'd have beat the Chicago Bears in the second half. We were unbelievably inspired. Texas Tech didn't know what hit 'em."

Arkansas won 17–0, securing the conference championship, a trip to the

Cotton Bowl, and a chance for a national title.

Or a piece of the title, anyway. The Associated Press and United Press International's final polls were taken before the bowls; Alabama and Arkansas were the only undefeated teams. The Crimson Tide, which was headed to the Orange Bowl to play Texas, was both polls' pick for number one.

Arkansas met 9-1 Nebraska in the Cotton Bowl. The Cornhuskers' only loss was to Oklahoma; they outweighed the Razorbacks by an average of twenty pounds per man.

Estimates were more than forty thousand Arkansas fans had purchased

tickets at $5.50 apiece. They'd started snapping them up in mid-October, after the win over Texas. And as the Razorbacks kept winning, the buzz grew to a full-fledged roar.

Businesses tried to capitalize, of course. Union Motors of Little Rock advertised Cotton Bowl Specials, listing several deals on used cars with the proclamation: "Any one of these cars will make the trip to Dallas on New Year's Day." A faint endorsement, perhaps, considering the journey was only 320 miles, all on Interstate highway. Anyway, a 1961 Volkswagen (maroon with white interior, heater, and white wall tires) went for $990. A 1960 Cadillac convertible (all power, green finish with matching interior and white top) went for $1,995. There was no word on whether the cars in fact made it to Dallas.

On an unseasonably warm afternoon, the Cotton Bowl was an all-red affair as Arkansas' darker shade mingled with Nebraska's happy, fire-engine color. The Hogs went ahead 3–0 on Tom McKnelly's 31-yard field goal in the first quarter. A second-quarter touchdown by Nebraska's Harry Wilson capped a ten-play, 69-yard drive and gave the Cornhuskers a 7–3 lead.

It was the first score allowed by Arkansas since the final minutes of the Texas game. For the longest time, as Nebraska played its best game and the Hogs delivered a stale effort, it appeared Wilson's score would be enough.

Though he had struggled earlier in the game, Freddie Marshall directed the touchdown drive that clinched the national championship. He was named the game's most valuable player.

Marshall had thrown an interception and missed several open receivers. He had lost two fumbles. In the Razorbacks' first ten games, he hadn't fumbled. At one point, Broyles had Bill Gray warm up, though the coach later said it was only a precaution in case Marshall was injured, or tired. At any rate, Gray wasn't needed on offense.

With 9:21 left, Arkansas took possession at its 20. Time for one last drive. In the huddle, the Hogs looked each other in the eye.

"We knew without question or doubt, 'This is it,'" Lindsey says. " 'We can't leave this on the field.'"

They didn't. Marshall needed nine plays for his redemption: "From the outhouse to the penthouse in one drive," he remembers. Marshall personally accounted for 71 of the 80 yards. He completed 5 passes in 5 attempts, totaling 61 yards, and scrambled away from a Nebraska blitz for 10 yards. Tailback Bobby Burnett managed the other 9 yards, including a 3-yarder for the winning touchdown with 4:41 left.

Lindsey might have turned in the biggest play. On third-and-6 from the Arkansas 47, Marshall threw quickly, before Lindsey had turned to look for the ball. As it whizzed by him, he reached and caught it with one hand.

"I just kind of flicked out and caught it," Lindsey said.

Later, Marshall hit Lindsey for 28 yards to the Nebraska 5, setting the stage for Burnett's score. Marshall rolled right on the option, then pitched to Burnett, who cut inside, and leaped for the most important touchdown in Arkansas history.

Fittingly, defense sealed it. Nebraska moved quickly to a first down at midfield, but got no closer. Jim Williams and Ronnie Mac Smith sacked quarterback Bob Churchich for an 8-yard loss. A pass netted 6 yards. An end around went for no gain.

On fourth-and-12, Williams walloped Churchich again as he looked to pass. A 15-yard loss. Arkansas' ball, and ballgame.

When Williams returned to the bench, he told teammates he hadn't been touched on the final play. On the play before? He held up his helmet: The facemask's vertical bars were mangled.

Marshall ran out the clock in three plays, and the Hogs had completed a perfect season. One important domino still stood.

Later that evening, Marshall attended the traditional Cotton Bowl banquet, held at the Marriott Motor Inn, but his mind was elsewhere. He had to be pried away from a television set in a men's restroom; it was tuned to the Orange Bowl, where Texas was playing Alabama.

Inside the ballroom, Marshall's absence was conspicuous. Finally, someone found him.

"You need to get back to the banquet," he was told.

"Well, why?" Marshall replied, his eyes still on the unfolding action in Miami.

"They just named you most valuable player of the game, and they can't find you."

Reluctantly, Marshall left the restroom to pick up the award. He understood what a Texas win in the Orange Bowl would mean.

So did his teammates. Many of them watched the game from their hotel, where a television had been set up in the lobby. They found themselves in an unfamiliar position: cheering for Texas. When Tommy Nobis stopped Joe Namath on fourth-and-goal, allowing the 'Horns to claim a 21–17 win, the Razorbacks celebrated.

Well, maybe they knew how it would happen.

"We'd had so many good things happen to us, I think we'd all have guessed what would happen [in the Orange Bowl]," Lindsey says.

When Broyles returned to Fayetteville, he went straight to athletic director John Barnhill's office, ready to share the warmth of the program's finest moment. Barnhill greeted him with something else: "You've just screwed up the best job in America." Broyles recoiled in surprise. "What do you mean?" And Barnhill told him winning eight and nine games was "perfect," because it kept fans hungry without overly raising expectations. But the damage was done.

About that time, a new tune hit the airwaves of Arkansas. Cecil Buffalo, a Little Rock University student, was backed by The Prophets on the ballad of "Big Red." The first line told the story: "Big Red, he is a number-one pig, uh huh." Initially released after the win over Texas, the group modified the lyrics to reflect the Hogs' Cotton Bowl success: "The moral of the story is easy to spot, Big Red's number one— Alabama is not. That's right. Uh huh. Sooiee!"

Alabama's national championship, as voted by the Associated Press and United Press International, was secure. But two organizations, the Football Writers Association of America and the Helms Athletic Foundation, hadn't yet named their champion. Texas' win cast

Frank Broyles points to the day his Hogs reached the pinnacle of college football. Arkansas athletic director John Barnhill told Broyles he had "just screwed up the best job in America."

doubt on Alabama's worthiness. And Arkansas was the only unbeaten team.

The Football Writers took their time voting. They didn't announce Arkansas as their national champion until January 6, five days after the Cotton Bowl. That afternoon, the Hogs met for a team photo. Though they were without Broyles and several players (some were with Broyles in Honolulu, Hawaii, for the Hula Bowl) and several assistants (on the road recruiting), they raised their index fingers and were all smiles.

"They said Coach Broyles made winners out of a bunch of boys, and he did," says Finch, a homebuilder who now lives in his hometown of Forrest City. "But he assembled a bunch of winners and put 'em together. And

that's the reason we won. Everybody had a desire to win."

The heart of the 1964 team departed: fourteen seniors, many of whom had played key roles. But they left behind a talented roster filled with players who had learned how to win, and who expected to do just that.

Lindsey returned, though because of injury, his playing role was greatly reduced. Bobby Burnett was at tailback. Harry Jones moved from safety to wingback and blossomed into a star. Jon Brittenum, who'd been part of the three-headed quarterback monster in 1963, had redshirted in 1964. He won the starting job in 1965, and quickly became a star, passing most often to All-American receiver Bobby Crockett.

Most important, the Hogs had talent and size in the trenches. Dick Cunningham, Glen Ray Hines, and Mike Bender helped form a solid offensive wall, protecting Brittenum and punching holes for Burnett and Jones. Defensively, Loyd Phillips was an All-American at tackle; he was one year away from winning the Outland Trophy. Jim

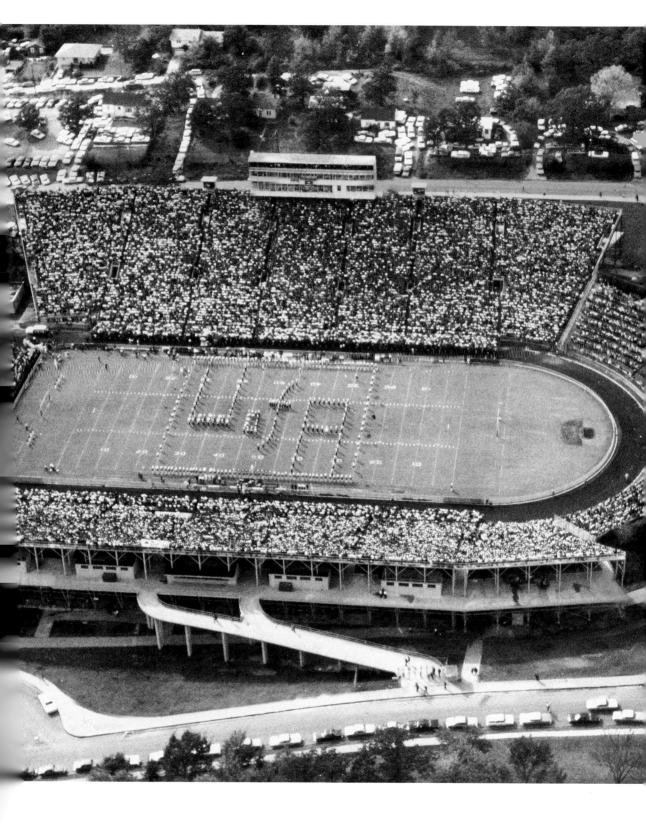

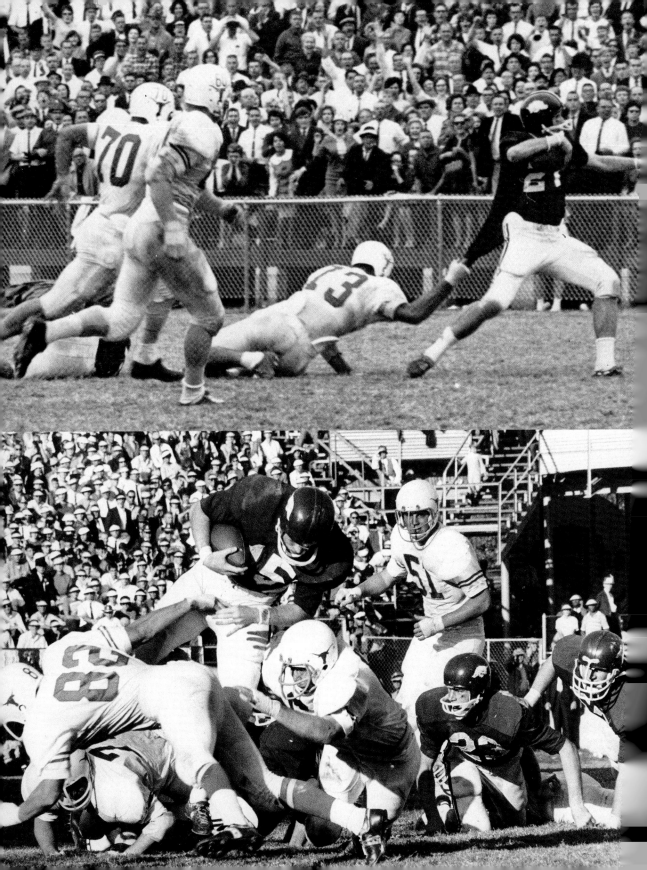

Williams and Bobby Roper returned, as well.

The Razorbacks' strength in 1965, however, was unquestionably the offense. In 1964, Arkansas led the nation in scoring defense; in 1965, Arkansas averaged 32.4 points a game, best in the nation.

The mental journey was also different. In 1964, the Hogs might have slipped up on some opponents; in 1965, they wore targets. Against no team was that more true than Texas. When the Longhorns traveled to Fayetteville that October, they were still smarting over their 14–13 loss a year earlier. It was their only loss in twenty-six games, and it had denied them a second straight national championship.

Fueled by two defensive touchdowns—safety Martine Bercher pounced on a fumble in the end zone after a mishandled punt, and Tommy Trantham plucked a fumble from midair and returned it 77 yards for another score—Arkansas grabbed the early lead. When Brittenum hit Crockett for an 11-yard touchdown, the Razorbacks led 20–0.

Texas pulled within 20–11 at halftime, though, then dominated the second half en route to moving ahead 21–20. With just more than four minutes left, David Conway's field goal stretched the Longhorns' lead to four points.

The Hogs took over on their 20.

And drove into legend once more. Before the possession started, Lindsey stepped in. Broken ribs had kept Lindsey from much playing time, as had Jones' surge to stardom. But with the season on the line, he assumed leadership.

"I hadn't been on the field at all, so I wasn't whipped in any way," Lindsey says. "I was just in a frenzy. I'd made an all-out commitment."

Lindsey called the offense together. He told his teammates Texas was not leaving Fayetteville with a win. Brittenum and Crockett would take care of the yardage, if they would take care of the blocking.

"My assignment," Lindsey told them, "is gonna be to block that end. I promise you he will not rush the passer. How about you?" And Lindsey pointed at a teammate. "And you? And you?"

During much of the drive, the Hogs kept nine blockers in and sent Crockett out on routes. Six times (for 64 yards), Brittenum connected with Crockett. The drive starter was a 22-yard toss. Several plays later, Crockett turned and snagged another pass just inches before it hit the ground.

"What a fantastic catch," Royal told reporters.

The last connection, on third-and-4 from the Texas 15, set up the winning touchdown. Crockett ran what the Hogs called a "squirrel pattern," racing directly at the defensive back as though on a fly pattern, then suddenly cutting

TOP, FACING PAGE
Senior wingback Jim Lindsey's determination was pivotal to Arkansas' rally for victory over the Longhorns.

BOTTOM, FACING PAGE
Jon Brittenum dove for the winning touchdown: Arkansas 27, Texas 24.

▶ FACING PAGE

The Razorbacks were favored to beat LSU and win their second straight national title.

to the outside. Brittenum feathered a perfect lob over two defenders. Crockett leaped for the catch and fell. He came to rest a few feet inbounds and inches from the goal line.

A flag had been thrown and the crowd fell silent, until the officials signaled a defensive penalty, which Arkansas declined.

With ninety-two seconds left, Brittenum punched into the end zone on a sneak. Razorback Stadium erupted. "We're number one in the nation right now," Brittenum yelled as he returned to the bench. (When the Associated Press poll was released two days later, the Hogs were number one.)

On the first play after the ensuing kickoff, Mike Jordan (playing the monster-man position in Arkansas' secondary) sealed victory with an interception. Brittenum ran out the clock, and the Hogs had beaten Texas for the second straight year, prompting spontaneous celebrations far beyond Razorback Stadium.

Not quite two-hundred miles away, normally thriving downtown Little Rock had been a ghost town all afternoon. After the final gun, traffic jammed the streets. Crowds honked their horns, screamed "We're number one" and, of course, called the Hogs. Students and fans celebrated late into the night in Fayetteville, as well.

"People said the entire state would be in orbit if we won," Broyles told re-

porters after the game. "I'm not sure we're not all in orbit now."

Royal proclaimed it Arkansas' best team. "They're outstanding on offense and defense. They have good passing and good running. They do everything well, everything a great team should."

After beating Texas, the Hogs rolled, outscoring their last five regular-season opponents 183–47. And they did it to music. After the Texas game, The Pacers hit big (in Arkansas, anyway) with "Short, Squashed Texan." That wasn't all. The Rivermen turned Brittenum into "Jon Brittenum, Quarterbackin' Man;" Harry Jones was "Light Hoss Harry." Throughout the proud state, radio stations were flooded with requests.

"It just went crazy," says Bobby Crafford, who sang lead vocal on "Short, Squashed Texan." "They were just blasting it."

The Razorbacks were a hit well beyond the state's borders, as well. Arkansas was the toast of college football. For the first (and so far, only) time, Arkansas moved to number one in the

Associated Press poll. *Sports Illustrated* featured Jones on its cover with the headline: "Arkansas: The New Dynasty."

It seemed Arkansas might just live up to that tag. At the Cotton Bowl, Arkansas was favored by 10 points over a 7-3 LSU team. It wasn't an attractive matchup. The Tigers had been preseason favorites to win the Southeastern Conference; their season had soured because of injuries to key players. During December, the injuries healed. LSU arrived in Dallas at full-strength, with something to prove, and did, winning 14–7.

Ironically, the Hogs were again bitten by the polls.

After the premature decision for Alabama in 1964, the Associated Press decided to wait until after the bowls to conduct its final poll. Had the former policy remained in place, Arkansas might have been declared national champion after finishing the regular season at 10-0; Michigan State and Nebraska were undefeated before the bowls, as well. Instead, after Arkansas' loss in the Cotton Bowl (and Michigan State's loss in the Rose, and Nebraska's in the Orange, to Alabama), Alabama slipped into the number-one slot and its second straight Associated Press and United Press International title.

Was Arkansas a bit complacent?

Slumped in a corner of the locker room, Frank Broyles' countenance reflects one of the most difficult losses in his career.

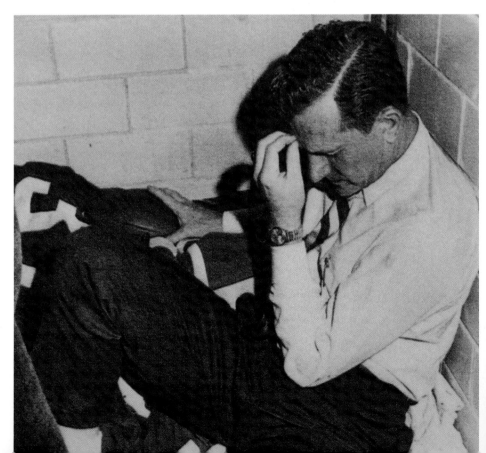

Perhaps. Several seniors had been drafted by professional football teams. Top assistant Jim Mackenzie had finally landed a head-coaching job; Barry Switzer was going with him to Oklahoma. Even so, the Hogs point to a more tangible issue.

Late in the second quarter, as Arkansas was driving for what would have been the go-ahead score, Brittenum suffered a separated shoulder. Though he returned, the arm numbed by powerful painkillers, he wasn't effective.

"It was courageous for him to even be out there," Lindsey says.

Two plays after Brittenum's injury, Arkansas fumbled, and LSU recovered at the Tigers' 34. The Hogs had lost just seven fumbles all season. Still, LSU wasn't able to do much in the second half. And with 2:35 left, the Hogs had one last chance.

As it turned out, there wasn't enough time. Arkansas moved 65 yards in nine plays. But the final play of the winning streak was a Brittenum-to-Crockett completion. Trying to get to the end zone, Crockett raced toward the middle of the field instead of the sidelines. He was brought down at the 24; the clock ran out before Arkansas could get off another play.

LSU 14, Arkansas 7. It was hard to believe, and harder to swallow.

"We should have beat LSU that day," Lindsey says. "We were better than LSU."

"We were the equal of LSU and we probably could have played better," Broyles says. "If I had been in the press box, I'd have jumped out and ended it all right there. It's about as blue as I've been in coaching."

Players felt the same way. Lindsey has made a fortune in real estate. He's a member of Arkansas' board of trustees. And he's remembered by most for his many highlight-reel moments. But he cannot shake the memories of his final game.

"I was crushed," Lindsey says. "I feel like I could have done a lot more. I really do, right this minute. You know in your own mind we could have done more."

With the healing benefit of time, Broyles fully understands how special 1964 and 1965 were, and what those seasons meant to Arkansas football. "For us to win twenty-two in a row, we were respected to a degree that most people—our neighbors and all—didn't think we could reach," he says forty years after the fact. "It was a special time for us."

Yet, to this day, Broyles recalls the loss to LSU as one of the two biggest disappointments in his coaching career.

The other came four years later.

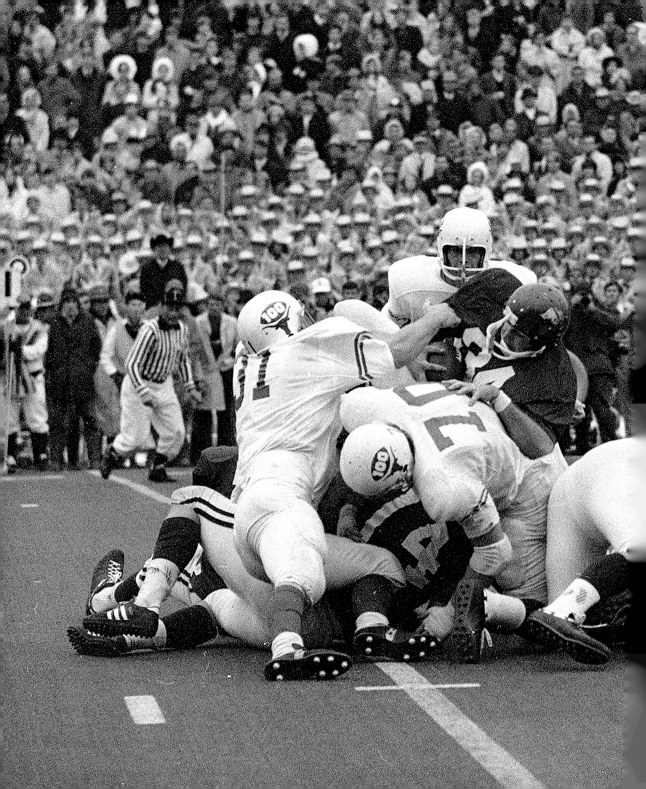

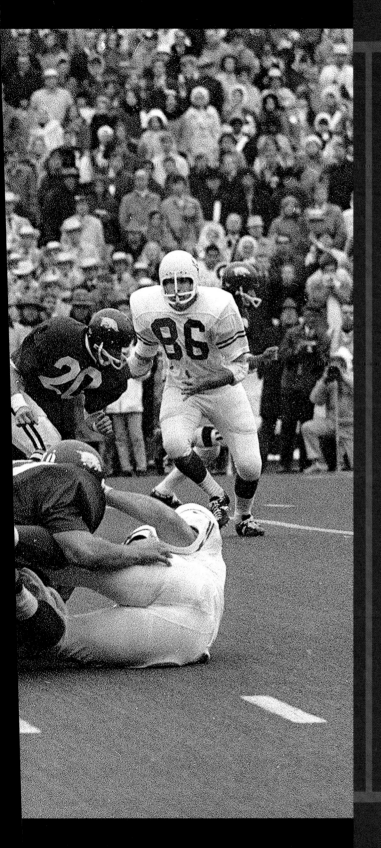

4

Pigskins
and Presidents

O NE QUARTER. Three plays.
In the end, that's what everything came down to. Together, fifteen minutes and three moments
combined to produce the most
heartbreaking loss in Arkansas
history—and that might be the
state's history, not just the football
program's.

▲ PREVIOUS PAGE
Arkansas fullback
Bruce Maxwell (no. 34)
finds himself in a pileup.
As the nation watched,
the Hogs and 'Horns
clashed in a classic.

The Big Shootout of December 6, 1969, is a game Arkansans would love to forget, but cannot help but relive. Texas 15, Arkansas 14 is burned indelibly into the Hogs' collective memory because, in a few heartbeats, what might have been their greatest triumph became their most bitter defeat.

To this day, Frank Broyles has not watched the game film. Should he pick up this book, he won't read this chapter.

"I wouldn't know why I would want to," he says.

In the final regular-season game of college football's one hundredth season, the Hogs and 'Horns played a made-for-TV matchup that lived up to its considerable billing. A president (and a future president) attended. Billy Graham gave the invocation. A national television audience watched, transfixed, as number one and number two battled for the national championship.

It's perhaps hard now, in the days of the Internet and 'round-the-clock cable sports coverage, in an age in which a multitude of college football games blast into living rooms each week, an era in which even humdrum midseason games are hyped into *best ever* status, to understand just how big was the Big Shootout.

Never before had unbeaten number one met unbeaten number two in the season finale, certainly not on national television.

"It was storybook," says Bruce James, who was a junior defensive end. "I doubt it could ever be duplicated again in college football. It was the end of an era."

Arkansas had not quite regained the status of mid-decade, when it won twenty-two straight games. But a Sugar Bowl win over Georgia to complete the 1968 season led to predictions the Hogs would seriously contend for the 1969 national championship. And by the time they hosted Texas on December 6, 1969, they had won fifteen straight games.

Texas had won eighteen straight. And together, the Hogs and 'Horns had dominated the 1960s. Texas finished the decade 80-18-2; Arkansas was 80-19-1. Only Alabama (85-12-3) had a better record. Arkansas and Texas won or shared eight Southwest Conference titles; Arkansas won one national title, Texas won two (including 1969).

And in the final regular-season game of the decade, the rivals battled in a game worthy of their near-even status.

Texas' win pushed the Longhorns to the national championship (they would win another the next year). It gave Texas bragging rights for the decade, and propelled them into dominance in the early 1970s.

It left the Razorbacks pondering what might have been.

"We had a jillion chances to win it, but didn't," says Terry Don Phillips, a senior defensive tackle that day, and now athletic director at Clemson University.

That made the outcome so much harder for the Hogs and their fans. Second-ranked Arkansas dominated most of the game. The Razorbacks led top-ranked Texas by two touchdowns as the fourth quarter began, but the Longhorns scored twice, helped by improbable long plays, to steal victory.

Bill Burnett was a junior tailback in 1969. Ever afterward, he has rarely gone more than a few days without hearing about the Big Shootout.

"People all over the state of Arkansas have told me they've never gotten over that game," Burnett says. "That they never have been affected by any game like that game. It was just the whole nature of the whole thing. The buildup and everything that was involved. Everybody's at an emotional peak. And other than those two plays, they didn't do anything all day.

"We basically won the game and then to have it just ripped right out from underneath us? If we hadn't even been in the game, it wouldn't have been such a crushing blow. But all of that came together to create such an emotional expectation and then to have it taken away in the last minute, the last few seconds, even."

Which is why Broyles has never reviewed the films.

"I think 99.9 percent of the fans feel like I do," Broyles says. "They don't want to discuss it. . . . It broke my heart."

Yet they understood its importance. Thirty years later, a poll of Arkansas fans ranked the Big Shootout number two all-time in sporting events in Arkansas history, just behind the Arkansas basketball team's 1994 national championship win over Duke. The *Arkansas Democrat-Gazette*'s staff reversed that order, but the point was made. The devastating loss ranked first or second in the state's sports history.

The events that conspired to build the moment began the summer before the 1969 season, when ABC sports publicist Carroll "Beano" Cook and executive Roone Arledge put their heads together, looking for a fitting matchup to televise as a capper for college football's first century. As Cook looked at the schedules of the powerhouses, he determined Arkansas and Texas had the best chance of reaching the end of the season unbeaten.

Arledge called Broyles, catching him between a round of golf in Little Rock and a speaking engagement at a Razorback Club in Lonoke, and made an unprecedented offer: Would the Hogs consider moving their tilt with Texas from its traditional mid-October slot to the first weekend in December? Bud Wilkinson, the former Oklahoma coach turned TV commentator, was also working for newly inaugurated President Richard Nixon. Wilkinson suggested the president might attend such a matchup.

Broyles called Royal, his good friend, and soon enough, the schedule had been altered. Arkansas athletic director John Barnhill offered one disturbing question: "What if," he asked Broyles, "you're only playing for the championship of Washington County?" That didn't happen. Instead, the season played out exactly as if according to a script. Arkansas and Texas rolled unbeaten through nine games. And when Ohio State was upset by archrival Michigan on November 27, Texas moved up one spot to number one in the Associated Press poll; Arkansas moved up to number two. Asked about the matchup, Royal unintentionally

coined its lasting moniker, saying it would be a "big shootout."

Only Penn State (ranked number two in the United Press International coaches' poll) could possibly dispute the legitimacy of the Arkansas-Texas winner's claim upon the number-one spot in the polls heading into the bowl season. Those ABC executives, Royal said, looked "wiser than a tree full of owls."

In the days leading up to the game, a divided nation had plenty of topics to capture its attention.

An investigation was proceeding into allegations of a horrific atrocity that had occurred many months earlier in South Vietnam. In the My Lai Massacre, as it was being called, more than one

hundred Vietnamese villagers—men, women, and children—had been killed during a raid by the U.S. Army in March 1968.

In Los Angeles, a drifter and cult leader named Charles Manson was questioned and then indicted for masterminding the murders of actress Sharon Tate and six others in two bloody nights the previous August.

Closer to home, there were issues, as well. Antiwar protesters planned, and ultimately staged, a peaceful protest on a hill overlooking Razorback Stadium, in full view of President Nixon. A planned protest by black students was canceled after the student government voted that week to cease playing "Dixie" at university events. And male students were concerned or relieved, depending upon their birthday, by the results of the first draft lottery in twenty-seven years; the first three birthdays called were September 14, April 24, and December 30.

Mostly, though, the talk was of the impending football game. In Fayetteville, BEAT TEXAS! banners were stretched across city streets. The Reverend Andrew Hall, pastor of the First Baptist Church, was in the spirit, as well. Four years earlier, Hall's message on the church's marquee had been:

FOOTBALL IS ONLY A GAME

ETERNAL THINGS ARE SPIRITUAL

NEVERTHELESS, BEAT TEXAS!

That message had been given nationwide attention when the Associated Press sent a photograph worldwide. In the weeks leading up to the Big Shootout, Hall received plenty of suggestions for a reprise. From Washington, D.C.: "Take no thought for tomorrow, but beat Texas today." From Missouri: "Love one another, bear one another's burdens, but clobber Texas." From nearby Tulsa: "Do unto Texas before it does unto you."

Hall pondered those, and others. He finally came up with this:

ATTENTION DARRELL ROYAL:

DO NOT CAST YOUR STEERS BEFORE SWINE

As before, the church marquee was photographed and distributed via newswire. Texas coach Darrell Royal was left to wonder aloud to reporters: "I thought the Lord was supposed to be neutral on this kind of thing."

Apparently not in Arkansas. A sign on the First Baptist Church of Dumas had that one answered:

GOD IS NEUTRAL

WE ARE HUMAN

BEAT TEXAS!

Similar sentiments sprouted all over the state, where the days before the game passed at an interminably slow pace. Arkansans could hardly wait for

Saturday, when their Hogs would whip the hated 'Horns and notch Broyles' second national championship. A popular bumper sticker proclaimed 1969 the YEAR OF THE HOG. Another sign read: GO HOGS! BEAT NOTRE DAME!, a reference to the winner's opponent in the Cotton Bowl (the loser's consolation prize was Ole Miss; yet another sign sarcastically wished Texas GOOD LUCK . . . IN THE SUGAR BOWL!).

One Little Rock furniture store ran an advertisement in the newspaper informing customers it would be closed Saturday afternoon, "in order that our employees might render their full support to the Razorback ascension to number one in the nation!" Another ad suggested fans could "relieve the pregame pressure" by enjoying a movie. The selection included *The Battle of Britain, The Wild Bunch,* and *Chitty-Chitty Bang Bang.* Airing on television that night was a Billy Graham crusade in Southern California, tape-delayed, obviously, since Graham already had plans for that day.

Arkansas' press box seated about fifty. More than twice that number requested credentials for the game. Many of the reporters arrived several days early. That didn't include the White House press corps, which arrived just ahead of President Nixon and was seated in folding chairs on the track around the field's perimeter.

"The people who started football

never intended for it to get this important," Broyles told reporters early in the week, though he later backtracked.

However, Arkansas' players and coaches remember the week before the game as being relatively relaxed. The hardest thing, Broyles recalls, had been getting to December unbeaten. Living up to ABC's hope was tougher than dealing with the resulting hype.

"With each game we played, that was in the back of my mind," Broyles remembers. "We were trying to fulfill the confidence that ABC had shown in the Razorback program. It wasn't surprising they had that for Texas, but for them to have that [confidence] in us was a compliment that we wanted to live up to."

Players felt much the same way.

"It was, 'Let's get to that game undefeated,'" says James, who would be an All-American at defensive end a year later. "The pressure was to win each week, more so than playing Texas at the end."

And so the Big Shootout, James said, felt like a "gigantic reward."

Even so, they felt the buzz building all week. How could they not? In Austin, twenty-five thousand fans attended a pep rally. In Fayetteville, the number was five thousand. A few days before the game, Arkansas quarterback Bill Montgomery tried to explain the situation by misquoting slightly a story from the cartoon strip *Peanuts.*

"Peanuts [*sic*] is telling Charlie

▲ ABOVE
Bill Burnett blossomed into a star, helping the Hogs rocket to number two in the nation.

▶ RIGHT
Burnett receives congratulations from teammates. Most of the season was a celebration for the Hogs.

Brown about the greatest football game he ever saw," Montgomery told the *Arkansas Gazette*. "He describes the seventy-yard run that won it, the scoreboard lighting up, the thousands of fans rushing on the field, and the players carrying the coach off and the celebrations.

"And Charlie Brown said, 'What'd the other team feel like? [*sic*]'"

President Nixon's visit to Arkansas became official on Tuesday with an announcement from the White House. Secret Service agents arrived in Fayetteville a day later; they set up shop on the fifth floor of a campus dormitory.

Game day dawned with overcast skies, temperatures in the thirties, and a mist, sometimes a drizzle. The weather wasn't nearly the issue it could have been. After the schedule change, and knowing of the possibility of wintry conditions, Arkansas had spent almost $300,000 to install Astroturf—a revolutionary new artificial grass that had gained worldwide fame when it was installed in Houston's cavernous Astrodome four years earlier. Three days before the game, workers shampooed the surface with fire hoses and a brush dragged by a tractor. And although afterward, players said the damp surface was a bit slippery, it was clearly better than rain-soaked mud would have been.

The game was much better than almost anyone could have hoped. Better, in fact, than Arkansas would have liked.

▶ FACING PAGE

Cotton Speyrer (no. 88) was Texas' go-to receiver in 1969, and a big-play threat in an explosive offense.

Texas had been installed by oddsmakers as about a touchdown favorite. It wasn't hard to see why. While both teams were unbeaten, Texas had been more impressive, especially against common opponents.

"We haven't made many people look bad," Broyles told reporters. "Texas has."

Although Arkansas' defense was allowing just 6.8 points per game, best in the nation, Texas' offense appeared unstoppable.

Before the 1968 season, Texas assistant Emory Bellard had tinkered and come up with something the Longhorns called Right-Left. Some called it the Y. Others, the wishbone-T. By 1969, Broyles understood the wishbone's impact on college football.

"This is the greatest scheme to come along in fifteen years," Broyles told reporters in the days leading up to the game. "It will be the rage within two years." As in so many other things, Broyles was correct. For much of the 1970s, it was the rage. Texas used the wishbone to great effect; others copied with similar success. Former Arkansas player and assistant Barry Switzer rode the wishbone to three national championships at Oklahoma.

In 1969, the attack was still a relative novelty, but Broyles understood the danger presented by the triple-option attack. Texas was piling up yards (a 482.8 yard average) and points (44.3).

And yet, Arkansas' defensive staff, led by Charley Coffey, cooked up the perfect scheme.

The coaches altered the Hogs' 4-3 defense (four linemen, three linebackers). Moving monster-man safety Bobby Field up near the line of scrimmage put eight players within a yard or two of the football. Arkansas' defenders would change positions at the last minute, hoping to confuse Texas quarterback James Street and the Longhorns' offensive linemen. And they would try to force plays to the inside.

Others had tried eight-man fronts, and failed. Street and standout receiver Cotton Speyrer could make teams pay for loading up against the run. Heading into the Arkansas game, Texas' first-team offense had scored on twenty-four of its last twenty-eight possessions.

The Longhorns would find the going against the Razorbacks to be much more difficult.

The weather didn't dampen the atmosphere, which was electric. An above-capacity crowd of forty-four thousand jammed into the stadium, arriving early. "It was the first time I ever felt the hair stand up on the back of my neck," Burnett says.

Arkansas kicker Bill McClard, as recounted earlier, believes the fans' hog call knocked the football off the tee before the opening kickoff, which came at twenty minutes after noon.

"It was so loud, it almost felt like

Bill McClard.

the Astroturf was vibrating from the sound, almost like a speaker was turned up too high," McClard says.

As McClard replaced the ball and kicked off, another sound entered. Just then, the presidential fleet of five helicopters touched down on the practice field just south of the stadium. *Air Force One* had landed in Fort Smith; President Nixon and his party had traveled the remaining fifty miles by chopper.

"It was a big, huge sound," remembers Phillips. "That was a big moment, when the helicopters came in."

The fans in the stands were making plenty of noise, as well, and not because of the president's arrival. Texas halfback Ted Koy had fumbled on the game's second play. Field fell on the ball. And Arkansas quickly capitalized.

Montgomery connected with John Rees for 20 yards, though whether he was inbounds was questionable. And Burnett scored from 2 yards out. Six plays in, Arkansas led 7–0.

Just then, President Nixon settled into his 40-yard-line seat on the west side, with a group of politicians including Arkansas governor Winthrop Rockefeller, senators William Fulbright and John L. McClellan, congressman John Paul Hammerschmidt and Texas congressman George H. W. Bush. Also in the party was Heisman Trophy winner Steve Owens. The running back from Oklahoma had been a guest on *Air Force One*.

Though they'd missed the first

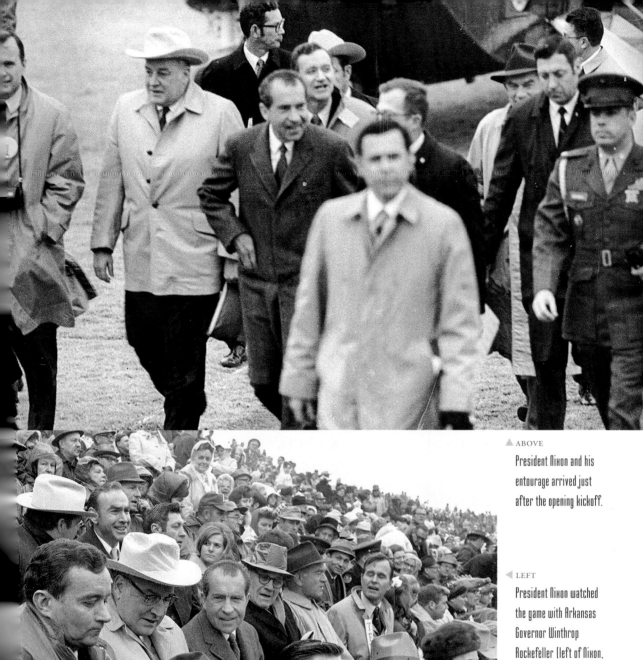

President Nixon and his entourage arrived just after the opening kickoff.

President Nixon watched the game with Arkansas Governor Winthrop Rockefeller (left of Nixon, in hat), and a future president: Texas congressman George H. W. Bush (three seats to the right of Nixon). The dignitaries had seats near the 40-yard line.

Chuck Dicus had 9 catches for 146 yards and a touchdown; another scoring catch was called back by penalty.

touchdown, or seen it while on the move toward their seats, the guests watched as a classic unfolded. Years later, players remember every play. And they remember how every play was played.

"I remember how brutal the hitting was," James says. "How literally the two teams went after each other. Every play was at full speed. No one was taking a play off on either side. It was two heavyweight championship boxers, just slugging it out.

"It was a sixty-minute ballgame. And everybody left everything they had on that football field."

Mike Boschetti, who was a junior linebacker, remembers it this way: "Usually, you get out there and the

pregame butterflies go away. But for some reason in that game, the butterflies never left me."

Looking back, the Hogs might wish it had been a forty-five-minute ballgame. Because midway through the third quarter, Montgomery threw to Chuck Dicus, the Hogs' All-American receiver, for a 29-yard touchdown that made it 14–0. And it might have been more. In the first half, Montgomery had connected with Dicus for an apparent 26-yard touchdown pass. Dicus had been wide open when, reading man-to-man coverage, Montgomery changed the play from a run to a pass before the snap. Rees hadn't heard the audible; believing the play was a run, he blocked the cornerback. Although the block occurred far from the action and had no effect on the play, Rees was flagged; the touchdown was erased.

As the third quarter ended, however, Arkansas held a two-touchdown lead. The Hogs appeared well on their way to their biggest victory.

Arkansas' defensive scheme, which amounted to six linemen, two linebackers, and three defensive backs, had baffled the Longhorns. Through three quarters, Texas' deepest penetration was the Arkansas 31. Texas had not managed a running play of more than 8 yards. Twenty-two running plays went for 2 yards or less, and when Street went to the air, Arkansas' defensive backs were waiting. Twice, they intercepted the 'Horns quarterback. The Hogs also pounced on four Texas fumbles.

As the fourth quarter began, Texas faced second-and-9 from the Arkansas 42. Street dropped back to pass, looking for tight end Randy Peschel. Feeling pressure, he scrambled.

Terry Don Phillips had a shot. When Street left the pocket, Phillips' assignment was to turn the quarterback toward the inside, where other defenders waited. Instead? Phillips had grown up with Street in Longview, Texas. He knew Street as a gritty competitor. And he wanted to make the tackle.

"I thought I could beat the blocker," Phillips says. "I'm trying to make the play on James. I could have

Cliff Powell.

feathered it and turned him back inside. I didn't beat the blocker, so he was able to turn it upfield and make the play."

Near the 35, All-American linebacker Cliff Powell met Street and delivered a big blow—with one problem.

"I hit him and I knocked him back about two or three or maybe four yards," Powell says. "But I didn't wrap up. He regained his balance and he was gone."

With some help. As Powell fell, he knocked down James, the defensive end, who thought he was going to make the tackle. Had he avoided Powell, James says, "there wouldn't have been a scoring run."

But as James watched helplessly, Street raced into the secondary. And it was a footrace.

At the snap, Boschetti had read pass and floated into short zone coverage, watching Texas halfback Jim Bertelsen. When the play broke down and Street took off, Boschetti took off after him. With an angle, Boschetti thought he was gaining. He also realized a Longhorn—Bertelsen—was coming up behind him.

"He got me on my right heel," Boschetti says.

For years afterward, Boschetti

Linebacker Mike Boschetti believes he was clipped on James Street's touchdown run.

showed films of the play, pointing to the clip by Bertelsen. Hogs assistant coach Harold Horton likes to kid Boschetti that he was too slow and wouldn't have caught Street.

"I really think there was a good chance I could have," he says.

The clip wasn't called, and Boschetti went down. And Street raced into the end zone, breathing life into the Longhorns.

Perhaps mindful of the 1964 game, Royal went for a two-point conversion after the touchdown. On the bus ride from Rogers to Razorback Stadium that morning, Royal had told Street if and when they tried for two, they would run a counteroption.

Street faked a handoff to the fullback and spun left. Powell charged through a gap. Slowed for a fraction of a second by a guard, he still hit Street at the 1. But the quarterback fell into the end zone, pulling the Longhorns within 14–8.

"I felt like if I'd got there a half-second sooner, he wouldn't have made

it," Powell says. "Or if I'd held on better."

Still, it appeared Arkansas would hold on to victory. After the kickoff, the Hogs moved smartly downfield, deep into Texas territory. Along the way, Montgomery, Dicus, and Rees riddled the Longhorns' secondary. Montgomery hit Dicus for 20, then 21 yards, and Rees for 13. Dicus would finish the game with 9 catches for 146 yards. A pass interference penalty gave the Hogs a first down at the 9.

Two plays later, it was third-and-goal from the 7. And here, Broyles and his offensive coaches arrived at a decision they would never forget, and would forever have second-guessed. A field goal would push Arkansas up 17–8, probably enough to win with little more than ten minutes left to play. Maybe a running play toward the middle of the field, which would set up a better angle for kicker Bill McClard?

Arkansas decided for something more. Instead of handing off, Montgomery rolled left, looking to pass.

Statistically, with this team and this quarterback, it didn't appear to be all that risky. Montgomery and backup quarterback John Eichler entered the game with an impressive streak. They had combined to throw 172 consecutive passes without an interception over a span of six games.

Before making the call, Broyles and offensive assistant Richard Williamson had quickly discussed their options.

"Dicus was convinced he could get behind and outside their cornerback," Broyles says. And there was one other possible factor. Although Broyles says he didn't make the decision for this reason, he remembered a bad snap on a field goal try during a previous game.

"I finally made the call: Roll out and let Dicus see if we could get the touchdown," Broyles says. "And he was open."

Dicus had found daylight as he cut toward the sideline. But Montgomery's pass was a tad underthrown.

"I hung the ball too much on the side," Montgomery said. "The halfback was very quick. It was a great call, and a great play. I just threw it badly."

"He was so wide open, [Montgomery] just aimed it," Broyles says.

Cornerback Danny Lester cut in front, stole the ball, and raced upfield to the Texas 20. The Longhorns moved to Arkansas' 38 before defensive tackle Dick Bumpas forced a Street fumble that was recovered by defensive end Gordon McNulty at the Arkansas 42. But Arkansas couldn't manage a first down, and was forced to punt.

With 5:51 left, Texas took over at its 36. Three plays later, it was fourth-and-3 from the 43. Texas called timeout. And Royal called "Right 53 Veer Pass."

It was enough of a surprise that Street double-checked. Royal, after all, was known for his conservative nature.

Coaches' confidence in the steady Bill Montgomery (no. 10) was a factor in their decision to eschew a fourth-quarter field goal that might have won the game. Instead, they tried for a touchdown. Montgomery was intercepted, preserving Texas' chances for victory.

But Royal sensed it was now or never for the 'Horns. Texas' wishbone wasn't built for speedy drives. And he wasn't sure his team could drive on Arkansas, anyway. Not counting Street's touchdown run, the Longhorns' longest drives had been 51 and 36 yards.

"We couldn't move the ball all day," Royal remembers. "Their defense confused us, and we hadn't had a drive. We never did drive the ball. To grind it out, I didn't feel there was enough time left on the clock. And I didn't feel like we could grind it out, because they had us confused defensively.

"I just felt it was all or nothing."

Thus Royal eschewed a run, which might have gained the 3 necessary yards but would have left Texas with more than 50 yards to go and not enough time to get there in small chunks. Peschel, not the speedy Cotton Speyrer, would be the only receiver on the all-or-nothing pass, with the option to cut the route short or to go deep.

The Arkansas defense lined up to play the run. The play call was "80 Short." At the snap, the defensive line charged ahead, trying to get underneath the blockers. Peschel faked a block, then bolted downfield. Cornerback Jerry Moore started forward, then recovered and raced step for step with Peschel. Safety Dennis Berner came over quickly. As Street's spiral descended, both Razorbacks reached for the ball.

"Our safety and our halfback were there, and [Peschel] came down with it," says Broyles, who calls the play "a stroke of genius."

"If they tried to throw that pass ten times, that's the only time they're gonna complete it," Phillips remembers. "We had good coverage. We had the guy covered."

Peschel agreed. He said after the game the Longhorns had tried the pass play three or four times earlier in the season. "That's the first time it's been complete," he said.

Peschel and the defenders tumbled to earth at the Arkansas 13. From there, Koy burst to the 2. And Bertelsen scored on the next play. Happy Feller's kick pushed Texas up 15–14 with 3:58 left.

The Hogs weren't finished, though. Behind Montgomery's passing, Arkansas moved from its 20 to the Texas 38. A few more yards would have them in field-goal range for McClard—who a year later would hit college football's first 60-yarder. But with 1:13 remaining, Montgomery's pass was intercepted by Texas cornerback Tom Campbell, who outwrestled Rees for the football near the 20-yard line.

"It was probably the greatest moment of my life," Campbell said moments later.

And maybe the worst of the Hogs' lives. Texas needed two plays to drain the final seconds from the clock, and the remaining spirit from the Hogs and their fans.

When Broyles and Royal met at midfield for a postgame handshake, the Arkansas coach was stoic. But Royal understood the depth of emotion felt by his friend—and, by extension, Arkansas' players and fans—because of the tears being shed by Broyles' eleven-year-old twin daughters, Betsy and Linda. Royal looked down, then embraced one of the girls.

"They were sobbing," Royal says. "You can't help but have a feeling about it. It took away a lot of happiness there for a short period."

The twins weren't the only ones crying. Inside the locker room, players and coaches sniffled. Some, like Boschetti, just plain sobbed.

"I sat over in the corner and just cried, really," he says. "President Nixon came in and a lot of the guys got up and went over and shook his hand. I could care less."

President Nixon had first visited Texas' victorious locker room and presented a plaque with the presidential seal and these words: "To the number-one college football team in college football's one-hundredth year."

Then, Nixon hurried to the home locker room, where hc found a very different atmosphere.

"I am honored to be here with a great team," Nixon told the Razorbacks. "I know how you feel, because in my political life I've lost some close ones and I have won some close ones. But I want you to know that Arkansas was magnificent throughout the game. Texas, in order to win, had to beat a great team."

Nixon greeted several players; television viewers watched as he told Dicus: "You remind me of [Lance] Alworth." And to Montgomery: "You have a lot of poise under fire."

Montgomery's reply: "Thank you for coming by, sir. It's quite an honor."

Royal told reporters, "Arkansas is as good a football team as we are, and maybe they played a little better most of today than we did."

Near game's end, a steady rain had finally settled in over the Ozarks. But it was nothing compared to the emotional gloom that lingered long over the entire state.

Consider this testimony from fan Fred Whistle of Paradise Valley, Arizona, as published in the *Arkansas Democrat-Gazette* in September 2003, not quite thirty-four years after the loss: "A part of me died that day. And it was a part that never had a chance to grow up. I was only twelve. . . . If I could only change one thing in my life, Randy Peschel would drop the ball."

And there was this, from George Burks of Cape Girardeau, Missouri: "To lose a game with those kinds of stakes on the line took the heart and soul out of an entire state for a long, long time. . . . To put so much into a simple 'game' sounds silly, but as we all know, it was more than a game that day in [Fayetteville]. It was us against them, good over evil, right against wrong, and it hurts to this day. It will always hurt."

Texas went on to beat Notre Dame in the Cotton Bowl, 21–17, and claimed the national championship (the 'Horns would win another in 1970) the Hogs had believed was theirs.

"We had to beat Notre Dame, but we felt we would have," Powell says. "They were big and slow, and Texas beat 'em pretty handily."

Texas barely won, but the point remained valid. Meanwhile, the Hogs moved on instead to the Sugar Bowl. Their bodies made it to New Orleans—their broken hearts remained somewhere else.

Led by Archie Manning, Ole Miss won, 27–22.

"We were as flat as we could be," Boschetti says. "We were devastated. It was sort of like going through the motions. . . . Granted, Archie Manning was an incredible quarterback, but we were much better than what we played in that game.

"We were just flat. That's all there was to it."

In the intervening years, the sadness has faded for many Razorbacks. During the 2004 season, when Texas played in Fayetteville, the 1969 Hogs hosted their Texas counterparts in a reunion. And their prevailing sentiment was this: It was a privilege to participate in the Big Shootout.

"We played well enough to win a national championship, and you really regret not winning it," Phillips says. "But you balance that off, I guess, with the perspective of age, with having the opportunity to play in a game of that magnitude. I think most of us have gotten to where it's a great thrill to have played in it."

"It was an incredible disappointment for everyone on the team, for everyone in the state," Burnett says. "Yet it was amazing that we were there, that we had the opportunity to play in that game for the national championship, the fact that it was all the things that it was, that everything had come together to make it such a unique game.

"There's never been one like it before or since. So it really is a wonderful thing to be able to be a part of all that."

It was, to be sure, a classic. The game lived up to its considerable billing. Broyles, for one, understands. Although he won't be reading this chapter, and would rather not revisit a bad memory, Broyles understands the Longhorns' late heroics catapulted the game to its status.

"That's the reason it ended up being a big game, a game to remember," Broyles says. "If we'd won it with that other touchdown, it might not have been the game of the century. If you want to look at it from that viewpoint

"I don't."

That is readily apparent. When asked about the Big Shootout, Broyles pauses. A pained look appears. He rubs his forehead as though battling a headache. But if the pain hasn't completely faded from Broyles' memory, he has found room for humor.

That Saturday morning, Billy Graham visited the Broyles' home at 1525 Hope Street in Fayetteville. Though Frank Broyles wasn't there (he was going through pregame preparations with the team), Barbara Broyles hosted brunch for the evangelist and his son, eleven-year-old Ned.

After the fact, the Hogs football coach learned an alarming detail about the visit.

"Our dog bit his son!"

Lady, the Broyles' gentle, white German shepherd, had indeed nipped young Ned. Though the injury wasn't serious, it might have had serious implications for the Razorbacks. Because all these years later, when Broyles tells of the incident, he leans forward conspiratorially: "That's why," he says, "we lost!"

5 ▸

Grand Saturdays

THERE HAVE BEEN plenty of glorious victories, of course. The Big Shootout was not Arkansas' only defining moment. Recall grand Saturdays of 1946 and 1954, of 1960 and 1964 and 1965, when the Razorbacks won championships with stunning upsets or dramatic rallies.

Remember all these, and so many more.

THE 1978 ORANGE BOWL

JANUARY 2, 1978

ARKANSAS 31, OKLAHOMA 6

Remember that stunning rout in 1974 of fifth-ranked Southern Cal, who went on to win a share of the national title. Recall a magical night in Miami, when a wiry, fiery first-year coach turned Oklahoma's championship dreams to dust, and a rainy day when an unranked bunch of Hogs ripped the top-ranked Longhorns. A pinball shootout with Houston in 1989. Clint Stoerner's redemption against Tennessee in 1999. The Y2K Cotton Bowl domination of Texas.

One December afternoon, Lou Holtz burst into his predecessor's office and breathlessly wondered: "If we win this game, will we be national champs? When we beat them by thirty, do you think we'll be number one?"

Ludicrous thoughts, since there was no way it could happen. Mighty Oklahoma loomed in the Orange Bowl. And adversity had already devastated the Razorbacks.

Which meant Holtz had the Sooners right where he wanted 'em. A few days later, Arkansas pulled off one of the biggest upsets ever in a bowl game, routing number-two-ranked Oklahoma 31–6.

The win shot Holtz, Frank Broyles' hand-picked choice as successor, to the top of the coaching profession. And it sent Arkansas fans into joyous celebration unseen since the national championship some thirteen years earlier.

"It was an unbelievable victory that put us right at the top of college football," says Broyles, who had received that unexpected visit from Holtz in the weeks before the game. "It was one of the outstanding coaching performances that I've ever seen."

Broyles had retired at the end of the 1976 season. And Holtz made an immediate impression on his new team. Spring practice of 1977 was long remembered for its intensity; players later wore T-shirts that read: I SURVIVED SPRING OF '77. Holtz's approach helped mold a talented core of Broyles' recruits into one of the best teams in Arkansas history. The Hogs' only loss was to Texas, by 13–9, and it was just that close (the Longhorns rolled unbeaten and ranked number one into the Cotton Bowl).

Still, not many gave them much of a chance against Barry Switzer's Sooners. The former Razorback player and assistant had won national championships in 1974 and 1975, and after Texas' loss to Notre Dame in the Cotton Bowl earlier in the day, the Sooners were in position to win their third title in four years.

It didn't turn out that way. The Razorbacks came to play. "We just got a thorough, thorough whipping," a stunned Switzer told reporters after the game. "I think we might have played the best team in the country tonight."

The shocking victory came after Holtz and Arkansas suspended three players—running backs Ben Cowins and Micheal Forrest and receiver Donny Bobo—for violating his Do-Right

Rule—and lost starting guard Leotis Harris, an All-American, to a knee injury suffered in a scrimmage. Cowins was the Hogs' leading rusher (1,192 yards, with 14 touchdowns), Bobo the leading receiver (22 catches, 454 yards, 5 touchdowns).

The three suspended players had allegedly taken off a girl's clothes in what became known as the "dorm incident." No charges were filed. During a hearing for a lawsuit quickly filed (and quickly dropped) by the three players for reinstatement, Cowins called the incident "a playful act," and said, "We all knew what was going on."

All three players returned the next season; Cowins remains Arkansas' all-time leading rusher (3,570 yards). However, immediately after the suspensions

Lou Holtz's magic helped the Hogs to a stunning Orange Bowl upset of Oklahoma.

were announced, a dozen of Arkansas' black players threatened a boycott. Though it didn't materialize, it was a real possibility. Assistant coaches spent part of their short holiday break calling players to ensure they were planning to report for the trip to Miami.

Given all the turmoil, it was no wonder oddsmakers took the Orange Bowl off the board for a while. When kickoff neared, Oklahoma was favored by as many as eighteen points, but Holtz and the Hogs were confident. The coach had taken the adversity and molded a talented team into a more tightly knit unit.

Looking back, the Hogs say they weren't surprised when they jumped to a 14–0 first-half lead. Ron Calcagni, a junior who had matured into a steady quarterback for Arkansas' split-back veer attack, was told to report to Holtz's office as soon as he returned from Christmas break. Holtz slid a manila folder across his desk. Inside was the game plan.

"Ron, this is how we're gonna win this game. And we're gonna win it big," Calcagni remembers Holtz telling him. The coach, who was notoriously hard on his quarterbacks, chose this moment to begin pumping up Calcagni. "This is how we're gonna do it. You and I are gonna win this ball game." And Holtz showed an opening sequence of play calls; they were mostly quarterback keepers.

"He knew what buttons to push," Calcagni says. "I had a big smile on my face because I knew he was going to rely on me."

Holtz pushed all the right buttons with everyone. Roland Sales, who had been a part-time starter at the other halfback position, stepped in for Cowins and rushed for 205 yards on 22 carries—for twenty years, it remained the Orange Bowl record. Sales scored on runs of 1 and 4 yards. And he set up two other touchdowns with runs of 38 and 35 yards.

"Roland Sales was outstanding," Holtz said after the game. "I'm not surprised he played well. But I'm truly shocked by his performance."

Sales had entered the game with 409 total yards on 69 carries; his previous career high was 71 yards, set earlier that season against Oklahoma State. Complicating matters, the quiet sophomore had spent part of the week before the game battling the flu.

When kickoff was delayed because the Rose Bowl ran long, Holtz told jokes. Several players did, as well. And then Sales stepped forward.

"I haven't been feeling well all week," Sales said.

Calcagni, a bundle of barely restrained adrenaline in a corner, thought: "Uh-oh. This is gonna be the guy in the backfield?" But Sales wasn't finished.

"I'm gonna give my all," he said. "I'm gonna give one hundred percent.

Unheralded sophomore running back Roland Sales ran for 205 yards, then an Orange Bowl record.

Lou Holtz designed a play that took advantage of Oklahoma's defensive tendency to react to offensive linemen's first moves. Arkansas rushed for 315 yards, many up the middle, on the false key tackle run.

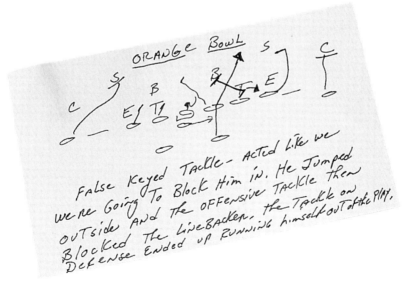

ORANGE BOWL

False Keyed Tackle - Acted Like we we're Going To Block Him in. He Jumped outside And The offensive Tackle then Blocked The Linebacker. the Tackle on Defense Ended up Running himself out of the play.

I'm gonna play my heart out for you guys, because I love you."

Arkansas' coaches devised a way to combat the Sooners' talented defensive front, which keyed on the first moves made by offensive linemen. In a play especially designed to foil the Sooners, Arkansas' tackles were taught to fake to the outside, as though they planned to block the defensive tackles to the inside. Then, when the defensive tackles jumped outside, the offensive tackles surged forward to block a linebacker. "The tackle on defense ended up running himself out of the play," Holtz later wrote, describing the scheme. Much of Sales' yardage came right up the middle, behind his tackles and through the spot vacated by the misreading defensive linemen. And Arkansas rushed for 315 yards.

"It was a great scheme that created some great gaps for their dive backs," Switzer remembers.

The strategic dominance continued. Arkansas' defense befuddled the Sooners' vaunted wishbone attack. Nose guard Reggie Freeman was delegated to contain Oklahoma quarterback Thomas Lott. For much of the game, he moved from his interior position to the outside. Five times, he corralled Lott behind the line of scrimmage. Overall, Freeman finished with 12 tackles.

"I got there a couple of times and Lott didn't know what was going on," Freeman said.

"They played a scheme we were not prepared for," Switzer remembers. "That gave us tremendous problems. And they had tremendous players, Dan Hampton and that crew."

Hampton and William Hampton and Jimmy Walker and Larry Jackson and . . .

"They had a great defensive football team," Switzer agrees.

The Sooners helped the Hogs. Billy Sims, who would win the Heisman Trophy the next season, fumbled on the game's third play—third-and-18 from the Oklahoma 12—and his fumble set up a quick Arkansas score.

After Walker's recovery, Calcagni carried the ball for 8 twisting yards to the 1. On second down, the call came in from the sideline: "Right 34." A handoff to Sales. Touchdown.

Years later, Calcagni discerned layers in Holtz's play call: "I had no idea what he was doing with Roland Sales," Calcagni says. "But he made sure [Sales'] first carry was a touchdown. And Roland Sales broke the Orange Bowl rushing record that night."

Later in the first quarter, Dan Hampton recovered another fumble. Arkansas moved 58 yards for another touchdown. The drive was keyed by Sales' 38-yard burst to the 2; Calcagni scored from there.

"Billy Sims fumbles, two plays later it's seven to nothing. And a little later it's fourteen to nothing," Switzer recalls.

"We never got back into the game from that point on."

Arkansas took the two-touchdown lead into halftime, then tacked on 10 points in the third quarter to lead 24–0. Oklahoma finally scored on the first play of the fourth quarter. But a quick kick—Steve Little slipped into the offensive backfield on third down, pretended to be tying his shoe, and then punted 63 yards—effectively ended the Sooners' chances.

Arkansas' reserves played the final minutes. And yet, third-team running back Barnabas White bolted 20 yards for a touchdown with 1:05 left to set the final margin and kick off a Hog-wild celebration.

Afterward, the Hogs lobbied for the number-one ranking. "I think we deserve it," Sales said. "We proved it." But it wasn't to be. Notre Dame's impressive win over Texas—the only team to have beaten Arkansas in 1977—convinced voters to make the Fighting Irish number one. Arkansas finished ranked number three in both polls, just behind Notre Dame and Alabama.

Afterward, a bumper sticker was briefly popular in Arkansas (and presumably, near the Oklahoma border): CALCAGNI WAS A "LOTT" BETTER. Looking back, Switzer says Arkansas was a lot better than the oddsmakers believed.

"Both of us had identical records, and we'd both lost to the same team, Earl Campbell's Texas, by nearly the same score," Switzer says. "When we looked at film, we knew they had a great defensive football team. Really good."

Adversity? Underdog status? Holtz had 'em right where he wanted 'em.

"A lot said we'd fall apart," Sales said afterward. "But we're probably closer than ever. We were ready to play the game. . . . We knew we were going to win."

Ron Calcagni's first-quarter touchdown was a catalyst in the rout of the Sooners.

NOVEMBER 9, 1946
ARKANSAS 7, RICE 0

There was only one highlight, but John Hoffman's interception return paved the way for so many more in Little Rock. As an overpacked house watched at a high-school stadium, Arkansas' 7–0 upset of fifth-ranked Rice pushed the Razorbacks to their first Cotton Bowl. And it provided the impetus to fulfill coach John Barnhill's vision of a large stadium in Little Rock.

As the veterans streamed home from World War II, many enrolled in colleges around the country. Barnhill, who had guided Tennessee's football team during the war years, was displaced when General Robert Neyland returned from active duty to again head the Volunteers program. So Barnhill—known as "Barnie" to many, if not most—moved on to Arkansas, where he immediately built a championship squad.

That championship squad built a stadium, and from there, the football program. Most seasons since 1906, Arkansas had been playing one game a year at Little Rock High School's ten-thousand-seat stadium. Barnhill understood the value of playing in the centrally located capital city. He believed the Hogs needed more of a presence there in order to build a statewide fan base.

"Barnie knew he had to have a larger stadium in Little Rock if the pro-

John Barnhill believed Little Rock— Little Rock— and the Razorbacks— needed a larger stadium. His Hogs' 7–0 win over Rice in 1946 paved the way for the construction of War Memorial Stadium.

gram was ever going to amount to much," says former *Arkansas Democrat* sports editor Jack Keady. "The Rice game proved it."

After a 3-0-1 start that included a tie with powerhouse Oklahoma A&M (later Oklahoma State), the Hogs dropped consecutive games to Texas and Ole Miss. But they rebounded to beat Texas A&M, setting up a date with Rice in Little Rock at Tiger Stadium (later renamed Quigley Stadium). Rice had beaten Texas and was favored by at least two touchdowns over the un-ranked Razorbacks.

Fans apparently believed. Extra bleachers were brought in. As many as seventeen thousand fans jammed into the high school stadium. "It was fes-tive," says Eugene "Bud" Canada, who was a sophomore end that day. "We had a chance to win the conference and go to the Cotton Bowl, so as many people as could get into the stadium showed up."

On a slick, muddy field, the only touchdown came in the fourth quarter, when Little Rock's own Hoffman re-turned an interception 32 yards.

That the only score came via de-fense probably shouldn't have surprised. Barnhill had built his one-platoon team to stop opponents, with speed being the most prized skill. Clyde "Smack-over" Scott was just one of several play-ers with extraordinary running ability. Arkansas shut out four opponents that

season, including LSU in a scoreless Cotton Bowl tie.

"We didn't beat anybody very much," Scott says, "but we didn't let anybody beat us. It was defense, de-fense, defense." Or, as Barnhill de-scribed the team to the *Arkansas Gazette:* "They'd hit you. When they hit you, you bounced. And they liked to see you bounce."

Arkansas had almost scored earlier in the game, after Steed White blocked a Rice punt, giving the Hogs possession at the Owls' 15-yard line. On fourth-and-goal from the 1, Ken Holland ap-peared to have crossed the goal line, but was hit hard and fumbled. Rice recov-ered; Holland did not. Unconscious, he was carried off the field.

Rice got as close as the Arkansas 10 but, for most of the game, the Owls' vaunted passing attack struggled; re-ceivers slipped and slid in the mud, and quarterback Virgil Eikenberg was inter-cepted four times. The winning inter-ception came with just less than six minutes left.

Hoffman was a superb, speedy line-backer (6-2, 195 pounds) who had grad-uated from Little Rock High School two years earlier. He would go on to play for the Chicago Bears. On this Sat-urday, however, he was an Arkansas sophomore. And he produced the lone highlight.

From his 25, Eikenberg uncorked a wobbly pass over the middle, perhaps in part because of harassment from ends Alton Baldwin and Canada. Hoffman had backed up and was waiting. "The pass was underthrown," he told the *Gazette.*

According to the *Dallas Morning News,* Hoffman "leaped high in the air and speared the ball in an open field." He rumbled downfield toward the front left corner of the end zone, picking up speed as he ran. Despite his above-average size for the times, Hoffman was reputed to run the 100-yard dash in just over ten seconds.

Years later, after Hoffman's death in 1987, the *Arkansas Gazette*'s Charles Allbright quoted a spectator's recollection of the play: "The great John Hoffman had the ball, was running free, thundering toward the south end zone, toward Sixteenth Street. Thundering. Thundering." He got several blocks along the way, with the most crucial being delivered by Baldwin.

Hoffman, by the way, didn't finish his career at Arkansas. After the 1946 season, he returned home to Little Rock and worked in the family brick-laying business. The Chicago Bears drafted Hoffman despite his not having played college football for two years. He played eight years for the Bears.

The touchdown was enough to provide victory and a tie (with Rice) atop the Southwest Conference standings and to send Arkansas to the Cotton Bowl for the first time.

"We beat LSU, zero-zero," says Canada, laughing as he recalled the frigid day in Dallas. It was the only tie in Cotton Bowl history. Arkansas took home the trophy after a coin flip at the postgame banquet.

Long afterward, the win over Rice was hailed as the catalyst for the building of War Memorial Stadium, which opened in time for the 1948 season.

"After the Rice game, people listened to me," Barnhill said years later.

"Without that game, I'm not sure it would have happened when it happened," Scott says. "It kind of got everybody not only thinking about having a stadium, but determined to have a stadium in Little Rock."

OCTOBER 17, 1981
ARKANSAS 42, TEXAS 11

Before the Razorbacks left the locker room, the master motivator had one last pregame instruction: "When the reporters come in here after the game," Lou Holtz said, "You tell 'em: 'This was not an upset.'"

And so, after Arkansas' 42–11 victory over top-ranked Texas, All-American defensive end Billy Ray Smith, Jr., dutifully sounded a note of defiance: "It wasn't an upset. That's the party line." And who would argue?

The blowout victory certainly

wasn't expected. Texas was coming off a 34–14 win over archrival Oklahoma. Arkansas was just two weeks removed from a 28–24 loss to TCU—an upset that broke a twenty-two-year victory streak over the Horned Frogs. But on a rainy afternoon in Fayetteville, forty-four thousand fans, and countless more via ABC's regional telecast, watched the unranked Hogs send the 'Horns to the third-worst defeat ever of a number-one-ranked team.

Four Arkansas starters had been injured in a 26–14 win at Texas Tech the previous week. The Hogs might have still been reeling from the TCU loss, which came after Arkansas held a 24–13 lead with five minutes left. Whatever it was, no one was particularly pleased with the Hogs' performance in Lubbock, the Hogs' third straight road game.

"Coming home to play Texas," Holtz said that week, "is like coming home with lipstick on your collar. There can be complications."

Former Razorback Fred Akers, a Blytheville native, was in his fifth season as Texas' head coach. After a dominating second half against Oklahoma, his Longhorns were thinking national championship, and so were others. Sooners coach Barry Switzer had suggested the Longhorns were too good for any remaining opponent. Holtz had watched the Oklahoma game, which was played in the afternoon, before Arkansas' night game at Tech.

"Texas put on an awesome display in the second half," Holtz said in the days leading up to the Longhorns' visit to Fayetteville. "They are playing as well as any Texas team I've seen, and maybe as well as any team I've seen."

The afternoon kickoff was conducted under a tornado watch, but the Longhorns clearly weren't prepared for the havoc that was to ensue. To a large degree, Texas self-destructed under the weight of three lost fumbles and four interceptions thrown by quarterback Rick McIvor, along with various other mental errors. Arkansas' average starting field position was the Texas 46; Texas' was their own 12.

"It was one of those games where anything that could go wrong, went wrong," remembers Vance Bedford, who started at cornerback for Texas. "You name it, it went wrong. They just embarrassed us."

"It was incredible," Akers said afterward. "I can't explain it. It is simply beyond my comprehension. . . . I never saw so many bad things happen, so many turnovers, so many mistakes by one team in one game."

To onlookers, the stage for the upset might have been set when Smith recovered McIvor's fumble on the Longhorns' first play. The turnover quickly led to Tom Jones' 1-yard sneak for a touchdown.

The Hogs had plenty to do with Texas' disintegration, however. The Razorbacks' defense swarmed McIvor and Texas' running backs all day. And the Hogs believed the offensive tone was set on the game's first play. All week, teammates joked with right guard Steve Korte about his upcoming battle with Kenneth Sims, Texas' All-American defensive tackle (who would become the number-one overall pick in the next NFL draft). Film study had showed Sims manhandling Oklahoma's offensive linemen.

"We teased Steve all week about how Sims was gonna make him a midget," says Marcus Elliott, a true freshman lineman who was out for the season with a broken leg.

On Arkansas' first play, fullback Jessie Clark blasted for 25 yards. He ran right through the hole created when Korte bulled underneath Sims. "Steve just gets under Sims and roots him out of there," Elliott says. "From then on, I think that set the tone for the day. We felt like we could block Sims, and we could beat Texas."

Two more Texas errors gave Arkansas a 15–0 lead after the first quarter. A snap sailed over the Longhorn punter's head and out of the end zone. After another fumble, junior tailback Gary Anderson scored from 8 yards out.

The most important play came in the final seconds of the first half. After Kim Dameron's interception, Arkansas had moved to the Texas 19, but appeared ready to settle for a field goal.

Instead, Jones dropped back and looked right, then threw left, where Anderson had sprinted out of the backfield and gotten past a linebacker. Jones' pass, unleashed an instant before Sims crashed into the quarterback, hit Anderson in stride for a touchdown.

"He put it just where he needed to put it, outside where only I could get it," Anderson says. "That was a good throw by Tom Jones."

And a crushing blow landed on the 'Horns. With twenty seconds left before halftime, Arkansas led 25–3.

Texas never got back into it; the

95

Gary Anderson proved too tough for Texas to handle. His 19-yard touchdown reception just before halftime pushed Arkansas up, 25–3.

Hogs scored touchdowns on their first two third-quarter possessions, stretching the lead to 36 points. As the second half continued, the Razorback Stadium scoreboard flashed: FANTASTIC! And Arkansas' third- and fourth-teamers got into the action.

In the final seconds, as Arkansas led 42–3 and the Longhorns threatened to score in the north end zone (they did, with fifty-five seconds left), fans mobbed the south goal post. "Be sensible," came the public-address announcement. "Clear the field, please. The game's not over." Holtz raced to the end zone and tried to prevent the fans from tearing it down, to no avail.

"The referee said he'd penalize us if we didn't get the people off the field," Holtz told reporters afterward. "So I ran down there to tell 'em we didn't need any more penalties."

And one other thing: "I chided them for their lack of confidence, their thinking that we wouldn't score again."

When it was over and the reporters flooded into the Arkansas dressing room, seeking to understand how the Hogs had upset the 'Horns, the Razorbacks were defiant: "No upset! No upset! No upset at all!" said senior tight end Darryl Mason.

Afterward, fans paraded the goal posts out of the stadium and onto nearby Dickson Street, the entertainment district. And the celebration lasted all night.

"It tore down Dickson Street," Anderson remembers. "You couldn't even walk. You sure couldn't drive nowhere. There were so many people in the street enjoying it."

The victory occurred seventeen years to the day after the Hogs had knocked off another top-ranked Texas team. In 1964, Arkansas went on to win the national championship. The 1981 team had more modest success, finishing 8–4 with a loss to North Carolina in a fog-shrouded Gator Bowl, but no one would ever forget the Hogs' biggest win over Texas.

"It's one of those things you don't want to remember," Bedford says. "If we had beaten Arkansas, we might have been playing for a national championship. Instead, it was a great victory for them."

That it was. But one thing it was not: "They call it an upset," says Anderson. "We don't call it an upset. It was something we were supposed to do. It was great."

OCTOBER 28, 1989
ARKANSAS 45, HOUSTON 39

Andre Ware was the headliner. The record-setting quarterback was on his way to a Heisman Trophy but, one evening in Little Rock, Houston's gunslinger was outdueled by Arkansas' Quinn Grovey.

The Razorbacks' 45–39 win in a pinball game disguised as football came largely because Grovey, who wasn't known as a passer, did a fine impression of one. And years later, he remembers most the sense of urgency the Hogs possessed.

"We knew we had to score every time we touched the football," Grovey says.

Coaches had pressed that imperative home during practices. And the Razorbacks had little problem believing it. Houston's run-and-shoot offense was a rampaging juggernaut. Led by Ware, who would finish the season with 4,669 passing yards and 46 touchdowns, the twelfth-ranked Cougars were blitzkrieging their way to fantastic scores, averaging more than 600 yards a game. A week earlier, they had edged SMU 95-21 and piled up more than 1,000 yards—that is not a typo.

Thirteenth-ranked Arkansas, meanwhile, was coming off a loss to Texas. The Longhorns had upset the Hogs 24–20 in Fayetteville, leading many to write off the Hogs' chances of repeating as Southwest Conference champions. One afternoon that week, the Razorbacks coaches rolled a coffin onto the practice field. "We thought we'd poke a little fun," Arkansas coach Ken Hatfield told the Associated Press. "Everybody said we were dead."

Far from it.

Arkansas piled up 647 yards, one of the best performances in school history, and certainly against a big-time opponent. It was the most yards ever given up by Houston.

Grovey, the overshadowed quarterback who had been recruited to run the wishbone, threw for a career-high 256 yards (11 of 14) and ran for 79 yards. He threw touchdown passes of 65 and 51 yards, both to receiver Derek Russell, and ran for three scores. Fullback Barry Foster had 125 yards rushing; tailback James Rouse added 114.

"They had a super game," Houston coach Jack Pardee said afterward. "We couldn't get them stopped."

Arkansas' touchdown drives were of 77, 69, 78, 81, 76, and 62 yards. The Hogs scored on seven of eleven possessions. And though the drives were mostly achieved on the ground, Grovey made his mark passing.

"All game long, we were on, all eleven guys on the offense," Grovey remembers. "And even though the defense gave up thirty-nine points, they were on. It was just a wild, wild game."

Houston piled up 571 yards, including 352 through the air. Fullback Chuck Weatherspoon had 143 yards rushing, 115 receiving.

The teams' combined total of 1,228 yards ranked second in SWC history. Mostly, Grovey and Ware punched and counterpunched, alternately landing roundhouse haymakers. "You didn't dare go get a hot dog," Hatfield recalls.

"You were liable to miss three scores."

No one expected the shootout. And if anyone had predicted a scorefest, they'd have chosen Ware and Houston as the winners. The first series showed why: Ware lateraled to Kimble Anders, who tossed a 60-yard touchdown pass to Patrick Cooper.

Grovey had an emphatic answer. On the Hogs' third play, he connected with Russell for a 65-yard bomb. And from that point on?

"I felt like Superman," he told reporters afterward. "There wasn't anything I thought I couldn't do."

That was Arkansas' fifth touchdown pass of the season. Ware had thrown five in a quarter against SMU. Houston led 21–17 at halftime and threatened to score again in the third quarter before Ware fumbled when he was hit by Hogs safety Kirk Collins. From there, Grovey moved the Hogs 78 yards for the go-ahead touchdown; Russell's 49-yard run on a reverse was the biggest play.

Although the lead changed hands again when Weatherspoon rumbled 37 yards after a short pass, Grovey struck again, hitting Russell for a 51-yard touchdown on the first play of the fourth quarter.

"Quinn Grovey keeps getting better and better," Hatfield told the Associated Press. "We knew we had to throw the ball against them. He threw the ball extremely well."

Rouse's 3-yard touchdown run with 9:54 left pushed Arkansas up 38–31. And when Houston, finally, had no answer, Grovey put the Cougars away with a 2-yard run.

On its last four possessions, Arkansas scored 4 touchdowns and racked up 317 yards.

"We clicked on everything," Grovey says. "I felt like I was just mentally drained, because I'd spent so much energy. Series in and series out, there was so much pressure, because we believed we had to score."

And they did.

The game wasn't on television because Houston was on probation for NCAA rules violations. Only the fifty-five thousand or so spectators at War Memorial Stadium got to see the highlights. At least one was plenty impressed.

Ware, the pilot of Houston's space-age offense, said of Grovey and the Hogs: "They were fun to watch."

NOVEMBER 13, 1999

ARKANSAS 28, TENNESSEE 24

When it was finally over, when he knelt one last time with the football, then watched the final seconds melt off the clock, Clint Stoerner allowed some emotion to escape. His face flushed. His eyes watered, just a bit. And as Razorback Stadium became Hog Heaven after Arkansas' 28–24 upset of number-three Tennessee, the senior quarterback continued to kneel, sharing a quiet moment of prayer with his girlfriend.

A year earlier, Arkansas had seemed well on its way to an even bigger upset of the Volunteers. Until the fumble. Until Stoerner's personal nightmare, which had played out on national television, and has been replayed countless times since.

This time around, Stoerner's 23-yard toss to Anthony Lucas with 3:44 left had provided the winning touchdown. This time around, he had hung on to the football.

"That's what makes this so sweet," Stoerner told reporters a few minutes later. "You put up with all that, and you hear it and hear it and hear it—so to end it like this is great. It felt good. It felt real good."

In 1998, led by Stoerner, Arkansas shot to a 21–3 first-half lead. Late in the fourth quarter, the Hogs needed to just run out the clock to hang on to a 24–22 victory, which would be their most important in many years.

It wasn't to be. With 1:43 left, Arkansas faced second-and-12 from its 48. Nutt called "Right Deuce Pass Force Sprint." Stoerner would roll left with the option to run or pass—mostly,

Clint Stoerner, a key ingredient in Arkansas' resurgence, gained respect for the way he handled himself after a costly mistake led to a disappointing loss to Tennessee in 1998.

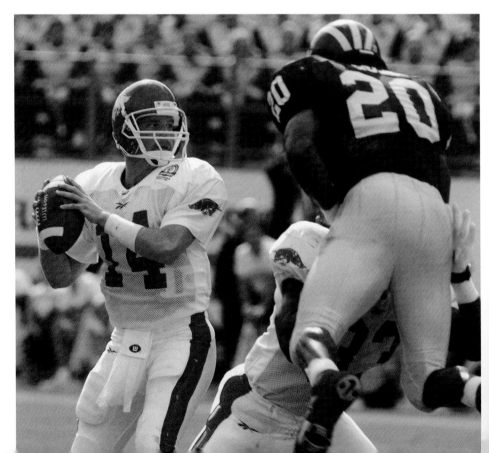

to run. The thinking was simple: Tennessee was stacking the middle against the high-percentage, run-out-the-clock running play. If Stoerner could get free, he'd have room to attain the clinching first down.

Instead, as he started away from center, he stumbled. His foot tangled momentarily with right guard Brandon Burlsworth's.

As Stoerner started to fall, he reached down with one hand—the hand holding the football. When the ball squirted away, Tennessee defensive tackle Billy Ratliff pounced on it at the Arkansas 43.

And 106,000 fans, who had quietly been pondering making an exit, exploded into full-throated sound. "That," says Arkansas offensive lineman Russell Brown, "was the loudest thing I'd ever heard."

Five running plays later, with twenty-eight seconds left, Travis Henry charged into the end zone. The Volunteers charged away with a 28–24 win, and continued on their way to the national championship.

And the Razorbacks? Dazed by the sudden turn of events, they walked off the field and into a locker room that was like a morgue.

"I was numb," Brown says. "I remember thinking, 'Oh, my gosh. This can't happen.'"

When reporters swarmed Stoerner, he took the blame for the loss. He had

passed for 274 yards, including 3 first-half touchdowns. He had been sacked just once.

"None of that matters," Stoerner said afterward. "We had the number-one team in the country beat and I couldn't hang on to the ball. It all boils down to that."

No one blamed Stoerner. In fact, he received much credit for the way he had led the Razorbacks in that game, and for how he handled himself in typically stoic fashion afterward. The next year was a trying one for Stoerner. Sure, he laughed when a friend gave him a football with a handle, but after Tennessee completed an unbeaten run to the national championship, his lowlight popped up on every highlight reel. The week of the rematch in 1999, reminders were everywhere: countless questions from reporters wanting to relive the 1998 game; grateful Tennessee fans wearing national championship T-shirts with a personal message: THANKS CLINT; an SUV with Tennessee flags and the word FUMBLE painted in orange on the windows; and so on.

By the time the Vols rolled into Fayetteville in November, Stoerner was plenty tired of hearing about the fumble.

Tennessee was ranked number three. Coming off a discouraging 38–16 loss at Ole Miss, Arkansas was unranked at 5-3. Trailing 24–14 in the third quarter, it didn't look good, but Stoerner connected with Boo Williams for a

53-yard touchdown, pulling the Hogs within 24–21. Then, after Tennessee moved to the Arkansas 13 and appeared ready to clinch victory, defensive back Ontraia Moss crashed into Vols quarterback Tee Martin, causing a fumble.

The turnover kept the Hogs close until, with 7:08 remaining, Arkansas took possession at its 20. In the huddle, Arkansas center Josh Melton looked at his offensive linemates: "We said, 'We are going to do this.' We got that fire in our eyes," Melton told the *Knoxville News-Sentinel* after the game. "We kept saying, 'We're going to do this. We're going to take it to the house. We don't lose here.'"

Seven plays later, the Hogs faced second down at the Tennessee 23. Sensing opportunity, Stoerner changed the play in the huddle. Faking a handoff, he pump-faked a short pass to freeze the safety, then threw deep to Anthony Lucas, who had cut in front of the cornerback. "I just threw it up there and let Luke go get it," Stoerner said.

With 3:44 left, Arkansas had the lead. This time, the Hogs would not lose it. The irony of the final score—28–24—wasn't lost on Stoerner, or other Razorbacks. It was the same as the year before, but the teams were happily reversed.

"It was déjà vu," Lucas remembers.

Anthony Lucas' touchdown catch gave the Hogs a 28-24 win over Tennessee in 1999— sweet redemption for the Hogs, and especially for Clint Stoerner.

"But in our favor. And we were emotional after the game."

Stoerner had run out the clock, kneeling three times with the football in a vise grip. Then, as students stormed the field—they tore down the goal posts for the first time since the 1981 Texas game—Stoerner remained in the position, praying with his girlfriend, a Razorback cheerleader. Sweet redemption.

"We really deserved this," Stoerner said. "What happened to us last year just wasn't right."

No one would have blamed him if he had substituted "I" for "we."

2000
COTTON BOWL

JANUARY 1, 2000

ARKANSAS 27, TEXAS 6

Y2K had finally arrived, and the lights were still on. Civilization remained intact. And the only worrisome mobs in Dallas were wearing cardinal or burnt orange.

The Hogs and 'Horns were hooking up for the first time in eight years. The irony of their meeting place was not lost on the Razorbacks: Where once they battled Texas to get to the Cotton Bowl, now they were battling the 'Horns *in* the Cotton Bowl.

Arkansas' 27–6 win sent the Razorbacks into that special level of Hog Heaven reserved for the most delightful of victories. Unfortunately, athletic director Frank Broyles, who had coached in so many of the classic matchups between the rivals, didn't get to see the game. He left the stadium after experiencing chest pains. When Broyles arrived at a local hospital, he asked, "Who won the game?" Given the happy news, he wondered: "Was it impressive?"

Was it ever.

"This is the kind of thing you dream about, beating Texas in the Cotton Bowl," Arkansas safety Kenoy Kennedy told the *Arkansas Democrat-Gazette* that day. "This is the best thing that could have happened to us."

With the advent of the Bowl Championship Series, the Cotton Bowl was no longer the ultimate destination for any team, but it remained a favored prize for the Razorbacks. And after an up-and-down regular season (which included an upset of then-number-three Tennessee), 7-4 Arkansas was somewhat of a surprise choice for the bowl, which had evolved to tie-ins with the Big 12's best non-BCS team and the SEC's second-best non-BCS team (and usually from the SEC West).

Hog fans were ecstatic with the destination, and especially with the matchup. They filled perhaps forty-five thousand of the seventy-five thousand seats at the old stadium. And although none of the Razorbacks had ever played

▶ FACING PAGE
Freshman tailback
Cedric Cobbs rushed for
98 yards in Arkansas'
Cotton Bowl win over
Texas. His 30-yard catch
and run for a third-
quarter touchdown gave
the Hogs the lead.
A 37-yard touchdown
run sealed a rout.

Texas, they understood the rivalry's history. It was burned into the collective psyche.

"I was so sick of hearing about the 'Great Shootout,'" senior wide receiver Anthony Lucas said after the game. "We lost that game. . . . We wanted to show the SEC was better than the Big Twelve and that we are the team rising in the new century, not Texas."

Lucas had just one catch in his final game, but it might have been the game's most important play. Midway through the third quarter, it helped unravel a tight contest. The game was tied at 3, but the Hogs faced third-and-12 from their 1-yard line—more precisely, from their 1-inch line.

On first down, quarterback Clint Stoerner had been dropped for a 2-yard loss; the Longhorns thought it was a safety. On second down, tailback Chrys Chukwuma made it out of the end zone by even less. Momentum was clearly shaded orange.

When Nutt called "stick-and-go," Lucas was stunned, but excited. Just twenty-two days after minor knee surgery, the senior was playing in his final game. And here came a crazy gamble.

"We're backed up on our one-inch line, and coach says, 'We're gonna run stick-and-go,'" Lucas recalls. "I'm all for it, because I wanted the ball in my hands. I knew Clint was gonna make a great pass, so I knew I had to catch it."

In a set designed for maximum pass protection, Lucas was the only receiver. He dashed straight ahead several yards, then stopped as though looking for a short pass. But as the cornerback bit—hard—Lucas turned and raced upfield.

Stoerner hit him in stride. Lucas was finally tackled after a 47-yard gain. The Hogs still had half a field to go, but they had jerked momentum away from the Longhorns.

"That took some wind out of our sails," Texas defensive end Cedric Woodard said afterward.

"It turned the whole ballgame," Lucas remembers.

If it didn't, this did. Six plays later, Nutt came up with another perfect call. Before the bowl, coaches had installed a play gleaned from film study of Texas' overtime win over Iowa State, and now was the perfect time. At the snap, Stoerner faked a handoff and rolled left. After avoiding a sack, he looked back to the right, where Cedric Cobbs was all alone. The freshman tailback grabbed the short pass and raced 30 yards for the touchdown, completing a 97-yard drive that actually covered 99 yards and 11 inches.

"That was the critical play of the game," Arkansas receivers coach Fitz Hill said.

Texas tried to answer, the Longhorns quickly reached Arkansas' 1, very nearly the same spot from which Stoerner and Lucas had launched the Hogs. But the Hogs denied the 'Horns

the end zone three times. Texas settled for a field goal.

"That just killed them," Arkansas defensive tackle D. J. Cooper told reporters.

"We knew Texas could not score on us then," Nutt said.

It was Texas' last score. And the Longhorns' last chance for victory.

"If you're on the one-yard line and can't score, you're probably not going to win the game," Texas coach Mack Brown said afterward.

However, if you're on your own 1-inch line, then drive for a score, you probably *are* going to win. After the goal-line stand, Arkansas rolled to 17 more points, turning the reunion into a rout. Michael Jenkins and Cobbs ran for touchdowns of 42 and 37 yards, respectively. Tony Dodson added a field goal.

And the Hogs rang in the new millennium by dominating their old rivals. The Hogs sacked the Texas quarterbacks 8 times. That led to an incredible

statistic: Texas finished the day with minus-27 rushing yards (a school-record low) and 185 total yards, 225 below its average. Arkansas, meanwhile, totaled 385 yards, with 254 coming in the last twenty-four minutes.

"You have to give them all the credit in the world," Brown said. "We just got whipped."

It was Arkansas' first bowl win since 1985, breaking a seven-game losing streak. In the final minutes, with victory secure, Arkansas' forty thousand faithful fans taunted the Longhorns with chants of "SEC! SEC! SEC!" referring to the Razorbacks' decision years earlier to depart the Southwest Conference and join the Southeastern Conference.

With the exception of the 1965 Cotton Bowl and the 1978 Orange Bowl, there may never have been a more satisfying bowl experience.

"To beat Texas in the Cotton Bowl is something our team and fans won't forget," Nutt said.

◀ FACING PAGE
Offensive lineman Bobbie Williams' jubilation was matched by teammates and fans.

6

Nevertheless, Beat Texas

NOTING the growing mania, Reverend Andrew Hall became alarmed. The signs of excessive obsession were everywhere. On the airwaves. In the newspapers. In offices and coffee shops and . . . and . . . well, even in churches.

It seemed everyone was

▲ PREVIOUS PAGE
When the Hogs and
'Horns go nose to nose,
intensity is guaranteed.

▶ FACING PAGE
On campus in Fayetteville,
Texas Week is special.
Pep rallies, then and now,
draw big crowds.

110 HOGS!

consumed by football, by the Razorbacks—by *Texas*.

So when the Reverend Hall, pastor of Fayetteville's First Baptist Church, sat down to construct a message for the church's marquee one day in October 1965, he wanted somehow to bring proper perspective, to emphasize what was truly important. Here's what he came up with:

FOOTBALL IS ONLY A GAME
ETERNAL THINGS ARE SPIRITUAL

Hall thought, Yeah, that's about right. That's the right message. But, how to finish? How to really make people understand?

And then, Hall caved in. The flesh overcame him. He penned this final line:

NEVERTHELESS, BEAT TEXAS!

In the following days, newspapers around the country ran an Associated Press photograph of the marquee.

The Razorbacks' 27–24 win a few days later sent fans into Hog Heaven. Four years later, as the Big Shootout neared, Hall received dozens of unsolicited suggestions for the marquee message, but settled on:

ATTENTION DARRELL ROYAL:
DO NOT CAST YOUR STEERS BEFORE SWINE

Sure, those were huge games; both affected the national championship picture. But Hall's writings serve to illustrate how important the Texas game was—and is, although Texas is no longer a regular opponent—to the Razorbacks. Arkansas football is always important, of course. "But there's a special passion when you play Texas," says Arkansas coach Houston Nutt, who participated in two losses to the Longhorns as a player, but is 2-1 against them as head coach.

Consider this anecdotal evidence: Ronnie Caveness helped Arkansas win the national championship in 1964. The outstanding linebacker was named an All-American. He moved on to professional football. And yet, asked for his fondest football memory, Caveness wasted little time.

"Beating Texas," he said, referring to the Hogs' 14–13 squeaker in Austin in 1964, which propelled them to that national title.

He had good reason, maybe, to count that day as a good memory. In the win, Caveness recorded 25 tackles, 4 shy of the school record (which he had set against Texas a year earlier). Hold on a minute; Caveness wasn't finished with the thought. "I only beat Texas one time. I lost two times."

That year, as so many others, the Texas game meant everything. That year, it propelled Arkansas to the school's only national championship. But even

when the outward stakes weren't as high, the passion to beat Texas—make that *Beat Texas!*—hummed at fever pitch.

Everything has changed, and maybe nothing has.

In 2003, when *Sports Illustrated* commissioned a poll of 422 Arkansans, seeking to divine the state's sporting mindset, the not-so-surprising results showed Texas remained Arkansas' biggest rival.

Perhaps the only real surprise was the percentage; twelve years after the end of regular meetings (football, basketball, and otherwise), the Longhorns polled only 23 percent. Still, that was better than the numbers for Southeastern conference rivals Tennessee (19 percent) and Alabama (16 percent). More telling, under the category "Most Hated Opponent," Texas drew 35 percent.

Any Arkansan would tell you the figures in both categories would be much higher had Arkansas and Texas remained regular competitors.

Beating Texas transcends football. It is state versus state.

Arkansas is the twenty-ninth-largest state by area (53,182 square miles), thirty-third-largest by population (just under 2.7 million, according to the 2000 census). And for years, Arkansans had labored with an inferiority complex, believing their national image was that of shoeless hillbillies. As for Texas? It's five times larger (268,601 square miles), with nearly eight times the population (20.9 million). As the state's own advertisements once proclaimed, "It's a whole other country." Big enough to be one, anyway. And proud enough—perhaps too proud, if you ask Arkansans.

"It's the David and Goliath attitude of Arkansas," says Bruce James, a standout defensive end in the late 1960s and early 1970s. "It was little ol' Arkansas against the big state of Texas. You knew you were playing the best when you played them."

And while it was true that every Southwest Conference school but Arkansas was located in Texas, meaning the Hogs were involved in Texas' intrastate battles every week, they took special satisfaction in beating the Lone Star state's flagship school.

"It's our identity," says Dick Hatfield, a Little Rock attorney who was an offensive lineman in the 1960s, and the deep snapper on the 1964 national championship team, who beat Texas 14–13 in Austin. "We were the stepchild of the Southwest Conference in a lot of ways. And [the University of] Texas pretty well personified the state of Texas."

It was a practical passion, as well. Though other teams rose and fell, Texas was the SWC's perennial powerhouse. "For us to get a piece of the championship, we had to beat Texas," says Harold Horton, who played for

Arkansas in the 1960s, then coached at the school. So, that's how the Razorbacks approached everything.

During the summer before the 1965 season, Texas linebacker Tommy Nobis was quoted as saying the Longhorns had tried to think a little bit about Arkansas every day, the better to avenge a 14–13 loss the previous season. Arkansas won in 1965, anyway. Problem for Nobis and his teammates might have been this: The Hogs *always* thought about Texas.

"It played on my mind all season," says Frank Broyles, who was 5-14 in nineteen games against the Longhorns. "There were seldom many days that we prepared and my thoughts weren't, 'Will this beat Texas?' Because if we beat Texas, we had a chance to be champion. So virtually everything we did was based on how it would work against Texas."

Often, it didn't work as well as the Hogs might have hoped.

Arkansas and Texas first played in 1894, in the Razorbacks' first year of football (and in fact, before they were known as the Razorbacks). The Longhorns won, 54–0. Thirty-nine years later, Arkansas finally notched its first win in the series. Okay, it was only the fifteenth meeting; but it had been a long time coming. And eleven of the Longhorns' fourteen straight wins were by shutout.

Through the years, the Hogs all too often found themselves on the wrong end of the scoreboard. Texas leads the series 55-21—lopsided, sure, and it was the Razorbacks' only losing record to a Southwest Conference opponent. However, in the programs' modern era, which we'll define as beginning when Frank Broyles (1958) and Darrell Royal (1957) became the schools' head coaches, it's 25-14. And even that number doesn't tell the entire story. Of those thirty-nine games, twenty-one came down to seven points, or fewer.

And, in the 1960s, Arkansas-Texas almost always decided the Southwest

Bobby Crockett's catches helped the Hogs edge Texas, 27-24, in 1965.

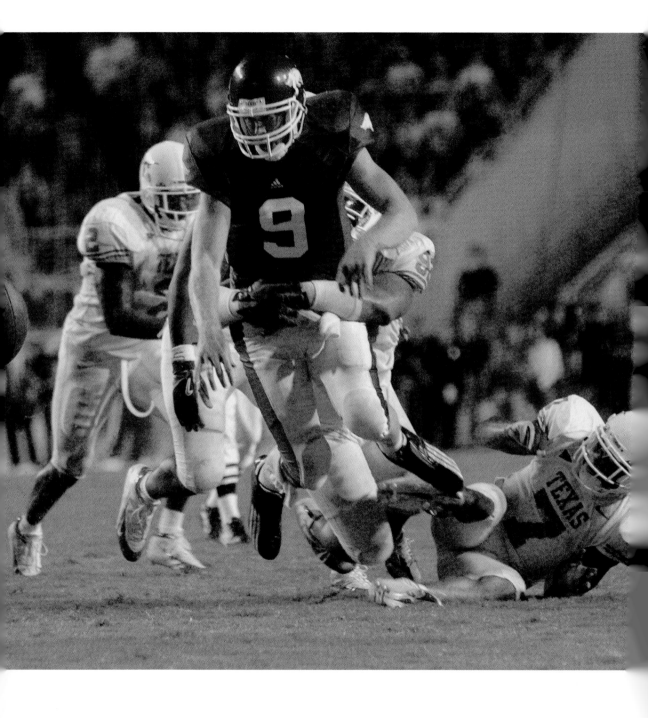

Conference race. Several times, it had serious national-title implications, as well.

"It was a great series," Royal says. "A Texas-Arkansas game"—and here, we'll forgive him for getting the correct order reversed; it's a Texas thing—"was one of those that was, in some years, the biggest game in the country. It was always a big game. For years, it seemed like one or the other was gonna be the conference champs."

Often, the worst part wasn't a loss to Texas, it was how the loss occurred. Start, as everyone must, with the Big Shootout of 1969, when Texas escaped Fayetteville with a 15–14 win, but understand the series featured plenty of other heartbreaking moments.

All too often, the Longhorns found a way to jerk the rug from beneath the Razorbacks, often in the final minutes.

"We'd always get close," says Nutt, a Little Rock native who has lived and died with all those Texas games for as long as he can remember. "But always at the end, Texas would find a way. And you'd feel bad the rest of the weekend. You'd feel sick."

The history of pain might have begun in 1939, when Arkansas lost a 13–7 lead in the final minute in Austin, giving up a 67-yard pass. Arkansas was looking for its fifth straight win over the Longhorns. Instead, Texas ended the Hogs' streak, and won the next eleven meetings.

- In 1959, Broyles' second season, Lance Alworth muffed a punt, leading to a late Texas touchdown in a 13–12 win. Though Arkansas tied for the Southwest Conference championship, the loss prevented the Hogs from reaching the Cotton Bowl.
- In 1962, Texas escaped 7–5 in Austin when, after a 20-play drive, Tommy Ford crashed into the end zone with thirty-six seconds left. The Hogs pointed to the loss as the only thing that kept them from winning the national championship.
- In 1977, after replacing the retired Broyles, Lou Holtz led Arkansas to a magical season. The only blemish was a 13–9 loss to the Longhorns. Typically, a late touchdown was the difference.
- In 1980, the Longhorns pulled an upset (unusual, since Texas was usually the favorite) of sixth-ranked Arkansas, winning 23–17.
- In 1987, Texas stole a 16–14 victory on the last play. Arkansas' top two quarterbacks were injured; with the lead, the Hogs tried to grind out the win. Instead, an 18-yard pass from Bret Stafford somehow found Tony Jones among three defenders in the front of the end zone, stunning the Hogs and a capacity crowd in Little Rock.

All those losses, and others that weren't as close, made the wins even more special. In 1960, Mickey Cissell's

◀ FACING PAGE
This fumble by quarterback Matt Jones in 2004 was one of many heartbreaks the Hogs have suffered against the 'Horns.

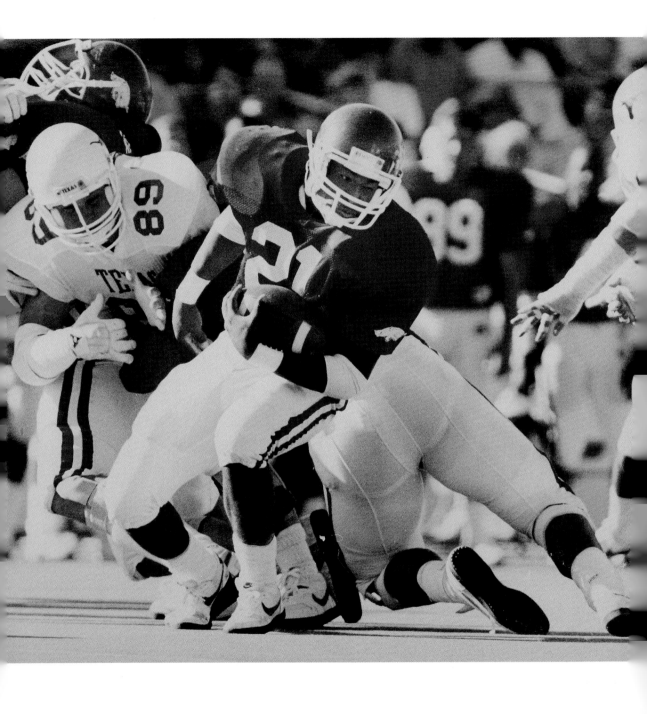

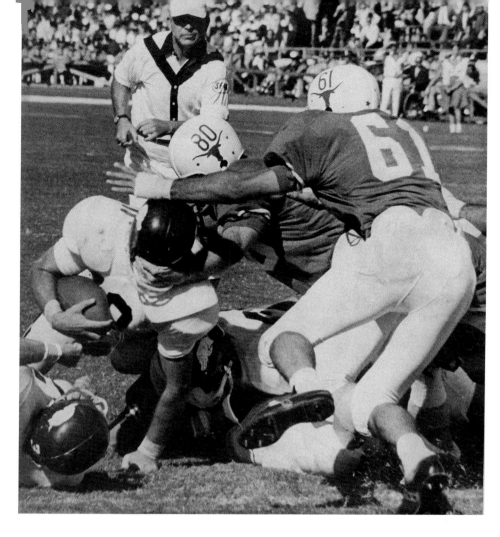

A 12–7 win over Texas in 1966 was Arkansas' third straight over the Longhorns.

late field goal propelled Arkansas to a win in Austin, and on to the SWC championship. In 1964, as noted earlier, Arkansas went on to win the conference and national titles. A year later, in Fayetteville, perhaps inspired by First Baptist's marquee, the Hogs rallied from a late deficit to beat the 'Horns, extending a winning streak that would reach twenty-two games. In 1966, the Hogs won again, by 12–7. In 1971, Joe Ferguson passed Arkansas to a 31–7 win

in the rain in Little Rock. In 1981, Lou Holtz's under-Hogs pulled off a stunning upset of number-one ranked Texas by 42–11.

Former Arkansas linebacker Cliff Powell recorded 24 tackles in the Big Shootout, but wishes he'd made one more: He had a clean shot at James Street on the quarterback's 42-yard touchdown run, which gave the Long-horns hope.

Still, Powell, a lifelong Hogs fan

◀ FACING PAGE

The Hogs found little room to run in 1987, then lost on the last play.

who grew up in Eudora, in the Delta near the Louisiana border, has a special Texas memory. As a junior in high school, Powell traveled with his father to Austin in 1964. They watched Kenny Hatfield bolt up the sidelines with that punt return, Freddy Marshall connect with Bobby Crockett for the eventual winning touchdown, and Jimmy Finch's defensive pressure force Texas' two-point conversion pass to fall short, preserving the Hogs' 14–13 win.

"I think that's the most excited I ever got at a game in my life, and that includes the ones I played in, anything," Powell says. "I was overjoyed."

It's quite possible a win in the Big Shootout would have displaced that

1964 memory, but the point remains. And Powell wasn't alone. Every Arkansas win over Texas, whatever the outward implications, sets off spontaneous celebrations across the small, but fiercely proud, state.

"You remember just what it did for your swagger, and how good it made you feel to beat 'em," says Merv Johnson, the former assistant coach under Broyles. "It hurts to lose to 'em, and yet they've got every advantage a college program could want. When you do beat 'em, it's a great, great feeling of accomplishment."

To really understand, consider two games. Neither meant much on a national scale. Conference and national ti-

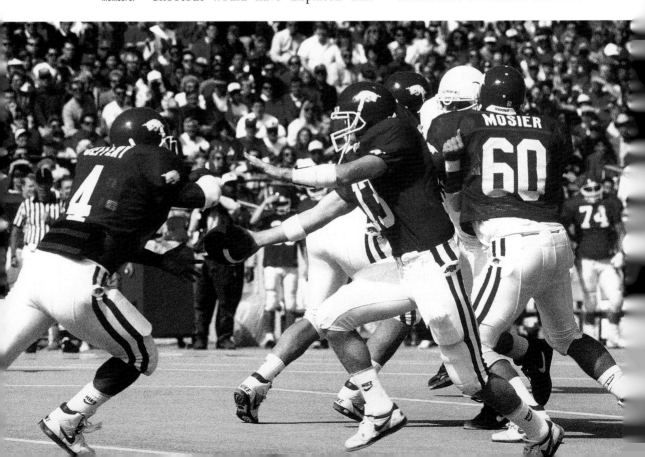

Jason Allen hands off to Tony Jeffery in 1991. A 14-13 win gave the Hogs a happy sendoff in the rivals' last meeting as Southwest Conference members.

tles did not hinge on their outcome. State pride? As always and, in these instances, perhaps more than usual.

October 1991. Arkansas was on its way out of the Southwest Conference, in its final season before moving to the Southeastern Conference. When the Razorbacks edged Texas 14–13, the crowd of 55,618 at Little Rock's War Memorial Stadium remained in the stands, unwilling to go home. The fans understood the meaning: It was the last scheduled game between the rivals; the series as anyone had ever known it was finished.

And so, ten minutes after the final gun, Arkansas coach Jack Crowe sent the Razorbacks back onto the field. According to the *Arkansas Democrat-Gazette,* Crowe told the team: "There is a lot of frustration in you. There is a lot of frustration in our fans. Go back out to the fifty-yard line and thank them."

The Hogs bolted crazily from the locker room, raced to midfield, and saluted the fans. And joined the revelry that ensues any time Arkansas beats Texas.

"It was a great feeling to win," Arkansas center Mark Henry told the *Democrat-Gazette.* "It's been a great rivalry. But who laughs last, laughs best. That's best."

That day, the newspaper took an informal poll of fan reaction to the end of the series: "It's the end of an era that goes back ninety years," said Jeff Hart

of Little Rock. "It's one of those games the whole country looks forward to seeing. I won't miss the [Texas A&M] Aggies, but I sure will miss Texas. They're a class act."

The Associated Press reported this yell from a corner of the Arkansas locker room, purportedly from an assistant coach: "Ain't no rematch! Best thing of all, ain't gonna be no rematch."

Except, of course, there have been rematches. Fast forward to January 2000.

Eight seasons after the end of the series, the old rivals met again. Instead of playing for the right to go to the Cotton Bowl, they were playing in the Cotton Bowl. Arkansas had adjusted to life in the SEC. Texas had moved on to the Big 12.

Perhaps forty thousand Hog fans made the journey to Dallas. They roared as Arkansas raced away in the fourth quarter to a 27–6 victory. Texas finished with minus-27 yards rushing, a record low for Arkansas' defense and Texas' offense.

And in the final minutes, as cardinal-clad fans celebrated, Nutt—who had played for Arkansas against Texas in the 1970s—was caught on camera doing what came naturally. Looking into the stands at the Razorbacks, Nutt inverted Texas' trademark hook 'em hand signal. With both hands.

"It was not like I was trying to rub

it in their face, but I have forty thousand people still in the stands," says Nutt, recalling the euphoric moment. "And they're all doing this! Well, we were raised, we were taught to do this."

Nutt pauses, then laughs.

"I just didn't want to do it on national TV."

No, of course not. Head football coaches are supposed to be reserved, stoic, above the fray (though the ever enthusiastic Nutt doesn't often fit into that mold). But how could anyone who understood the unique environment in which he was raised have objected? Really, the gestures only served to fur-

ther endear Nutt to Hogs fans. He was simply sharing their sentiments.

The Texas mania again swept the state during September 2003 and a year later, when the Hogs and 'Horns hooked up for two nonconference football games. Texas coach Mack Brown agreed to a temporary resumption of the series in part to honor former coaches Royal and Broyles, and the history and tradition between the two football programs. Perhaps Brown and the modern-day Longhorns didn't fully understand what the game would mean to the Razorbacks until it was too late.

The Hogs rolled the 'Horns, win-

◄ FACING PAGE
Arkansas' defense sacked Texas quarterbacks eight times in the 2000 Cotton Bowl.

In the delirium after Arkansas' 38-28 win over Texas in 2003, De'Arrius Howard expresses every Hog's sentiment. In time-honored tradition, he inverts the Longhorns' traditional "Hook 'em" hand sign.

ning 38–28, and it wasn't nearly that close.

Afterward, Nutt grabbed someone's helmet and held it aloft toward the four thousand or so Razorback fans who had journeyed to Texas. With his hands thus occupied, he wasn't able to flash the inverted hook 'em. Hey, whatever it takes to conquer an addiction.

"It's a special feeling to beat Texas," Nutt said a few minutes later. "It's an awesome feeling. It's up there."

Still, even Nutt said he was surprised by how immediately the fans' intense passion returned. "I knew it was gonna be big," he says. "But immediately, it was as if we'd never left [the Southwest Conference]."

The fans' desire and the Hogs' ferocity that day certainly didn't surprise Royal, who was on hand for the game.

"I don't ever recall Arkansas coming into a game sleepy-headed against Texas," he says.

Before the game, Brown and others familiar with the rivalry had tried to explain that reality to the Longhorns. It wasn't until the final gun had sounded and the Razorbacks were celebrating as though they had won the national title that the Longhorns finally figured out how seriously the Hogs took the game.

"I didn't understand the rivalry before," Texas defensive tackle Rod Wright told the *Austin American-Statesman.*

To be fair, even when the teams played every year, Arkansans' passion wasn't reciprocated, at least not consistently.

"Texas never ever saw Arkansas the same way we saw them," says Bill Burnett, who starred at tailback for Arkansas in 1969 and 1970, when Texas won the Big Shootout and the not-quite-so-Big Shootout II. "The Arkansas game to Texas was not a big deal. . . . They didn't have the same emotional investment we did."

Texas' biggest rival through the years was (and remains) Oklahoma; it never hurt the Hogs that their date with Texas usually fell a week after the annual Red River Shootout in Dallas. The Longhorns also had a special rivalry with Texas A&M. And, in fact, to almost every opponent, Texas was the Big Game. Royal put it best, saying, "We've got our fans and then we've got seven other groups of fans that hate us."

Pick any other team in the Lone Star state, and chances are Texas is its most hated rival; and the same is true of another border state. Quinn Grovey, the Hogs' standout quarterback of the late 1980s and early 1990s, grew up in Duncan, Oklahoma. There, the Sooners share Arkansans' view of the Longhorns.

"I already hated 'em growing up," Grovey says.

And yet, upon his arrival in Fayetteville, Grovey discerned a different

Amid a rivalry's maelstrom, a warm relationship blossomed. While Arkansas and Texas fans fought, their head coaches became lifelong friends.

Frank Broyles and Darrell Royal arrived at Arkansas and Texas at about the same time (Broyles in 1958, Royal a year earlier). They quickly set about establishing their teams as the Southwest Conference's powerhouses, helping create and fuel the intense rivalry. Especially in Arkansas, fans grew to hate the Longhorns. Despite their collision course, however, Broyles and Royal didn't hate each other. Far from it.

Over the years, they and their families grew close. During the offseasons, they vacationed together, playing plenty of golf. During the seasons, they called each other once a week—except, of course, for that *one* week. Even today, the ex-coaches find time for regular visits, either by phone or in person.

There was but one rule then, and now. Perhaps to preserve the peace, Broyles and Royal agreed never to talk about their games and with one exception, they have stuck to that pledge.

Shortly after both retired in 1976, they traveled together to speak at a coaching clinic. Unable to resist, Royal turned to Broyles with a long-nagging question: "Were you picking up our defensive signals in nineteen-seventy-one?"

"Darrell, before I answer that, were you picking up our offensive plays in nineteen-sixty-two?" Broyles replied.

"Yes," Royal said. "Yes," Broyles said.

"That's the only time we've ever discussed football," Broyles says. "And it will be the last time."

When Broyles decided to hang up his whistle after nineteen seasons, Royal did, too. A few weeks before their game (which had been moved to the end of the season for television), Broyles told Royal he was retiring, but asked him to keep the news to himself.

Royal had his own news. He was ready to call it quits, too. It wasn't planned that way—not really. "That's way too important to say, 'Let's do it together,'" Royal says. "It's important to each individual to decide exactly what time he wants to step out of it."

Planned or not, their simultaneous exits were fitting. After the final gun (Texas won, 29–12) of their final game, the coaches met at midfield, as they'd done eighteen times before. This time, a handshake became an embrace.

"I love you," Broyles said.
"I love you, too," Royal replied.

Two coaching legends and close friends retired on the same day in December 1976.

level of intensity. "When I'd go to class, everybody was talking about Texas. Beat Texas bumper stickers. That's all there was all year long. . . . There is definitely a bigger hatred for Texas here in Arkansas than it is in Oklahoma."

Well, maybe. But not many would argue the intensity is very similar. While at Arkansas, Grovey beat Texas once, in 1988. In 1987, 1989, and 1990, the Longhorns won.

"You knew you were letting a lot of people down if you lost that game," he says. "You were letting a lot of people down. You just knew how important it was."

After the 2003 game, and the rematch a year later in Fayetteville (as a stadium-record crowd of 75,671 watched, the Longhorns escaped with a 22–20 victory), the series ended, again. There aren't any future games scheduled, but the two-game resumption of the series proved one thing: Arkansans remain addicted to the rivalry. They probably always will be.

"It's the big, ol' state of Texas against little, ol' bitty Arkansas," Nutt says. "When you play Texas, it's a special week. Always, the biggest, strongest athletes on the orange side. The fighting Razorbacks on the other side."

◄ FACING PAGE
To the Razorbacks, nothing is better than beating Texas. Wide receiver George Wilson's 2003 touchdown helped Arkansas do just that.

7

Fantastic Moments

SOME SEASONS, teams are defined not by wins and losses or games but by a moment. In an era when highlights are replayed on continuous cable TV loops for twenty-four hours, then forgotten for the next play of the day, it's sometimes hard to distinguish the truly meaningful

Preston Carpenter outraces Ole Miss defenders to the end zone in what would become known as the Powder River play. It gave Arkansas a 6-0 win over the highly ranked Rebels.

plays from the mundane. But some have staying power. Because of their significance, some remain in our memories. While many of these plays were spectacular, all are etched into the rich tapestry of Razorback history.

THE POWDER RIVER PLAY

OCTOBER 23, 1954
ARKANSAS 6, OLE MISS 0

They have argued for years. Buddy Bob Benson remembers the most important pass in Arkansas history, which he hurled, as a spiraled thing of beauty. Preston Carpenter remembers the toss, which he gathered in stride, as something less.

"He says it was an end-over-end pass," Benson says, laughing. "I say it was a perfect pass."

The teammates agree on the important thing, though: The results of the 66-yard touchdown pass were sheer perfection.

Their connection, known ever after as the Powder River play, provided the only score in the biggest win in the program's history to that point. That win might have meant more than any other, before or since. It sent coach Bowden Wyatt's 25 Little Pigs on to the Hogs' most successful season in years. That season laid the foundation, according to

Wyatt's successor Frank Broyles, for a powerhouse program in the next decade.

"It was a victory that really transformed the future of the Arkansas program," Broyles says.

After a 20–7 win over Texas, Arkansas was 4-0. And here came fifth-ranked Ole Miss, a perennial powerhouse and a seven-point favorite over the surprisingly, seventh-ranked Razorbacks. On an unseasonably warm autumn afternoon (sunny and 75 degrees), thirty-eight thousand fans jammed Little Rock's War Memorial Stadium—the first sellout in the stadium's six-year history and the largest crowd to see a sporting event in Arkansas. Eighteen newspapers, far more than the norm, sent reporters for what was suddenly billed (at least locally) as Dixie's Game of the Year.

The Rebels brought the nation's top-ranked offensive unit: averaging 423.4 total yards and also leading the nation in passing (189.4 yard average). They had outscored their first five opponents 171–35. But other than a drive to the Arkansas 5 in the first quarter, Ole Miss didn't threaten.

As the fourth quarter progressed, it appeared the teams were headed for a scoreless tie, which would have been a victory of sorts for Arkansas. On third-and-6 from the Arkansas 34, the Hogs gambled for everything.

Benson, a transfer from Oklahoma who was from DeQueen, was the Hogs' second-team tailback, which in the single wing was equivalent to quarterback. He wasn't known as a passer; those duties typically fell to starting tailback George Walker, and Arkansas didn't do much passing, anyway.

"We used to have a saying: 'Two-four-six, move the sticks,'" Carpenter says. "That's the way it was. We didn't pass it."

Even on a running team, Benson was known as a runner, not a thrower. He had been running sweeps all day, moving great distances horizontally just to get a yard, maybe two. And that's exactly what the coaches were counting on when they sent in the play designed for Benson and named for Wyoming's Powder River, which Wyatt (who had come to Arkansas from Wyoming) had told his team was a mile wide and six inches deep.

Arkansas had worked on the play several times in practice, but not that week; still, assistant coach Dick Hitt called down from the press box and told Wyatt the play would work.

Benson took the snap and ran left toward the sideline, following his blockers. The Rebels' defensive backs surged toward the line of scrimmage, anticipating the sweep.

"I just ran hard and then stopped and threw the football," Benson says. "I looked up and boy, they were coming. I saw Preston down the field, and I just threw the ball. I threw it off my back foot."

Coach Bowden Wyatt, the mastermind behind the 25 Little Pigs' surprising success in 1954, designed the Powder River play to resemble a run.

Carpenter, the Razorbacks' best receiver, was normally a first-teamer at blocking back. However, earlier in the game, he had suffered a shoulder injury while making a tackle. At the beginning of the fourth quarter, Arkansas had reached the Ole Miss 22. But the threat ended when Carpenter dropped Benson's fourth-down pass. This time, Carpenter made the grab.

He was behind both defensive halfbacks, Earl Blair and Billy Kinard, and safety Houston Patton.

"Buddy Bob just threw it up and I caught it," says Carpenter, who came to Arkansas from Muskogee, Oklahoma, but lived in West Memphis for much of his childhood.

Carpenter caught the pass in stride

between the 30 and 35, a step ahead of Kinard. He outraced Kinard into the end zone, then flipped the ball high into the air. With 3:45 left, Arkansas led 6–0.

A writer from the *Arkansas Gazette* suggested the "roar must have made the lions of the nearby zoo cower in their cages." Benson missed the extra point, but it didn't matter; Ole Miss didn't get close to the end zone in the final minutes.

When the game ended, the fans rushed onto the field. Carpenter was carried to the locker room on their shoulders.

"It was pretty wild stuff," he says.

It was Arkansas' sixth straight win (dating back to the final game of 1953), the longest winning streak since 1929. Ironically, although it was a nonconference matchup, it counted as a South-

Preston Carpenter waits on Buddy Bob Benson's pass. The pass traveled about 33 yards, and Carpenter raced the final 33.

eastern Conference game for Ole Miss, thus causing some to wryly suggest the Razorbacks' first SEC win came thirty-eight years before they joined the league. Though the victory didn't impact the Southwest Conference race, it signaled the Hogs were genuine. Arkansas went on to win the conference and finished 8-3, losing to Georgia Tech in the Cotton Bowl.

Everything started with the Powder River play.

"It was just a wonderful play that clicked against the odds when you needed it most," Wyatt said. "It might not go again all season, but the boys made it go for the big one."

The biggest one, probably.

JUST BARELY

OCTOBER 15, 1960
ARKANSAS 24, TEXAS 23

Mickey Cissell was never a kicker. Not as the position has come to be understood, anyway. He arrived at Arkansas from tiny Wilson as a fullback, with hopes of glory. But Cissell kicked his way into Arkansas history, though just barely.

On an unusually warm afternoon in Austin, Texas, the sophomore's 30-yard kick with fifteen seconds left provided the Hogs with a stunning, come-from-behind win over Texas. It was Frank Broyles' first over the Long-horns, and it propelled the Hogs to the Southwest Conference championship.

The kick cleared the cross bar by perhaps a foot.

"I knew it was hit well," Cissell says, "but I didn't know if it was gonna make it."

Cissell almost didn't make it, either. After piling up big statistics at the small school in the Mississippi County town hard by the Mississippi River, he had found life in Fayetteville tough as a fourth-team fullback.

Before the season, Cissell told Broyles he wanted to transfer. "I felt like the thing for me to do was to go somewhere else where I might get to play and run the football," Cissell says. Broyles talked Cissell out of it, telling him he could contribute as a kicker.

"I just said, 'Well, I'll be a part of the team and kick and do what I can,'" Cissell remembers.

Cissell worked as a reserve fullback and a kicker, which mainly meant he started practice thirty minutes earlier than the rest of the team. When called on to beat the Longhorns, he had hit 13 of 14 extra-point attempts, but hadn't tried a field goal.

At the 2 P.M. kickoff, the temperature was 85 degrees (it would reach 87). As a regional television audience watched, the Longhorns grabbed a 14–0 lead, only to see George McKinney throw two touchdown passes to tie it.

Then, after Texas moved ahead 23–14, McKinney tossed a third touchdown pass. And late in the fourth quarter, Arkansas got the ball back with time for one last drive.

With just more than three minutes left, reserve halfback Harold Horton returned a punt 15 yards to the Texas 37. Lance Alworth (hampered by a leg injury and playing at 85 percent, Broyles said before the game) carried four times for 18 yards during the drive. Alworth's last carry was crucial. Facing fourth-and-2, Alworth got perhaps 2 yards and 1 inch for the first down at the 17 with 1:40 left.

McKinney fired incomplete into the end zone, then he kept the football for 5 yards, moving left and toward the middle of the field to set up a straight-on angle for the field-goal attempt.

Arkansas called timeout to stop the clock. And Cissell ran onto the field, "scared like a bunny," he told reporters afterward.

Cissell wasn't normally a nervous type, but as the Hogs moved downfield, Broyles had paced the sidelines. Wanting the kicker nearby, he took Cissell with him. Up and down, the sophomore followed the young head coach. And by the time his name was finally called, the kicker was a basket case.

Broyles actually sent Cissell in one play too early, perhaps contributing to the jangling of Cissell's nerves. McKinney knew he had enough time for one more play, so he sent the kicker back to the sidelines, then kept the football for the run toward the middle.

When the time finally came, Cissell set up directly behind the ball (soccer-style kicking was still many years away) and made his run. Against a slight wind, the ball never got far off the ground. Witnesses said it fluttered and seemed to take forever to cover the distance.

"I knew it was going to go straight," McKinney told the *Austin American.* "I wasn't worried a bit about that. So I just kept looking at the referee wondering if it was long enough."

Mel Allen, doing play-by-play for ABC, said the kick had been blocked. That wouldn't have been unprecedented. A year earlier in Little Rock, Texas had blocked a field goal (not by Cissell) and escaped with a 13–12 win.

Cissell says he was "just being ultracareful." He had not taken a big backswing. He realized he was sacrificing distance, but wanted to ensure the kick went straight. And he wasn't sure if it was long enough, but he knew it was hit well.

"It's kind of like hitting a half-wedge," says Cissell, likening it to golf. "If you don't draw it back too far, then you don't hook it or shank it. It barely cleared the crossbar, but I was gonna make sure it went straight. It wasn't gonna go left or right."

The football sailed straight and true. It dropped just over the bar, giving Arkansas the biggest victory of Broyles' young career.

"It was a tremendous victory," Cissell says. "Any time you beat Texas, it's a tremendous victory, and particularly in Austin."

Three games later, Cissell nailed another game winner. His 26-yarder with thirty seconds left gave Arkansas a 3–0 win over Rice. And a year later, he kicked a field goal in the Hogs' 10–3 loss to Alabama in the Sugar Bowl.

Still, nothing topped the kick that beat Texas. That was enough to secure Cissell's place in history. Weeks later, he got a write-in vote for governor. And a few days after the game, he received a letter with a photograph of "Mickey Wayne," an infant named after Cissell and Arkansas linebacker Wayne Harris. "There's one good thing about being a former Razorback," Cissell says. "You get to talk about it all the time. And so I've been talking about it since nineteen-sixty-one."

KENNY HATFIELD'S PUNT RETURN

OCTOBER 17, 1964
ARKANSAS 14, TEXAS 13

Every day during that summer of 1964, Kenny Hatfield ran sprints on the ballfield in his hometown of Helena. Lots

LEFT
Kenny Hatfield's 81-yard
punt return gave Arkansas
momentum for a 14-13 win
over Texas.

RIGHT
Kenny Hatfield.

of them. And every day, he finished with a special visualization. Cradling the football, he took off, pretending he was returning the opening kickoff against Texas.

He always scored.

So why would anyone be surprised a few months later, when Hatfield's 81-yard punt return helped propel Arkansas to a 14–13 upset, and from there to the national championship?

"Everybody knocked everybody down, and it was easy," says Hatfield of his bolt into legend.

Teammates aren't quite so modest in their descriptions.

"Ken was an unbelievable punt returner," says Jim Lindsey, whose initial block helped set the play in motion.

"Ken was not the fastest punt returner that ever was, but I think he may have been the best."

There was truth in both statements. Hatfield, who was also a starting defensive halfback, wasn't especially fast, but the president of the senior class had an uncanny knack for returning punts. He'd make one man miss, or maybe two—he was once described as a knuckleball. Then, helped along by blockers who typically executed to perfection, he'd pick a lane and bolt.

Ronnie Caveness, an All-American linebacker that season who was nonetheless impressed by his teammate's special ability, once asked Hatfield how he was so often able to find and exploit creases. Hatfield explained that after locating the football on its descent, he would quickly look downfield.

"He wanted to get a Polaroid picture of where that lane was," Caveness says. "I thought that was pretty neat."

Hatfield had led the nation in punt returns as a junior in 1963. The week before Arkansas played Texas, he set up a touchdown with a 39-yard return against Baylor. The Longhorns were determined Hatfield would not break free against them.

"I can remember reading the paper," he says. "It was something like, 'I can guarantee you one thing. Hatfield will not run a punt back today.' "

When Arkansas coach Frank Broyles and Texas coach Darrell Royal spoke during pregame warmups, the subject of Hatfield came up.

"He said, 'Boy, we've worked hard to try to be ready for Hatfield,' " Broyles recalls. "I said, 'You know, the kid doesn't have any speed at all. It's amazing what he does. He's slow.' "

Some time later, Royal brought that conversation up to Broyles.

"He wasn't very slow on that play," the Texas coach said.

Never was there a more important time for Hatfield to break free. The game was scoreless when he gathered Ernie Koy's long punt midway through the second quarter. Koy's 47-yarder didn't hang up much, either, which gave Hatfield room to dance.

"Ernie just flat outkicked his cover-

age," Hatfield remembers. "He got into a boomer."

His first move was to slide left, then forward, and then quickly left again. He kicked free of the hands of a diving Longhorn and headed for the visitor's sidelines.

"Kenny's little wiggle there at the start set it all moving," says Jimmy Finch, a defensive end who watched the play from the sidelines. "Then, all he had to do was run. Those other guys were knocking 'em down."

And indeed, when Hatfield got to the sidelines, he had a wall of blockers. But to get there, he needed a crucial block from Lindsey on Texas' standout linebacker Tommy Nobis. And Lindsey, a junior wingback, paid for it.

"I got kicked in the chin and had a tooth broke off," he says.

Lindsey gave much of the credit to Hatfield, whose style, he said, made it easy to block. Hatfield would run right at a defender, then jitterbug away at the last instant.

"Ken would so set up the block that all you had to do was be willing to throw yourself in there," Lindsey says. "He didn't give 'em an angle. You'd have had to almost want to miss the guy not to get him. As soon as he gets the block, he makes that move and then kicks his feet free."

Down the sidelines went Hatfield, past cheering teammates on one side, blocking teammates on the other. Koy,

▶ FACING PAGE
Hatfield led the nation in punt returns in 1963 and 1964.

better known as a standout tailback, had the last, best chance to get him. Koy hoped to turn Hatfield inside. Had he done so, another Longhorn with an angle would probably have caught Hatfield, but two Hogs—Mike Bender and Jerry Lamb—combined for just enough of a block to allow Hatfield to slip past Koy. He raced alone the last 30 yards into the end zone.

"I wasn't watching the blocker," Koy said after the game. "I was trying to make him cut back in from the sideline. I had two of them coming at me. I knew if they got to my left, I was gone. I pushed one, but the second one took a shot at me. It rocked me back, and I couldn't get to him.

"It doesn't take much for ol' Hatfield. He was off and running."

So were the Razorbacks.

During Broyles' tenure as head coach, the Hogs finished each practice by working on punt returns. Hatfield would go on to be the nation's leading punt returner for the second straight season. It was the fourth time in five years a Razorback led in the category.

"We took pride in it," Broyles says. "We worked on it and we developed an attitude that we were gonna average more than ten yards per return for the season. That was our goal."

The return was the fourth of Hatfield's career of more than 70 yards. And easily the most important. With 5:36 left in the first half, Arkansas led a stunned bunch of Longhorns 7–0. Although it would take another touchdown, then a defensive stop to secure victory, Hatfield's return was the game-defining moment.

"It turned the whole game around," Broyles said. "Up 'til then, we hadn't done much. But that one gave us the momentum."

For the win over Texas. And for a national championship.

THE IMMORTAL TEDDY BARNES

DECEMBER 6, 1975
ARKANSAS 31, TEXAS A&M 6

Nowadays, they'd call it taking a deep shot. "Back then, it was 'throwing into coverage,'" says Scott Bull, laughing. But it worked. Bull's 28-yard pass to Teddy Barnes was the catalyst in a 31–6 upset of number-two-ranked Texas A&M. The Aggies were favored, but with thirty-four-seconds left in a scoreless first half, Bull tossed a 28-yard pass toward Teddy Barnes, a senior from Lepanto. The 5-9, 174 pounder outjumped two bigger defensive backs for the football and came down with it in back of the end zone.

Arkansas coach Frank Broyles quickly dubbed him the Immortal Teddy Barnes.

"Someone asked me the other day,

'Teddy Barnes was immortalized, why weren't you?'" Bull says. "I said, 'Well, did you see the catch?' The catch was the big deal. The throw just gave him the chance to do it."

And sent Arkansas to the Cotton Bowl for the first time in ten years.

Texas A&M was 10-0 and brought the nation's top-ranked defense to War Memorial Stadium. After beating Texas, the Aggies believed they had a legitimate claim to the number-one ranking held by Ohio State. Arkansas, meanwhile, had lost early in the year to Oklahoma State, then by 24–18 to Texas—a familiar result, even though the Hogs believed they were better than the 'Horns.

The Razorbacks realized consistent drives would be tough to come by against Texas A&M's fierce, talented defense, which would send several starters to the NFL. The Hogs, better known for their running game, had determined they would need to take shots downfield. They believed they could make plays because of the Aggies' reliance on man-to-man, a strategy that usually worked because of the speed and talent of their secondary combined with a formidable pass rush. In the first half, the Razorbacks tried two halfback passes and another deep ball, but couldn't connect. Twice, Barnes was open deep; a halfback pass fell short and strong safety Lester Hayes intercepted Bull's underthrown pass.

With 1:21 left in the second quarter,

Arkansas took possession at the Texas A&M 41 after a 15-yard shank of a punt. The Razorbacks managed a first down, but seemed to be preparing to settle for a field-goal try from stellar kicker Steve Little.

Instead, Broyles gave permission for one more try at the end zone. At the snap, Bull sprinted left, behind blockers. He spotted Barnes with a step on Hayes and free safety Jackie Williams. As other Aggies rushed, Bull lobbed the football downfield in the receiver's general direction.

"I had people in my face," Bull says. "I saw Teddy somewhat break open. I felt like he would have a chance for the ball. . . . I just put it up where he should be. . . . I put it up the way the pros and college players do today, where they just depend on the wide receiver to fight for it. Back in my day, that would be called throwing into coverage. But anymore, it's just what you do with great receivers."

Not that Barnes had the physique of a great receiver. He was short and stocky. Although he had deceptive speed, he functioned more often as a downfield blocker than a pass catcher. "Barnes is your all-time hustler," Broyles told the *Arkansas Gazette* the next day.

Hayes and Williams each had several inches on Barnes. They had bitten on a short route, but recovered and nearly caught up with Barnes by the

Teddy Barnes' touchdown catch, just beyond two Texas A&M defensive backs, propelled the Hogs to a 31-6 rout of the second-ranked Aggies in 1975.

3

4

time the ball arrived. They leaped for the ball, but too soon. Then Barnes leaped, turned sideways in the air, caught the pass and came down, dragging his feet in bounds in the back of the end zone.

▶ FACING PAGE
Scott Bull's touchdown pass to Barnes sent the Hogs to the Cotton Bowl, where they beat Georgia 31–10.

"It was just luck," Barnes told reporters afterward. "It was a comeback play. I thought they were going to knock it down, but I think they hit each other."

"Teddy was at the top of his jump and the two defenders were on their way down," Bull says. "They mistimed it and he timed it perfectly."

Bull says this after seeing the highlights countless times over the years. He didn't see the catch in real time. "I was on my back," he says, put there by a would-be sacker, but Bull "heard the catch."

War Memorial Stadium erupted in sound. "There was no question what had happened," Bull says. "The fans let me know what the result was."

The Hogs mobbed Barnes in the end zone, and went into halftime with a 7–0 lead that felt much bigger. The touchdown, Broyles said, was worth millions to the Hogs' confidence.

"It changed the game around," Broyles recalls.

"There's no way to estimate what a lift [the touchdown] was to go back to the dressing room ahead seven to nothing in a game like this," Bull told reporters. "Being ahead, I mean, just being ahead."

The second half was all Arkansas. Arkansas managed 267 yards, well above the average allowed by the Aggies. Looking back, Broyles says, "Bull won that game for us with his throwing and running. It was Scott Bull's performance."

Bull rushed for 47 yards on 20 carries, many on unpredictable quarterback sneaks. And he completed 4 of 9 passes for 103 yards, including the most important completion of the season.

Arkansas' was the dominant defense, holding Texas A&M to 2.4 yards per play, intercepting a pass, and recovering five fumbles. Defensive end Johnnie Meadors recovered two fumbles, setting up a field goal with one and scoring a touchdown with the other. Those recoveries, along with Micheal Forrest's 7-yard touchdown run (set up by Bull's 35-yard pass to tight end Doug Yoder), were part of a 17-point third quarter that put the game away.

"The team was ready," Broyles says. "It was one of those games where everything just fell into place. We played nearly a perfect game."

As the fourth quarter wound down, the fans reveled in the rout, chanting over and over: "Hey, hey, ho, ho, Arkansas to the Cotton Bowl!" The Razorbacks' win left the SWC standings in a three-way tie. Arkansas, Texas, and Texas A&M were each 6-1. The Hogs got the Cotton Bowl nod because they had been away the longest; Arkansas

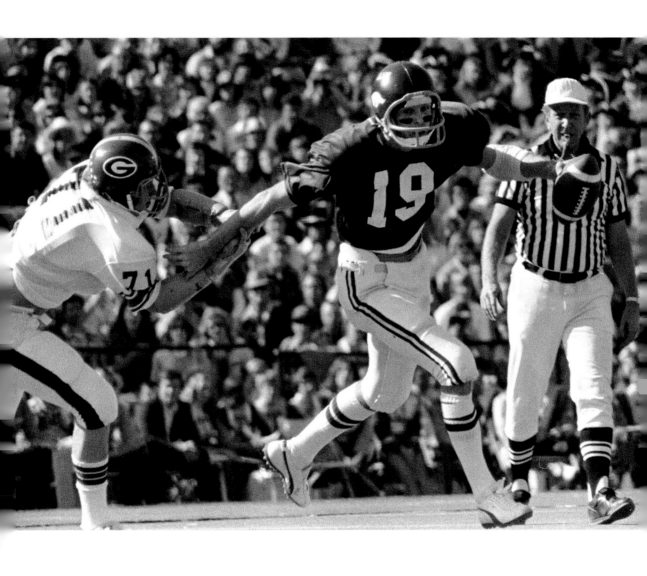

► FACING PAGE
Barry Lunney's late
heroics helped get
the Hogs into position
for an upset.

hadn't played there since 1965, Texas A&M since 1967, and Texas since 1973.

Arkansas met 9-2 Georgia in the Cotton Bowl, and won easily, 31–10, to finish 10-2. Without Bull's pass and the catch by "the immortal Teddy Barnes," the Hogs wouldn't have gotten the chance.

LUNNEY TO MEADORS, TOUCHDOWN

SEPTEMBER 16, 1995
ARKANSAS 20, ALABAMA 19

All these years later, Barry Lunney has come clean. No, he really didn't intend to throw so low that only five-foot-six J. J. Meadors could catch the football, as he claimed after Arkansas' stunning 20–19 victory at Alabama.

"A bad ball," Lunney calls it now.

But, oh, so good. Lunney's short pass to the shortest guy on the field was almost too short, but with 6 seconds left, when Meadors scooped the football just before it hit the ground near the goal line, Arkansas had a benchmark victory—its biggest since moving to the Southeastern Conference four seasons earlier.

It was Arkansas' first win over Alabama, and was a springboard to more victories. Since joining the SEC, the

Razorbacks had just missed on several breakthrough opportunities.

"For us to go down there to Tuscaloosa and just be in position to win was a huge deal for our football program," Lunney says. "But if J.J. had not made that catch and we hadn't punched it in down there, it would have been another one of those close-but-no-cigar deals."

The Hogs went on to win the SEC West Division championship.

"We won and we thought, 'We might be pretty good. We can do this deal,'" Lunney says. "It was kind of a point where we were able to say, 'Hey, we do belong.' When I think about that game, I think destiny, fate, what have you. It was just meant for us to win that game. Just the way it unfolded."

With 3:13 left, Arkansas took possession at its 43. An incompletion followed by a sack, and it was third-and-24. Lunney got 16 yards back with a pass to running back Madre Hill. Still, on fourth-and-8, some Alabama fans were heading for the exits. And who could blame them? Arkansas had played well, but the favored Crimson Tide was going to escape with a win.

But maybe not. Almost sacked again, Lunney scrambled away from pressure, then spotted Anthony Lucas running free down the sidelines. "I was just standing there all by myself," recalls Lucas, who was a freshman in 1995. "I

was waving my hands. He saw me and I just made the catch."

The 31-yard gain gave the Hogs new life. "That was a miracle in itself," Lunney says.

A 16-yard strike to Meadors gave Arkansas first-and-goal at the 3. Three plays later, it was fourth-and-goal from the same distance. The play call was an option route—"backyard football," Meadors called it. The left-handed Lunney rolled left. Given a block by Dexter Hebert, he had time to look for Meadors, and only Meadors (although three other receivers went out). Looking back, Lunney called it "the perfect call."

Arkansas expected and got man-to-man coverage. Split wide left, the diminutive receiver went in motion before the snap. He had the option of cutting inside or out, based on how the safety played him. When Cedric Samuels jumped inside, Meadors cut toward the sideline.

"He went inside and I went out, and I saw Barry running," Meadors told the *Arkansas Democrat-Gazette*. "He did a great job of keeping the play alive and getting the ball away. I remember seeing it coming in and thinking, 'Get your arms around it.'"

Meadors was wide open; it almost didn't matter. Throwing on the run, Lunney didn't get enough on it. The football started high and began descending rapidly. Meadors jolted forward, dropped to his knees and then closer to the ground. Did he get his arms beneath the football?

"I was so tired that when I first got the ball, it didn't really click what had happened," Meadors said. "Then the ref signaled touchdown, and it hit me."

The catch was redemption for a costly mistake. Midway through the third quarter, Meadors signaled fair catch on a punt. When he didn't field it, Alabama downed it at the Arkansas 1. From there, Hill was tackled in the end zone; the safety gave Alabama a 19–10 lead.

"I was thinking I had pretty much lost the game for us," Meadors said.

Instead, he won it with what Lunney called a "fantastic catch."

With six seconds left, it was tied at 19. Kicker Todd Latourette calmly drilled home the victory.

Ever afterward, Alabama fans complained about two things. On the play before the touchdown, Arkansas had twelve players on the field, but no flag was thrown. The fans also wondered whether Meadors might have scooped the ball on one hop.

"I did make the catch," Meadors said. And Alabama linebacker John Walters backed the claim: "I saw the catch. . . . It was a touchdown."

In the moments afterward, Lunney suggested he "threw it low on purpose. I knew J.J. could get down and catch it." But Lunney has finally come clean.

◂ FACING PAGE
Anthony Lucas' 31-yard catch and run on fourth down set up the winning touchdown.

FACING PAGE

DeCori Birmingham gathers
in the winning touchdown
pass as Arkansas
stuns LSU.

"No, it was a real bad pass, truthfully," Lunney said.

But, oh, so good.

MIRACLE ON MARKHAM

NOVEMBER 29, 2002
ARKANSAS 21, LSU 20

Houston Nutt was concerned. It wasn't so much that his Razorbacks trailed LSU 20–14 with thirty-four-seconds left, or that they were 81 yards from the end zone with no timeouts. It wasn't even that Matt Jones had misfired on 11 of 13 passes, often badly. No, what bothered Arkansas' coach was the quarterback's nonchalance.

During a television timeout, Nutt walked over to where Jones was sitting. All around him, on the home sidelines and in the War Memorial Stadium stands, anxiety had tied stomachs into knots. Yet, when the head coach arrived to give some last-second encouragement, the sophomore, apparently oblivious, was . . . "Humming! He was humming!" Nutt says. "You just wanted to say, 'Man, what are you thinking?'"

With Jones, there was no telling. Nutt forged ahead, explaining the situation: "Matt, there's thirty-four seconds left. We've got a hurry-hurry situation, our two-minute drill . . ."

"Coach, I got it."

He did. Twenty-five seconds later, his 31-yard dart found DeCori Birmingham in the end zone. The "Miracle on Markham," as the play was quickly dubbed (referring to the stadium's location), gave Arkansas the SEC West title, and sent the Hogs to the SEC championship game.

"Can you say 'SEC West champs?'" said tailback Fred Talley in the raucous moments afterward. "I can. And it's all good."

The pass established Jones' place in Razorback legend. And it immediately joined a select number of never-to-be-forgotten highlights.

"I think it will go down as one of the greatest, if not the greatest, of all time," Arkansas athletic director Frank Broyles told the *Arkansas Democrat-Gazette.* "A finish like that is so rare, I can't remember one like it."

Midway through the season, Arkansas was 3-3 overall, and 1-3 in SEC play. Then, the Hogs reeled off five straight wins to set up a showdown with eighteenth-ranked LSU for the division title. Most figured the winning streak would end that day in Little Rock, and Jones' play for fifty-nine minutes, twenty-six seconds didn't indicate anything different.

In just two seasons, Arkansas fans had come to know Jones as either fantastic or frustrating. His 2-of-13 performance (for 46 yards) fit squarely into the latter category. Jones had also

thrown an interception in the end zone. At one point, fans had booed their Hogs—a rare occurrence. They finished by roaring for them.

Talley's 56-yard touchdown run pulled the Hogs within 17–14, but LSU added a field goal with forty seconds left. Considering Jones' previous ineptitude, "We didn't think he could beat us throwing the ball," LSU linebacker Bradie James told the *Baton Rouge Advocate.*

Maybe the Tigers should have been more concerned.

After humming a while longer, Jones trotted out to the huddle. The call was for a short out route; the Hogs wanted to get a few yards and get out of bounds, stopping the clock. However, when Jones dropped back, he found Richard Smith deep, well beyond the LSU defensive backs. A blown coverage had left him wide open.

"I couldn't believe Richard Smith got behind that guy," Jones told the *Democrat-Gazette.* "They let him get behind them. I threw it as far as I could."

The 50-yard pass pushed Arkansas to the LSU 31 with twenty-six seconds left. War Memorial Stadium, long known for its volume level, reached ear-splitting decibels.

Jones' next pass was off the mark. Second down; seventeen seconds left. Three receivers split left, all went long on post patterns; another wide right slipped underneath. While rolling right

to avoid pressure, Jones saw Birmingham just ahead of LSU cornerback Randall Gay.

"You see a little opening, but . . . you've just got to give him a chance and hope he comes down with it," Jones said.

The football somehow eluded several Tigers' arms and nestled safely into Birmingham's as he collapsed in the back of the end zone.

"There may have been ten guys covering me, I don't know," Birmingham said. "I just had one thing in my eyes and that was making the catch. . . . All I was thinking was, *touchdown.*"

The catch touched off a wild celebration in the stands. War Memorial Stadium may have never been louder. The game wasn't won, though, not yet. The players' spontaneous joy as they mobbed Birmingham included several fans and some Hogs from the sidelines. The officials flagged Arkansas for excessive celebration, pushing the all-important extra-point try from a chip shot to a 35-yarder.

Not until David Carlton hit the suddenly tricky kick was the victory assured. And then, the celebration could continue, flag free. Afterward, Birmingham considered the miracle comeback to be a lesson about Arkansas football.

"We don't give up," Birmingham said. "We're the Razorbacks. We don't quit for nobody. We fight 'til it's over."

Later, some remembered that, on a

◄FACING PAGE
The unflappable Matt Jones had not passed well all day, but he found Richard Smith for 50 yards, setting up the Miracle on Markham.

cloudy afternoon, the sun broke through just as Arkansas lined up for that last drive. One Baton Rouge writer summed it up: "Pigs indeed can fly."

Ascribing supernatural means might demean the accomplishment of one unflappable player, which brought Nutt back to those tense moments before the final possession, to his quarterback's carefree demeanor.

"I'll tell you what, you never want anybody else in that situation," Nutt says. "This guy has ice water in his veins. He throws two of the most perfect passes in perfect stride. That's what this guy does. He makes big plays."

◀ FACING PAGE
Birmingham holds on for the touchdown, despite LSU's last-gasp attempt at breaking up the pass.

KEN HAT
F
GOV

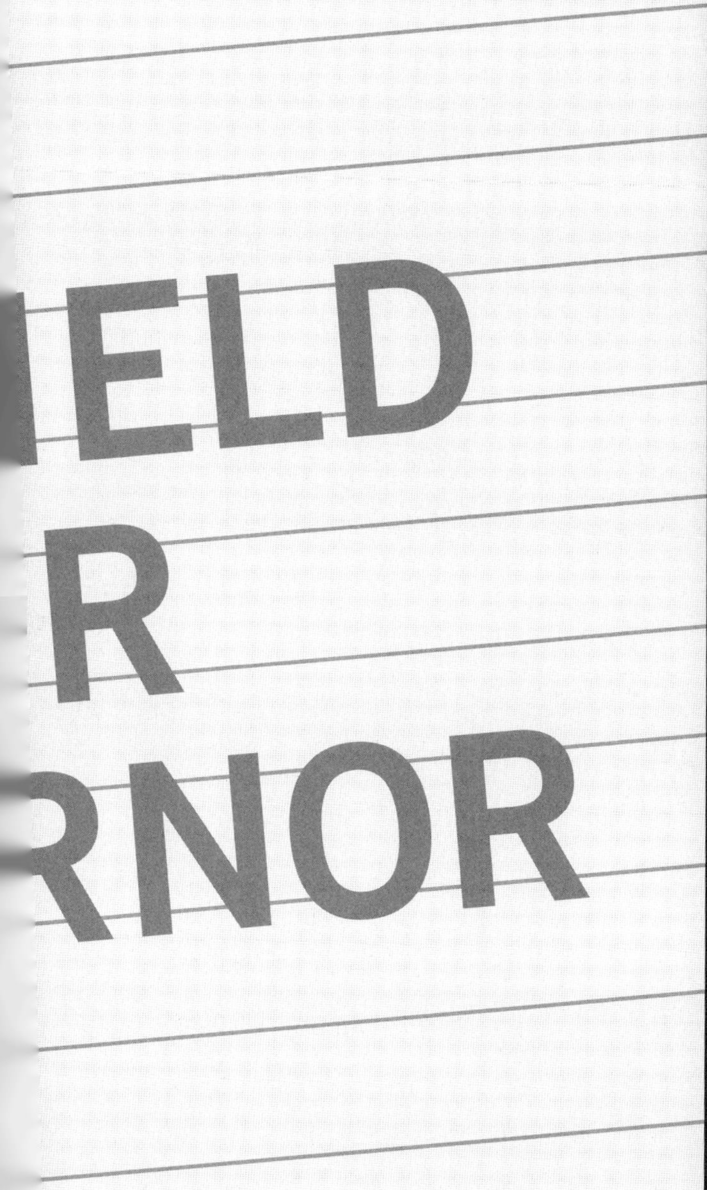

IELD
R
RNOR

8

Following Frank

THE DAY AFTER Arkansas'
win over Texas in 1964, which
paved the way for the Razorbacks' national championship, a
Little Rock drive-in restaurant
had this message on its marquee:
KEN HATFIELD FOR GOVERNOR.

Nice sentiment, of course.
And understandable, since

Hatfield's 81-yard punt return had sparked the 14–13 victory. Nineteen years later, however, Hatfield ascended to a higher office: Arkansas' head coach. It was also a more precarious post.

After Frank Broyles' retirement following the 1976 season, first Lou Holtz and then Hatfield coached the Razorbacks. Each produced plenty of highlight-reel moments. Both had better winning percentages than Broyles. Yet, ultimately, neither found the fit comfortable.

Holtz, a wiry, bespectacled little Ohioan with a quick wit, fiery temper, and an undeniable talent for getting the most out of players in the biggest games, burned brightly but then faded, wearing out his welcome as he appeared to lose interest. He was fired after six seasons.

Hatfield, a returning hero from Helena, built championship teams but earned a reputation that he didn't win the big ones. Detractors seized upon his reluctance to schmooze with boosters, his stubborn determination to cling to a conservative offensive style, and his unapologetic devotion to his Christian faith. He jumped for Clemson in January 1990, shortly after Arkansas' second straight Cotton Bowl appearance.

Both coaches found it was not easy following a legend. Especially when the legend works in the same building, which also bears his name.

After nineteen seasons, Broyles announced his retirement on December 4, 1976, the day Arkansas finished a disappointing 5-5-1 season with a loss at Texas. Longhorns coach Darrell Royal retired that night, as well. The two coaching legends, rivals and friends, walked off the stage together.

Broyles simply moved on to another stage. He had become athletic director three years earlier, and his choice

Quick-witted and fiery, Lou Holtz was Frank Broyles' choice to succeed him.

of successor was a sharp departure in style. Broyles had gotten to know Holtz during golf outings, and he'd learned more about Holtz from Bo Rein, whom he had hired away from Holtz's North Carolina State staff.

By the time Broyles began contemplating retirement, he was convinced Holtz would become "one of the giants of the profession. I knew that when I stepped down, he was the one I wanted."

Holtz had moved from North Carolina State to the New York Jets in 1976, but quickly realized it was a mistake. When Broyles offered the "best job in America," Holtz took it, leaving the NFL after thirteen games, and saying he wasn't going to look back. "That's why the Good Lord put eyes in the front of your head instead of in the back," Holtz said at the news conference to announce his hiring.

Holtz also suggested it would be his last coaching job. "There isn't going to be any more moves," he said. It was his fourth head-coaching stop (he coached at William and Mary before North Carolina State). After Arkansas, he coached at Minnesota, Notre Dame, and South Carolina. In 1999, when he brought his South Carolina team to Arkansas for the first time, Holtz insisted that was more than a line.

"I did think I would spend the rest of my life at Arkansas," he said. "I really thought I could do that and do that very comfortably."

The new coach, who turned forty soon after his arrival, was five-foot-ten and 150 pounds. He could do magic tricks and fire off funny one-liners and, man, could he coach football.

The Hogs won thirty games in Holtz's first three seasons. After spending several seasons off the radar, Arkansas was back on college football's short list of elite programs. In retrospect, Arkansas peaked during Holtz's first season.

As Broyles had predicted, Holtz swept the state with his engaging personality, firing one-liners at offseason Razorback Club functions. His quips were frequent enough; newspapers regularly published his best lines from postgame interviews. One of his best came late in the 1977 season, after fans threw oranges onto the field to signify their pleasure at an Orange Bowl bid.

"I'm just glad we weren't going to the Gator Bowl," Holtz said.

After an upset loss to Rice in 1980, Holtz opened his television show: "Welcome to the *Lou Holtz Show.* Unfortunately, I'm Lou Holtz."

Much more important than Holtz's wit was his success. Upon arrival in Fayetteville, Holtz molded a talented bunch left by Broyles into winners. Picked to finish sixth in the conference, the Hogs instead rolled through the 1977 season, losing only to Texas, 13–9. Then, after losing an All-American offensive lineman to injury and suspend-

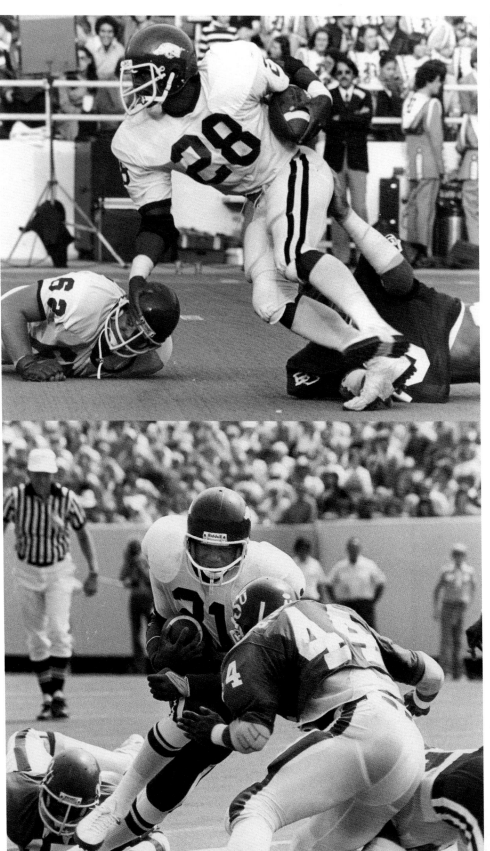

Ben Cowins, Arkansas' all-time leading rusher, was a key part of the Razorbacks' early success under Holtz, but was suspended and did not play in the 1978 Orange Bowl.

Roland Sales filled in for Cowins and set an Orange Bowl rushing record. Arkansas beat Oklahoma, 31-6.

ing three key offensive players for disciplinary reasons, Holtz led Arkansas to a stunning 31–6 win over Oklahoma in the Orange Bowl.

"One of the best coaching jobs that's ever been done in a bowl game, strategy and preparation," Broyles says.

"That kind of put Arkansas back in the limelight," says Ron Calcagni, who quarterbacked the Hogs in 1977 and 1978. "And it gave Lou Holtz his mark of, 'Stand by your guns and do right.'"

Shortly afterward, Holtz appeared on *The Tonight Show* with Johnny Carson, performing a magic trick and quipping of Fayetteville: "It's not the end of the earth, but you can see it from there." That one stung Arkansans, but the Razorbacks were riding high.

And so, as Holtz's national Q (recognition and appeal) rating grew and he became a sought-after banquet speaker, flying out frequently to collect nice checks for after-dinner remarks, fans' adoration for Holtz remained.

He was *their* coach, and the Hogs were back on top.

"Coach Holtz didn't get famous until he came to Arkansas," Arkansas offensive lineman Leotis Harris told the *Arkansas Democrat-Gazette*. "But he was what we needed. He brought a lot of fire."

For a while, Holtz's in-state popularity was unrivaled; he was the only football coach in Arkansas history (before or since) to have his own doll. After the Orange Bowl, the Lou Holtz

Hog fans express their appreciation for Holtz after an Arkansas victory in Little Rock.

wore those as part of their game-day ensembles.

In 1978, with the bulk of the team back, *Sports Illustrated* featured Holtz, Calcagni, and running back Ben Cowins on the cover of its preseason college football issue. Arkansas was the magazine's choice for number one.

When the issue came out, Holtz called Calcagni into his office. The quarterback still remembers the diminutive coach, swallowed by a large chair, slapping the magazine down onto his desk.

"You ruined the picture!" Holtz said.

"What do you mean?" Calcagni asked.

"Look at your shirt," Holtz said, referring to the home red jersey Calcagni had worn for the photograph.

"What's wrong with my shirt?"

"Look at that string hanging out of your shirt! You ruined the picture."

Calcagni remains convinced Holtz was serious. "Attention to detail," Calcagni says. "The little things. I learned so much from Lou Holtz—things to do. But I also learned a lot of things not to do."

That perfectionism showed in game plans, especially on offense. Holtz was as good as anybody at preparing for one big game. Of course, perfectionists exact a price. The vast majority of Holtz's practice time was spent with the offense. And often, the offense stayed

HOGS!

How many football coaches have their own doll? Lou Holtz dolls were briefly popular; now, they're collectors' items.

doll was briefly a hot seller. It looked something like Barbie's Ken, a nerdish Ken with glasses, a red V-necked sweater, and horrid red-and-white checked polyester pants with a folded game plan in the back pocket. The pants (think of the familiar picnic tablecloth pattern) were perhaps the most true-to-life item; Holtz's 1981 staff

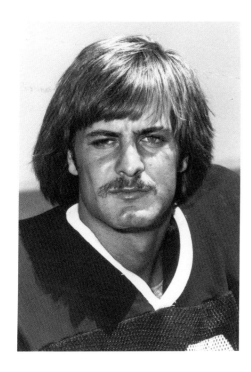

Ron Calcagni.

on the field long after the defense had finished, as Holtz waited for perfect execution.

Some players saw him as distant and unapproachable, others as a stern father figure. He was notoriously hard on quarterbacks, but Calcagni said no one was better at finding and pushing motivational buttons. In the Orange Bowl, Calcagni says, "Holtz and his staff did a remarkable job of making the exceptional players play at their peaks, where they needed to play, and making the ones just filling in believe they could play."

"Lou was extremely intense and demanding, and just totally committed to winning," says former offensive lineman Marcus Elliott. "You had to do

everything right, even putting the uniform on right. He was into doing the little things right. But we had success, and that was the reason.

"He knew exactly what he wanted to accomplish and how he wanted to accomplish that. He was a great coach. And we were so prepared. We knew what to expect, every game. He was tough. And he was demanding. And he was uncompromising. All of those words come to mind."

Holtz delighted in coming up with new wrinkles, sometimes razzle-dazzle. "He always had tricks or something up his sleeve," says Gary Anderson, who starred as a versatile running back from 1979 to 1982. Again, the Orange Bowl serves as a prime example: Arkansas whipped Oklahoma with specially installed schemes. Offensive linemen faked blocks one way, drawing the quick-reading defensive tackles to the outside and opening big holes up the middle. And Arkansas' defensive front used nose guard Reggie Freeman as a free-moving, standup rover who keyed on quarterback Thomas Lott. Freeman collected five tackles behind the line of scrimmage.

At least once, Holtz's attention to detail bled from game plan to pregame plan. In 1981, Arkansas played at Texas A&M, and before the game, Holtz became intrigued by the Fightin' Texas Aggie Band, with its militarily precise execution of incredibly intricate ma-

neuvers. Holtz then designed a special pregame warmup to reflect a similar precision. That week, in addition to practicing for the game itself, the Razorbacks spent time working on the warmup.

Forget six lines of six players for calisthenics, or whatever. Players were assigned letters and numbers, the better to properly shift in unison.

"Here we are trying to prepare for A&M, and he threw that at us," remembers David Bazzel, then a freshman linebacker. "We've got enough to fool with as it is. But he wanted to implement this showy thing."

The day before the game, the Hogs spent almost their entire walk-through practice running through the new warmup, and not well. "It was like the *Bad News Bears,*" Bazzel remembers. Holtz grew frustrated, then angry.

"Lou just loses it," Bazzel says. " 'Hey, if you don't get this right, if there's one person that messes up, you're not dressing out tomorrow. You're not dressing out.' Sure enough, there were a couple of guys that messed up and he ran 'em off the field, told 'em to go get on the bus.

"I think he allowed 'em to play the next day. But it was just the fact that here we are to play this game, and Lou wanted to have this intricate, A&M-esque warmup deal."

The next day, the Hogs pulled off the new warmups without a hitch: "A

miracle," Bazzel says. "We pulled it off, and it wasn't too disastrous. But why would Lou want to put that in there just to do something different?"

Arkansas won, 10–7.

In 1978, the Hogs didn't live up to the number-one ranking. Texas upset unbeaten Arkansas, 28–21. The next week, Houston won 20–9. Arkansas finished with five straight wins before tying UCLA, 10–10, in the Fiesta Bowl on Christmas Day; the bowl hadn't yet achieved big-time status.

A year later, with a new quarterback in Kevin Scanlon, the Hogs started 6-0 and finally beat Texas. Only Houston, with a 13–10 win, kept Arkansas from an unbeaten regular season. Though Arkansas earned a share of the Southwest Conference championship, Houston went to the Cotton Bowl, sending Arkansas to the Sugar Bowl to face one of Bear Bryant's best Alabama teams and, ultimately, to a crushing loss.

After winning thirty games in the first three seasons, Holtz's teams won thirty in his last four. With a 7-5 record in 1980, Arkansas matched the loss total of the previous three seasons. It didn't help that the Southwest Conference was going through a period of renegade status; several programs, including SMU, were at their peak while committing numerous NCAA violations.

In 1981, the Hogs were maddeningly inconsistent: A 42–11 upset of

◀ FACING PAGE

Versatile running back Gary Anderson provided a big-play threat.

number-one-ranked Texas was sweet, but losing to TCU (snapping a twenty-two-year winning streak over the Horned Frogs) was not. Arkansas finished 8-4 and lost to North Carolina in a fog-shrouded Gator Bowl.

In 1982, with a team loaded with talent, including All-American defensive end/outside linebacker Billy Ray Smith, Jr.; versatile running backs Gary Anderson (a waterbug) and Jessie Clark (a smasher); receiver Derek Holloway; and the quarterback tandem of Tom Jones and Brad Taylor, Arkansas appeared primed for a run at the conference championship. However, an upset loss to Baylor quenched national title thoughts. And two weeks later, a mis-

gotten tie ended the Razorbacks' conference hopes.

Arkansas led powerful SMU—which had running backs Eric Dickerson and Craig James, along with a host of other future NFL players—17–10 in the fourth quarter. That's when Lance McIlhenny threw deep—way too deep—for receiver Jackie Wilson. Arkansas defensive back Nathan Jones was beyond Wilson; if anything, it looked as though he were the receiver. Wilson knocked Jones down from behind. "He tackled him, just tackled him," remembers Elliott, who watched the play unfold from the sideline.

As the overthrown ball sailed by harmlessly, a yellow flag landed. The

Razorbacks were certain the game was over. It was, but not the way they thought. The official, Horton Nesrsta, called *defensive* pass interference.

Back then, pass interference was marked off to the spot of the foul. The Hogs were penalized 40 yards; SMU had a first down at the Arkansas 17. McIlhenny ran for the tying touchdown, which preserved SMU's unbeaten season and sent the Mustangs to the Cotton Bowl.

Still reeling, the Hogs traveled to Austin, Texas, for the regular-season finale. The game had been moved from October for television. The Longhorns remembered the Razorbacks' 42–11 rout of the previous year, when Texas had been number one.

Texas rolled, 33–7.

"It destroyed us," says Elliott of the pass-interference call. "I'll be honest with you: We were so flat in Texas. They were always a great team, very talented. But we were a better team that year, and they beat us like a yard dog. We couldn't get over that loss."

Arkansas went on to the Bluebonnet Bowl, and beat Florida. But that was the last hurrah of the Holtz era. With the nucleus of the 1982 team gone, the Razorbacks struggled in 1983, needing a win in the season finale against Texas Tech to finish with a winning record.

When the season ended, Holtz fired three defensive assistants. Holtz himself would soon go. Over the years, the one-liners had lost some of their appeal. There was a growing perception that Holtz was more interested in speaking at faraway banquets than in wooing recruits.

Holtz was unable to match his early success, or the expectations it created.

When Holtz decided to make television commercials for Senator Jesse Helms, who was actively opposing a bill to create Martin Luther King, Jr., Day, several black recruits became upset and went elsewhere.

And at those speaking engagements though the years, Holtz had continued to make statements similar to his *Tonight Show* quip about Fayetteville's remote location. A variation: Fayetteville, he said, was "fifteen minutes from Tulsa by phone." And when the Hogs weren't winning as much, those zingers stung a lot more.

The sizzle of 1977 was long gone. In the end, 60-21-2 wasn't good enough. Not when Holtz started at 30-5-1. Not when the magic act had worn thin.

"It was obvious that a change needed to take place there," Bazzel says. "You could tell that whatever was there with coach Holtz wasn't working and there were some problems there."

That December, the change was made. While it was obvious Holtz had been fired, he and Broyles maintained he had resigned, saying he was "tired and burned out." On the morning he was fired, Holtz had interviewed a candidate for one of the defensive coaching vacancies. A few days later, Holtz resurfaced at Minnesota, apparently refreshed (and the candidate for that assistant job was hired there). Two years after that, Holtz moved on to Notre Dame where, in 1988, he won a national championship.

Twice afterward, Broyles tried to rehire Holtz. Both times, Holtz said thanks, but no thanks. After an eleven-year career at Notre Dame, he eventually wound up his career at South Carolina. He wasn't given an especially warm reception in 1999, when he brought the Gamecocks to War Memorial Stadium (Arkansas won, 48–14).

In the winter of 2005, a few months after his retirement from South Carolina, Holtz flew to Fayetteville to spend the day with the Arkansas coaching staff, imparting coaching wisdom.

"It was really, really good," says Houston Nutt, who orchestrated the visit.

"We had seven winning seasons, went to six bowls," Holtz told the *Greenville News* in 2002. "One thing about coaching is that there's cycles and sometimes things just don't fit. I don't care what you do, they just don't. It's like a car that you have, and you get a flat tire and you get that fixed and the generator goes out. Sometimes it just goes that way."

After the meteoric experience with an outsider, Broyles went looking for a family member. He considered Oklahoma's Barry Switzer and Texas' Fred Akers, both of whom withdrew from consideration. He interviewed Jimmy Johnson, then at Oklahoma State.

Broyles instead hired another member of the 1964 national championship squad. Ken Hatfield understood what it meant to be a Razorback, and what the Razorbacks meant to Arkansas. He'd grown up in Helena, listening to games on the radio, and occasionally traveling the two hours to Little Rock for games. At Arkansas, Hatfield had served as senior class president and ROTC brigade commander. His 81-yard punt return for a touchdown against Texas had helped pave the way for that national title.

When Broyles called, Hatfield wasn't altogether sure he wanted the job.

After graduating with an accounting degree, Hatfield had left the state and forged a successful career; after stints as an assistant at Army, Tennessee, Florida, and Air Force, he had been promoted to head coach at Air Force

for the 1979 season. There, he had taken the wishbone, with slight adaptations, and built a consistent winner despite having service-academy talent (or lack thereof). The Falcons were 10-2 in 1983, including wins at Notre Dame and in the Independence Bowl over Ole Miss, and Hatfield was named national coach of the year.

After returning to Colorado Springs after his interview, which was Hatfield's first visit to Fayetteville in fifteen years, he and his wife, Sandy, talked and prayed long and hard. He had a great situation at Air Force, and he would have been content to stay there, but there was something about going home.

"I loved Arkansas with all my heart," Hatfield says.

His initial goal was to pull everybody together. For the first few seasons, Hatfield did that. His enthusiasm was contagious. Players and fans alike found him to be approachable and down to earth.

Hatfield didn't easily mix with the powerbrokers. And in a day when pro-style passing offenses were becoming the rage, fans weren't enthralled with the flexbone, his version of the wishbone. Also, the high visibility of his Christian faith, while undeniably the bedrock of his coaching success, was troubling to some.

Add a stubborn streak, and you had potential for conflict. But all this didn't

Nineteen years after graduating from Arkansas, Ken Hatfield was happy to return home.

James Shibest emerged as a go-to receiver in Hatfield's flexbone attack.

surface until after a few losses in big games.

In 1984, Arkansas scrapped to 7-4-1 and a berth in the Liberty Bowl. Along the way, the Hogs developed a reputation as gritty overachievers. Several times, they scrambled back from deficits to victories, or near misses. Trailing 24–6 at Texas, Arkansas rallied. The Hogs had possession at Texas' 4-yard line when time ran out, and lost 24–18.

"That was a fun year," says James Shibest, who's now an Arkansas assistant coach but was then the Hogs' go-to receiver. "We turned a lot of things around. You could kind of feel the momentum swinging back. You could see the future was gonna be good for us."

In Hatfield's eyes, they were true Fightin' Razorbacks, like the teams he'd grown up watching and then playing on. And Hatfield recruited, too. His philosophy was simple: "You had to get everybody out of the state of Arkansas, and then you had to supplement it with players from the adjoining states."

He'd found the cupboard mostly bare of talent, but lured to Fayetteville big-timers like halfback James Rouse and fullback Barry Foster, offensive lineman Freddie Childress, defensive lineman Wayne Martin, and safety Steve Atwater. One of the biggest "gets," especially considering Hatfield's wishbone attack, was quarterback Quinn Grovey, who came from Duncan, Oklahoma. He chose Arkansas over Oklahoma because of the Sooners' abundance of quarterbacks.

"It was an easy sell for me," Hatfield says, "because I'd been there through good times and tough times. I could believe in the little things about Arkansas that made Arkansas a special place."

In 1985 and 1986, the Hogs showed improvement. They missed the Cotton Bowl by a game each year. For 1987, Hatfield's fourth season, expectations had risen. Arkansas had played in the Orange Bowl after the 1986 season. And although Oklahoma won big, 42–8

(Barry Switzer admitted he wanted revenge for the stunning upset of nine years earlier), it appeared the Hogs were on the verge of a breakthrough.

Unfortunately, the Razorbacks disappointed.

It started with scheduling. Johnson, the former Hog, had moved from Oklahoma State to Miami, where he had assembled a powerful roster full of future NFL players. When Oklahoma dropped Miami from its schedule in the spring of 1987, Arkansas signed up for a two-year series.

"I looked at the schedule and thought we needed a really tough team before we played Texas," Hatfield recalls.

So, en route to the national championship, the Hurricanes traveled to

Little Rock and left plenty of storm damage: 51–7 was the largest margin of defeat for an Arkansas team in forty-four years.

"They beat the dog out of us," Hatfield says. "They just killed us."

Hatfield's practice of opening his television show with a Bible verse had rankled some. When, after the loss, he quoted John 11:35, "Jesus wept," the whispers boiled over into controversy. Folk on both sides of the divide were unhappy with the reference. And with the loss, of course. Three weeks later came something less forgivable. Trailing 14–10 in Little Rock, Texas came up with a last-second touchdown pass to win 16–14.

"Not only was it the last play, it was Texas," says reserve quarterback John Bland, neatly summing up the import.

Favored by nine points, Arkansas led 14–7 at halftime, but didn't attempt a pass in the final three quarters. Never mind that quarterbacks Greg Thomas and Quinn Grovey were battered, or that Hatfield was following a time-tested philosophy of playing conserva-tively with the lead. Forget that Arkansas appeared to have come up with a fumble near midfield with less than two minutes left, which would have sealed victory, only to have officials award the football to Texas.

What everyone would forever re-member was this: On the game's last play, after Arkansas had called timeout to set its defense (Texas didn't have a timeout), Longhorns quarterback Bret Stafford somehow found five-foot-seven receiver Tony Jones between two de-fenders for 18 yards and a touchdown. The ball was thrown slightly behind Jones, but the diminutive receiver reached back and got it even as safety Steve Atwater and cornerback An-thoney Cooney crashed into him.

War Memorial Stadium fell sud-denly silent.

"The fans were so quiet, you could have heard a pin drop," Grovey says. "And all of the sudden, they were mad."

As the stunned Razorbacks trooped slowly up the ramp toward the locker room, an apparently inebriated fan

James Rouse is corralled by a Longhorn defender. Texas' last-second upset of Arkansas in 1987 was bitterly disappointing.

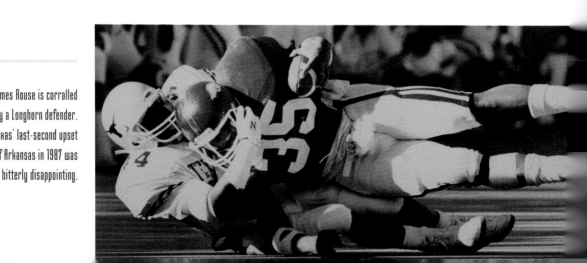

began cussing Hatfield, then spat at him. Their eyes locked for a moment. Hatfield didn't say anything, he just kept moving.

Moments later, when asked about the incident, he said he had "hide like an alligator." Hatfield now says he wondered: "Why do you think you hurt worse than we do? We're playing the game. We put a heck of a lot more into this game."

Arkansas would win the Southwest Conference the next season, and the next. The Hogs would make two straight appearances in the Cotton Bowl, with the first breaking a thirteen-year drought.

Yet, the Texas game was the turning point in Hatfield's tenure. Everything afterward was an uphill battle. An overwhelmingly negative buzz developed after the loss. The *Gazette*'s Orville Henry quoted a fan as saying after the game, "He won't pass. He's always preaching at us. And he can't beat Texas."

The criticism wasn't entirely fair.

Hatfield hadn't really preached, at least not much, but he certainly wasn't about to apologize for his faith.

His faith was clearly evident to players. Bible verses were posted on bulletin boards. Hatfield kept them from being considered for the *Playboy* All-American team, because he believed that the magazine's message was immoral. All of that was in-line with Hat-field's belief that his job was "teaching kids to win in life and win in football."

"He talked about his faith," Grovey says. "He coached us that way in regards to making sure we were doing the right thing. He wasn't just a football coach. He talked about life situations and being a better person and not always relying on football. . . . That's what coach Hatfield believed. He wasn't ashamed. He was going to do it his way. You have to respect a man that's going to do things his way."

There was also the issue of passing. There was no doubt Hatfield coached a conservative style. However, his teams had passed, to an extent. Quarterback Brad Taylor and Shibest had set school passing records in 1984, Hatfield's first season, even while operating from the 'bone.

During the Texas game, quarterbacks Greg Thomas (shoulder) and Quinn Grovey (strained groin, among other things) were severely banged up.

"We had two quarterbacks who could barely take a snap," Hatfield said after the game, "if they weren't so gutsy, they would not even have been out there."

Among the few passes thrown was an interception, which led to Texas' first touchdown. It's also ironic to note that two years later, Arkansas' chances to beat Tennessee in the Cotton Bowl were waylaid when Grovey forced a pass at the Vols' 2-yard line.

Known as an option quarterback, Quinn Grovey was an underrated passer. The Hogs passed under Ken Hatfield, but not much.

Arkansas finished the 1987 season 9-4, including a win in an extra game at Hawaii. After the season, Broyles asked Hatfield to fire three assistant coaches. He refused, and went into the 1988 season believing the Razorbacks had to win the Southwest Conference in order to keep his own job.

And so, they did. The years 1988 and 1989 were as successful as any in the Hogs' recent history. In 1988, Arkansas rolled unbeaten through the SWC. Included was a 27–24 win at Texas that was keyed by a fantastic catch by backup receiver Tim Horton on a throw by

backup quarterback John Bland, who had replaced an injured Grovey.

"That was the springboard to the championship," Horton says of the win.

Ranked eighth, the Razorbacks were 10-0 when they headed to Miami in late November. The Hurricanes had been beaten by Lou Holtz's Notre Dame team earlier in the season, but still had designs on their second straight national championship. (It was not to be; Holtz's Fighting Irish went unbeaten and reached the pinnacle.)

Despite Arkansas' perfect record, the

Barry Foster finds the
end zone in a 27-24 win
over Texas in 1988. The
Hogs won their first of
two straight Southwest
Conference championships.

Hog fans flocked to Dallas and packed the venerable old stadium for the 1989 and 1990 Cotton Bowls.

▶ FACING PAGE
Grovey led Arkansas to 568 yards against Tennessee, but three turnovers prevented the Hogs from winning.

memory of the 1987 debacle caused most to discount the Hogs' chances against Miami, which was installed as a seventeen-point favorite. Led by fullback Barry Foster, who broke free for an 80-yard touchdown run and caught a 16-yard pass from Grovey for another score, Arkansas led 16–15 into the fourth quarter.

Miami moved 74 yards in ten plays to win. Carlos Huerta's 20-yard field goal with 5:38 left, his third of the game, gave the Hurricanes an 18–16 win. Just barely. On the preceding play, Arkansas safety Steve Atwater, who would be a first-round draft pick and an all-pro with the Denver Broncos, had a misfired pass from Miami's Steve Walsh in his hands in the end zone, but dropped it.

"It was a little high, but I should have had it," Atwater told reporters afterward. "I don't know what happened. I had it, and then I didn't have it."

Kind of like the Hogs that day. Miami's escape dashed Arkansas' national title dreams. Still, Arkansas headed to the Cotton Bowl for the first time in thirteen years, accompanied by as many as fifty thousand fans.

"The state was just on fire," Grovey says. "And we were just elated."

UCLA's Troy Aikman left the Hogs deflated in a 17–3 win, picking them apart with precise passing. Aikman, who would soon be the number-one overall pick in the NFL draft, was one thing. When Arkansas managed just 42 yards of total offense, the naysayers came out again.

The Razorbacks, meanwhile, were motivated by the loss.

"We knew we had dropped the ball against UCLA," Grovey says. "We really wanted to get back to the Cotton Bowl and take care of some unfinished business."

After the offensive meltdown, Hatfield hired Jack Crowe away from Clemson to be his offensive coordinator (Broyles had suggested it). The Hogs dropped the wishbone and implemented the I formation. Although Arkansas actually ran more and passed less in 1989 than in 1988, the offense produced 4,926 yards, then a school record.

En route to Dallas, Arkansas lost only to Texas (another upset, this one by 24–20 in Fayetteville). Grovey had perhaps his finest day in a 45–39 shootout win over Houston's run-and-shoot, led by Andre Ware (who went on to win the Heisman Trophy). Against Tennessee in the Cotton Bowl, Arkansas piled up 568 yards (361 on the ground).

Still, the Razorbacks couldn't overcome three devastating turnovers in a 31–27 loss. Arkansas lost two fumbles inside the Tennessee 15. And, from the 2, Grovey tossed that interception into the end zone.

"I saw him wide open, but I just laid it out there," Grovey says. "[Tennessee's] Carl Pickens made an exceptional play. I should have stuck it in

there to [the receiver], and I didn't. That play changed the game."

If it didn't, this did. Two plays later, Tennessee quarterback Andy Kelly tossed an 84-yard touchdown pass, pushing the Vols up 10–6; they would extend the lead to 31–13 before the Razorbacks roared back with fourteen fourth-quarter points.

"I'd like to thank our fans for coming," Hatfield said after the game. "We were glad to be here, and we'll do all we can to get back here next time."

There wasn't to be a next time. Though fans were perhaps mollified by the consecutive Cotton Bowls, Hatfield's relationship with Broyles had deteriorated to the point the coach believed the rift wouldn't ever be healed.

A year earlier during the run-up to the Cotton Bowl, Hatfield had talked with Georgia's Vince Dooley about replacing the legend as the Bulldogs coach (Dooley, who as athletic director had the same ability as Broyles to choose his successor, instead tabbed Georgia assistant Ray Goff).

Broyles had offered Hatfield a new contract after the 1988 season. After a year of wrangling, Hatfield had been set to sign it, but noticed a few wording errors. A few days after the Cotton Bowl loss to Tennessee, he said he planned to sign it as soon as he received the corrected version.

Instead when Clemson called three

it was one of those things. I knew it wasn't gonna get any better. I wasn't gonna be there too much longer. I don't think there was any doubt something was gonna happen from the other end that I probably wasn't gonna be there too much longer."

"I didn't want to leave Arkansas," Hatfield continues. "There wasn't any doubt about that. If there was any way it could have happened. But there wasn't. It was the right decision at the time."

After four years at Clemson, Hatfield moved on to Rice. He's been there since 1994, and says he has no regrets about his time at Arkansas.

"Very few people are fortunate enough to be able to coach at your own school," he says. "Because I loved Arkansas with all my heart, I put everything I had into it for six years. Nobody could see it better than I did. We did it with our whole heart, and we never backed down.

"I'll always be a Razorback. I couldn't have given any more to the state or to Arkansas Razorback football."

The 1990 Cotton Bowl was Hatfield's last game as Arkansas' coach.

weeks after the Cotton Bowl, Hatfield took the job. Even though the Hogs had just played in their second straight Cotton Bowl, Hatfield says it was just a matter of time until he would have been forced out.

"Coach Broyles and I were not on the same page," he says. "It was very evident it was not gonna be that way, ever. . . . When the opportunity came,

9

Homegrown Hogs

THEY GREW UP Hogs, dreaming of a day when they might pull on the cardinal jersey and run through the A. There's something special about a home-grown hero, those players who can't remember when they learned to call the Hogs, just that they've always known how.

▲ PREVIOUS PAGE
Many an Arkansas boy has dreamed of playing for the Razorbacks.

Brandon Burlsworth developed from a walk-on into an All-American.

And who understood what it meant to be called.

Barry Lunney, Jr., who played quarterback in the 1990s, remembers a night in Little Rock in 1995. In the final minutes before kickoff against Auburn, the Hogs were in their locker room beneath the stadium. And they couldn't help but hear the roar as the fans called the Hogs.

"It was just like, 'Man, listen to *that!*'" Lunney remembers. "There were moments like that when you thought, 'I can't believe I'm actually running out on that field.' I think a lot of the kids on the team from Arkansas thought that.

"It was just so special . . . to know how important that game is to those people in the stands, to know they're there to support you, it's a little bit overwhelming."

Over the years, they have come from Little Rock and Lake Village, from Fort Smith and Fayetteville and Fordyce, from Hot Springs and Helena, from the Delta and the piney woods and the Ozarks . . . from every nook and cranny of a small, wonderful state. So many homegrown Hogs have thrilled us, for so many different reasons. Here are just a few of the best.

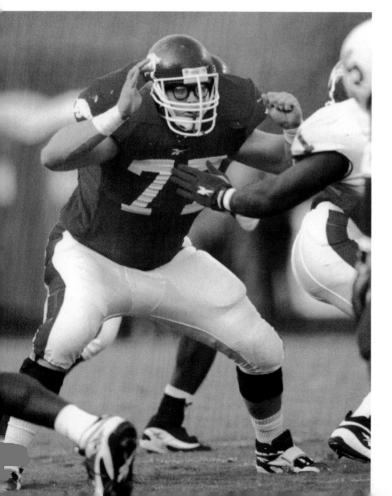

BRANDON BURLSWORTH

LETTERED: 1995–98
POSITION: OFFENSIVE GUARD
HOMETOWN: HARRISON

After a long day of practice, then meetings, Houston Nutt and his staff wrapped up. As they prepared to head home, an unusual skittering noise stopped them. It was coming from the indoor practice area.

"You could hear these feet moving on the turf," Nutt says.

This was 1998, several days before Arkansas would play Alabama. The Hogs hadn't practiced well. When Nutt flipped on the lights, there was Brandon Burlsworth. In the darkness, he had been shuffling his 6-3, 309-pound frame back and forth across the artificial turf.

"What are you doing?" Nutt asked.

"Coach, we had a bad practice today," Burlsworth said. "I'm walking through the plays."

If ever anyone embodied the Razorback ideal, it was Burlsworth. After walking on at Arkansas, he became a three-year starter on the offensive line, and an All-American as a senior in 1998. His work ethic was legendary.

Three weeks after the Indianapolis Colts drafted Burlsworth in the third round in the 1999 NFL draft, he died in an automobile accident. Arkansas retired Burlsworth's jersey. No future Razorback will wear number 77.

"There wasn't a better person than Brandon Burlsworth," Nutt told the *Arkansas Democrat-Gazette.* "He left something behind that nobody will ever forget. He does everything the right way.

"You talk about special, that doesn't even say enough."

The first time Russell Brown set eyes on Burlsworth, in August 1994, he thought: "There's a walk-on. He'll never make it." Burlsworth hid out in the weight room, Brown says, and emerged as a different player.

"He made himself into a man," says Brown, who started with Burlsworth on the offensive line.

He was an eccentric, too. He moved into a dorm room in 1994, and never moved out.

"He wouldn't step on cracks in the tile, used the same soap in the shower, wore the same undershirt," Brown remembers. "The year he graduated, he had the same workout shoes he wore as a freshman. Five years old. Worn out. Toes hanging out the side. That was Brandon."

So yes, Burlsworth, who became known for his thick, black glasses, was a creature of habit. And they were good habits. A devout Christian, he didn't drink, smoke, or cuss. He was a regular at his home church in Harrison. He was the only Razorback to earn a master's degree while still a player.

Burlsworth expressed delight and surprise after his selection in the draft. "I couldn't have dreamed of this happening when I first got here," he said. "I thought I'd be able to play for the Razorbacks, but the NFL was the last thing on my mind. The way things have gone, it's like a storybook.

"I don't think I could have written it up any better than how it's all happened."

Two weeks later, as Burlsworth drove a winding highway between Fayetteville and Harrison, he was killed in a head-on collision with an eighteen-wheeler.

Burlsworth's death stunned his teammates. This didn't: At the time of the accident, Arkansas' football players

Brandon Burlsworth.

were participating in a ring ceremony for their 1998 accomplishments of tying for the SEC West title and reaching the Citrus Bowl, while Burlsworth was headed home to attend Wednesday night worship services.

Burlsworth's locker remains encased in plexiglass, the better to remind the Razorbacks to go about things "Burls' way."

"The legacy he left," Nutt says, "was the commitment and the passion and the attitude."

JIM BENTON

LETTERED: 1935–37

POSITION: END

HOMETOWN: FORDYCE

Jim Benton.

It's a measure of Jim Benton's greatness that his receiving marks, set in the mid-1930s, stood as Arkansas' best until the 1970s.

The six-foot-four end was courted by LSU, but chose Arkansas, where his brother, W. R. "Footsie" Benton, had played a few years earlier. He became the Razorbacks' second All-American (Wear Schoonover, in 1929, was the first).

Playing in the era before Frank Broyles, before Bowden Wyatt, even before John Barnhill, Jim Benton was the receiving half of a potent passing combination.

Under coach Fred Thomsen's advanced schemes, Arkansas was briefly known as the Passing Porkers. In 1936 and, especially, 1937, quarterbacks Jack Robbins and Dwight "Paddlefoot" Sloan threw and threw and threw. Benton caught and caught and caught.

In 1936, Benton had 35 catches. A year later, as a senior, he put together astronomical numbers for the times: 48 catches for 814 yards and 7 touchdowns.

The Southwest Conference record he set stood until 1963. Not until 1971, when Mike Reppond caught 56 passes from Joe Ferguson, did Benton slip from the top of the Arkansas receiving charts.

Benton finished his three-year career with 83 catches, 1,303 yards, and 13 touchdowns. The yardage total remains the eleventh best in school history.

His most important highlight might have come a year earlier. Fittingly, it was against Texas. The Hogs needed a victory to secure their first SWC championship. Texas was only 2-6-1. In the series' history, however, Arkansas had beaten the Longhorns just twice in eighteen games.

On a rainy day and a muddy field, just one touchdown was scored. Late in the third quarter, Sloan hit Benton with a 13-yard touchdown pass. Arkansas won 7–3 and claimed the championship.

A year later, Arkansas went 6-2-2 and was ranked fourteenth in the final Associated Press poll. After Benton's departure, the Hogs went nine years without a winning season.

The Cleveland Rams made Benton the number eleven overall pick in the draft in 1938. Known as pro football's first split end, Benton had 10 catches for 303 yards in a game against Detroit in 1945; that mark still ranks third all-time in NFL history. He led the NFL in receiving yards in 1945 and 1946, becoming the first pro player to total one thousand receiving yards in a season, and retired after the 1947 season. At the time, Benton ranked number two on the NFL's career receiving chart with 388 catches, 4,801 yards, and 45 touchdowns.

When Benton died in April 2001, at eighty-four, the *New York Times* said he "was overshadowed in his day only by Don Hutson of the Green Bay Packers. . . . [Benton] was tall for his era, had large hands and displayed a penchant for making difficult catches."

Benton later coached at Arkansas A&M (now Arkansas-Monticello) and in 1953, his team won the Arkansas Intercollegiate Conference championship.

"I've been all around, and he's one of the greatest heroes that this state's ever had," said Larry Lacewell, fellow Fordyce native and former Dallas Cowboys front-office man.

CLYDE "SMACKOVER" SCOTT

LETTERED: 1946–48
POSITION: TAILBACK/WINGBACK
HOMETOWN: SMACKOVER

The Razorbacks have Miss Arkansas to thank for the services of the state's Athlete of the Century.

Clyde Scott, a Smackover native who was an All-American in football and track for Arkansas (and a silver medalist in the 1948 Olympics), was so named by readers of the *Arkansas Democrat-Gazette* in 2000. He got to Fayetteville only after falling in love with a beauty queen.

Scott had accepted an appointment to the Naval Academy, where he was an All-American in football and track. When Lake Village's Leslie Hampton visited Annapolis en route to Atlantic City and the Miss America pageant, Midshipman Scott was assigned to be her escort.

It was the beginning of the end of his career at the Academy.

"I invited her back up for the Army-Navy game," says Scott, eighty, who is retired and living in Little Rock, "then I went back home that summer and we decided to get married."

And that meant he had to leave the Naval Academy, which didn't allow

Clyde Scott.

midshipmen to marry. Although Scott had his pick of prime football destinations, his wife had just finished her sophomore year at Arkansas.

"That was a big reason I came back," Scott says.

As a running back and defensive back, Scott was a three-time All-Southwest Conference player (1946–48), and an All-American in 1948. As a sprinter and hurdler, he blazed to two world records.

He ran 13.7 seconds in the 110-meter high hurdles in the NCAA championships (and later won a silver medal in the same event in the 1948 Olympics). Scott ran a world-record time of 9.4 seconds in the 100-yard dash. He threw the javelin 197 feet.

"He's the greatest athlete I've ever seen," says Bud Canada, an end on those Arkansas teams. "He was the fastest football player in the country at the time, easily. He was so fast."

From 1946 to 1948, Scott rushed for 1,463 yards. He won All-American honors in 1948 after rushing for 670 yards on 95 carries, a 7.1 average.

Scott's biggest impact was consistently at defensive back. His most important contribution probably came during the 1947 Cotton Bowl, when his tackle at the 1-yard line preserved a scoreless tie with favored LSU.

Scott's best sport might have been track. He'd noticed as a child in the south Arkansas oil-patch town of Smackover "that he was a little bit faster than most people."

Make that a lot faster. Simply put, Scott had another gear. On Arkansas' 440 relay team, he ran the anchor leg. Canada ran the third leg, then handed off to Scott.

"I was continuously hollerin', 'Wait! Wait! Wait!' " Canada says.

In setting that world record in the 110-meter high hurdles in the NCAA championships, Scott nipped Northwestern's Bill Porter. Later, in the 1948 Olympics, the order was reversed:

Clyde "Smackover" Scott had world-class speed, and was a threat on offense or defense. He set a world record in the 100-yard dash and won a silver medal in the 110-meter high hurdles in the 1948 Olympics.

Porter won the gold medal, Scott the silver.

Scott played four seasons in the NFL (three with Philadelphia, one with Detroit), retiring after a knee injury.

Soon after his college career was finished, Arkansas retired Scott's number twelve. It's one of just two retired numbers in the program's history. Only one other Razorback has worn it; in 1974, university officials asked Scott if heralded Steve Little, the focus of a hot recruiting battle, could have the number.

BUD BROOKS

LETTERED: 1952–54

POSITION: OFFENSIVE GUARD/
DEFENSIVE TACKLE

HOMETOWN: WYNNE

They didn't lift weights in those days, but William "Bud" Brooks sure looked like he did.

The two-way lineman was the first of two Razorbacks to win the Outland Trophy, presented annually to the nation's best lineman. In 1954, he was one of the leaders of the 25 Little Pigs, who won the Southwest Conference and set the stage, many observers say, for the modern era of Arkansas football.

"Physically, Bud was just different than the rest of us," former Arkansas quarterback George Walker told the

Arkansas Democrat-Gazette in January 2005, shortly after Brooks' death at age seventy-four. "He was built like a rock. He was the first player I'd ever seen like that, that when you touched his arm or his neck or his shoulder or anything, it was just like a rock."

Brooks was named the outstanding lineman in the 1955 Cotton Bowl, even though Georgia Tech won 14–6. Weeks later, he was the most valuable player in the Senior Bowl.

Brooks, who played on a state championship team at Wynne, packed 200 pounds on a 5-11 frame. He might have carried more weight, but coach Bowden Wyatt's strenuous conditioning drills kept the Little Pigs lean. There wasn't much doubt Brooks was mean.

"As a blocker, he would pull and go around the end and you never had to wait for him," Walker said. "He was always out there when you got there. On defense, he could chase people down. Running backs would be going away from him and he'd go all the way across the field to make a tackle."

Said Buddy Bob Benson, who played quarterback and defensive back on the same team: "It wasn't hard to pick him out, because he was in on nearly every tackle. He was just one of the great players of his time."

Brooks' performances helped the Hogs edge Texas A&M for a key victory in 1954. With the game tied at 7, the Aggies were driving, but Brooks hit

Bud Brooks.

Nicknamed "Thumper"
because of the sound
his hard hits produced,
undersized Wayne Harris
remains the standard
by which Arkansas
linebackers are measured.

A&M's Elwood Kettler and knocked the ball loose. The Razorbacks recovered and drove for the winning touchdown.

Wyatt later explained Brooks' prowess this way: "He had as much speed as linemen ever have, and an amazing ability to get to the ball." Frank Broyles, who was a Georgia Tech assistant, said the Yellow Jackets were forced to make a halftime adjustment just for Brooks. Trailing 6–0, Georgia Tech began double-teaming Brooks on every play.

"We had to stop him from making the plays," Broyles said. "He was like a linebacker in that he could make plays all over the field. He knew where the play was going instinctively and he could get to the ball on either side."

In 1955, he was a fifth-round pick (number sixty overall) for the Detroit Lions, and played briefly for the Lions and New York Giants before returning home to Arkansas.

WAYNE "THUMPER" HARRIS

LETTERED: 1958–60
POSITION: LINEBACKER/CENTER
HOMETOWN: EL DORADO

He was too small, even back then, to play the game. Until he hit you.

Just ask SMU's Don Meredith, who probably doesn't remember meeting Wayne Harris one day in 1959. At six-foot, 185 pounds, Thumper packed a serious punch.

Harris, who was inducted into the College Football Hall of Fame in 2004, was an All-American in 1960, when he helped the Hogs win the Southwest Conference. That year, he tallied a school-record 174 tackles. Most of them probably left bruises.

"It was hard to understand how at his size he could hit that hard," says Mickey Cissell, who was a reserve fullback and kicker in 1960.

Harris had been given the nickname Thumper as a sophomore at El

Dorado High School. His tackle caused an assistant coach to say, "You can hear that thump up in the nickel seats." The nickname stuck, and it went with Harris to Arkansas, where no one saw any reason to change it.

"Wayne Harris was too little to play linebacker, even when little guys played," says former Arkansas assistant Merv Johnson, "but he was a great player. He was a heavy hitter. He was tough, smart, and fast. And he had such quickness, you couldn't block him."

If you had the football, you sure didn't want to meet him, which brings us back to 1959, and that SMU game in Dallas. Arkansas won 17–14, clinching a share of the Southwest Conference title. The Hogs' cause was greatly aided by Harris' crushing crash into the Mustangs' splendid quarterback.

With Arkansas clinging to a lead, Meredith dropped back to pass, then bolted up the middle. Bad move. Harris charged forward. When they met, the full-speed collision was like a car wreck—for Meredith.

Harris hopped up. They carried the woozy quarterback from the field (he later returned).

"It's hard to see your receiver when your eyeballs are in the back of your head," Arkansas assistant coach Wilson Matthews said.

Teammates remembered other collisions. It seems Harris never went half-speed in practice. "Everybody on the team, everybody that carried the ball remembered those licks," Cissell says. In fact, Cissell found himself on the wrong end of Thumper's punch during a Red-White scrimmage in Little Rock.

"I was kicking off for the white team, and he was on the red," Cissell remembers. "As soon as I kicked off, he hit me in the chest and knocked me down. I jumped up. He knocked me down again."

Coach Frank Broyles took film of the play and made it into a highlight sequence for recruits. "He was featuring Wayne Harris," Cissell says, "but I was the one getting knocked down twice."

Harris went on to an all-star, twelve-year career with the Calgary Stampeders of the Canadian Football League; in 1971, he was the Most Valuable Player in the Grey Cup (the CFL's version of the Super Bowl). Later inducted into the CFL Hall of Fame, he resides in Calgary.

Although other linebackers were larger, Harris remains the standard by which the Razorbacks' big hits are measured.

"I don't think anybody that's ever played linebacker had more ability than Wayne to make plays all over the field," said Broyles, who coached Harris. "He weighed one hundred ninety, but when he tackled you, you thought a two-hundred-sixty-pounder had hit you."

Dan Hampton.

DAN HAMPTON

LETTERED: 1975–78
POSITION: DEFENSIVE TACKLE
HOMETOWN: JACKSONVILLE

Dan Hampton, an All-American defensive tackle at Arkansas, went on to a twelve-year NFL career with the Chicago Bears. In 2002, he was inducted into the Pro Football Hall of Fame.

During the summer of 1973, however, as a sophomore at Jacksonville High School, Hampton was a 6-5, 240-pound saxophone player.

"The coach would be coming off the field after getting beat 30–0 at halftime, and I'm standing there, ready to assault those white lines with my sax, and he's thinking, 'What a sissy,'" Hampton told espn.com. "They really sold me on it. Why not try it?"

Why not, indeed? The career change, which Hampton made the next year as a junior, worked out pretty well. To be fair, Hampton had been a pretty fair athlete in grade school. He hadn't tilted toward music until he was twelve, when a thirty-foot fall from a tree put him in a wheelchair for six months. His heel, ankle, and wrist were broken; after inserting pins and screws in various places, doctors suggested Hampton might be better off without sports.

Hampton said the sax was cool. He also learned how to play the guitar. He joined the marching band. And, then, Jacksonville coach Bill Reed noticed Hampton and eventually talked him into playing football. After switching to the Red Devils' football team, Hampton moved on to Arkansas.

"From where he started to where he ended up," says Arkansas quarterback Ron Calcagni, who enrolled at Arkansas in 1975, same as Hampton, "it's just unbelievable how he progressed."

Hampton's late start in football was matched by a late start in maturing. He entered school a long, lanky athlete. "But he just developed into a man," Calcagni says. "Our strength coaches got a hold of him."

Hampton grew into a three-year starter at defensive tackle, a 260-pound force who anchored outstanding defensive lines. In 1978, his senior season, he was an All-American with 98 tackles (70 solo), including 18 tackles for loss.

"Nobody could block him," Calcagni says. "He was always penetrating and screwing up your [offensive] play. When we chose sides for the spring game, you always wanted him on your side."

Hampton was the number-four overall pick by the Bears in 1979. Playing end and tackle, he thrived despite constant double-teaming. He earned the nickname "Danimal" for his play as the linchpin of the Bears' 4-6 defense in 1985, when they won the Super Bowl.

In twelve seasons, he was credited with 57 sacks.

Not bad for a saxophone player.

BRAD TAYLOR

LETTERED: 1981–84
POSITION: QUARTERBACK
HOMETOWN: DANVILLE

He wasn't heralded, just a small-town boy who wanted to play for the Hogs. Brad Taylor, pride of tiny Danville, lived every young Arkansas boy's dream.

Taylor had led the Danville Little-johns to the 1980 Class A state championship. Other quarterbacks—Lance McHan (son of former Arkansas standout Lamar) and Mark Calcagni (brother of former Arkansas standout Ron Calcagni) got more publicity, however. No one was quite sure what to make of Taylor.

"Most people thought, 'Danville, Arkansas. How's he going to compete?'" remembers David Bazzel, former linebacker, who was a member along with Taylor of the 1981 freshman class.

Taylor understood. He'd heard the whispers he might punt, or play defensive back, but that there was no way he'd play quarterback. And that was fine with him. "That just motivated me, more than anything," Taylor says. "But I'd always wanted to be a Razorback. I'd have been a waterboy if they'd wanted."

The Hogs, and their fans, quickly figured out one thing: This country boy could chuck the football, and then some. He finished his career as Arkansas' passing and total offense leader (the numbers have since been surpassed).

"He wasn't just awe-inspiring with the looks," Bazzel says. "But when he would throw it, nobody wanted to play

Unheralded coming out of Danville High School, Brad Taylor became a folk hero for his passing skills.

catch with him, because he could rifle the ball."

It didn't take long for the Hogs to realize Taylor could play. As a freshman, he helped the Hogs to wins over Rice, Baylor, and Texas A&M. Hogs fans well remember the bombs he threw to Derek Holloway in that foggy 1981 Gator Bowl.

Taylor alternated with Tom Jones.

"But whenever we needed to throw the ball, [coach Lou Holtz] would put Brad in there to throw it," says Marcus Elliott, who as an offensive lineman was charged with protecting Taylor. "He had a gun."

As a senior, Taylor adapted to Ken Hatfield's flexbone attack. Although he wasn't suited to be a wishbone quarterback—he lacked speed—Taylor and James Shibest, his favorite target, hooked up often.

"Brad just wants to win," said David Lee, who was Arkansas' quarterbacks coach in 1984. "Brad would run the single wing if we asked him to and try his heart out at executing it."

Perhaps Taylor's best, or at least, his most gutsy, performances came in two 1984 losses. Trailing Texas 24–3 in Austin, Taylor had misfired on all 10 passes he had attempted, with four interceptions. In the fourth quarter, Hatfield turned to the quarterback and asked, "Brad, how would it feel to win this game?"

Taylor was a passer, not a runner, but he adapted to Ken Hatfield's flexbone.

"Great," Taylor said.

And then, he went out and almost did it, completing 12 of 22 passes for 201 yards in the last thirteen minutes. On the final play, Taylor eluded pressure, threw off his back foot and hit Jamie Lueders; Texas tackled him just shy of the goal line, then exhaled with a 24–18 win.

"We just couldn't get it in," Taylor told reporters after the game. "You feel bad about losing, but you can hold your head up. You never can count us out."

Later against SMU, Taylor completed 20 of 28 passes—13 passes went to Shibest, who tied a school record—for 248 yards and 3 touchdowns. It wasn't enough to prevent a 31–28 loss.

"He wanted to win, to be the best, so bad," former Arkansas assistant coach Ken Turner once said. "He was as great a team player as I've ever known. Those are two things the Razorbacks are all about."

MATT JONES

LETTERED: 2001–04

POSITION: QUARTERBACK

HOMETOWN: VAN BUREN

When Matt Jones arrived, Arkansas' coaches weren't sure what to do with him. Quarterback? Receiver? Something else entirely? Soon enough, Arkansas' coaches passed the dilemma on to op-

Matt Jones eludes the Longhorns for a touchdown in 2003. His speed and uncanny instincts combined to make Jones a big play waiting to happen.

posing defensive coordinators. Matt Jones might have defied easy description, but he also defied easy tackling.

"There's probably never been coordinators sleep less during the week worrying," says Harold Horton, the former Arkansas player and assistant coach.

Alternately fantastic and frustrating, Jones wasn't a prototypical quarterback, but he could improvise at whim. He finished his career as the SEC's rushing leader for quarterbacks, and as a dangerous passer. Want another barometer? His first pass went for a touchdown. His first basket—yes, he played basketball, too—was a dunk.

By the time Jones' career ended after the 2004 season, it was apparent he was one of the best athletes to ever play for the Razorbacks.

"He's the most unusual athlete I've ever coached in my life," says Arkansas coach Houston Nutt. "He just made unbelievable plays. He's the best playground quarterback in America. That's the best way to describe him, I think."

NFL scouts described Jones as a "freak." How else to define a 6-6, 242-pounder who ran a legitimate 4.40-second 40-yard dash? Not even on the radar screen on most draft boards before the 2004 season, Jones was the twenty-first overall selection by the Jacksonville Jaguars in April 2005. He was slated to play wide receiver, but surely the Jaguars were salivating for special quarterback packages.

SEC coaches were glad to describe Jones, finally, as *gone.*

"You never know how long you're going to have to cover a receiver," said South Carolina's Lou Holtz, the former Arkansas coach, to the *Arkansas Democrat-Gazette,* "because he's going to run around until he finds one, and he's amazingly accurate."

"I don't know if there's a single player that I could say has done more for his team and their success than Matt Jones has done over the last four years for Arkansas," former LSU coach Nick Saban said. "That guy is a phenomenal athlete and a phenomenal player. He finds ways to win regardless of what his physical circumstance is.

"If he can run, he runs. If he can't run, he passes."

Saban should know. Jones' last-minute heroics in 2002 gave the Hogs a 21–20 win over LSU, pushing Arkansas past the Tigers into the SEC championship game. He tossed passes of 50 and 31 yards to produce the Miracle on Markham.

Jones' talents were never more evident than in overtime situations. He had an uncanny knack to get the Hogs into them, then through them, with victory.

As a true freshman in 2001, he led the Hogs to a 58–56 win over Ole Miss in seven overtimes. It was the longest game in NCAA history.

"I got so sick of seeing him out

there," Ole Miss quarterback Eli Manning said afterward. "Every time he just came up with more big plays, scrambling around, finding the open guy and hitting him."

A year later, Tennessee outlasted Arkansas in six overtimes. In 2003, Jones pushed the Hogs to victory over Kentucky in seven more extra periods. He also helped Arkansas beat Alabama in two overtimes.

"If you're playing sandlot football," said former Texas defensive coordinator Carl Reese, "you want the guy on your side."

Jones could frustrate, as well. He'd have three or four good plays, then one awful mistake. His iconic status at Arkansas was a result of his home-run potential. At any moment, fans never knew what he might do. And often, he created a highlight.

"He's a rallying point for our fans," Arkansas quarterbacks coach Roy Wittke told the *Democrat-Gazette*. "He has a magnetism about him."

10

Building
a Program

T HEY COMMEMORATED
their friendly rivalry with a coin
toss. On that September day in
2003, Frank Broyles and Darrell
Royal stood together at midfield,
just as they had done so many
times before.

It was the happy, if temporary, resumption of the Arkansas-

Texas series, which had ended in 1991 when Arkansas left the Southwest Conference for the Southeastern Conference. Broyles and Royal, the former coaches who had lifted the rivalry to its greatest heights, were being honored before kickoff.

The visiting Razorbacks won the rematch, pounding the higher-ranked Longhorns 38–28 as a capacity crowd watched at Darrell K. Royal/Memorial Stadium in Austin, Texas. Don't count Broyles in the attendance. He wasn't there.

Shortly after the coin toss, Arkansas' athletic director left the stadium on foot. He walked halfway to the airport—a far piece through questionable neighborhoods—before catching a ride. He learned of the final outcome only when he saw some Texas fans returning to fly home.

"I could tell by their faces we'd won," he says.

This pedestrian journey wasn't unusual for Broyles. Since leaving coaching after the 1976 season, he has watched few games. He has walked away—literally—from many. Partly, it's a physical issue: His heart might not be able to take the excitement. Mostly, it's learned behavior.

For years when he played, then coached, Broyles suffered terrible pregame anxiety. The butterflies in his stomach seemed more like pterodactyls. "I remember throwing up in the morn-ing of a big game while brushing my teeth," he says. During the last fifteen years he coached, Broyles says his standard pregame meal was frosted corn-flakes topped with ice cream. "They were cold and sweet," he says, "and I could get those down."

"I got nervous as a player; I got nervous as a coach," he adds.

And as an athletic director, which is why he rarely watches football games, choosing instead to leave early. But Broyles has never been able to walk away from his passion of promoting Arkansas' athletic program.

In a thirty-two-year journey as athletic director, he has built a program to rival any other university's, anywhere.

"I think he's proven over time that what he does goes as the absolute best in his field," says Jim Lindsey, who played for Broyles' 1964 national championship team and is now a member of the university's board of trustees. "He may not have been the greatest coach in the field. But I think he's the best athletic director in history."

"There's never been a better combination of head football coach and athletic director," says Barry Switzer, who played and coached under Broyles before winning national championships at Oklahoma and the Super Bowl with the Dallas Cowboys. "There's never been a guy that accomplished so much in both areas.

"He *is* the Arkansas program."

Consider that, in nineteen years, Broyles' football teams won or shared seven Southwest Conference championships and one national title. In the twenty-three years (1950–73) before he became athletic director, all of the other Razorback sports teams combined for twenty-two SWC crowns.

From the time Broyles took over the reins through spring 2005, Arkansas claimed forty-one national championships and ninety-nine conference titles in sports other than football.

Although Broyles and others are quick to point to John Barnhill, his predecessor, as the original architect, there's no doubting Broyles' impact. "Progressive," some call him. "A visionary," others say.

"Coach Barnhill laid the foundation," says Arkansas executive associate athletic director Bill Gray, who played quarterback and defensive back on the Razorbacks' 1964 national championship team. "Coach Broyles has built the building on that foundation."

Quite literally, in a sense. More than $220 million has been put into building or renovating the school's athletic facilities.

"All you've got to do is look at that valley," says Ronnie Caveness, the former All-American linebacker from the 1964 national championship squad, referring to the venues that line Razorback Road on the southwestern edge of the campus. "If you want to see what coach Broyles has meant to the University of Arkansas, you start with that baseball stadium and keep driving. You've got the basketball facility, a football stadium that's state of the art. An indoor practice field, a new weights facility."

Caveness left out the indoor and outdoor track facilities, and tennis, and soccer, and softball, and so on, which also grace the downslope on the southwestern portion of the university's campus, but his point is well taken. The oldest athletic facility on campus is now Bud Walton Arena, a jewel that opened for the 1993-94 basketball season.

Caveness says the facilities, which rival those of any other school, are a reflection of Broyles' abilities as a master salesman fueled by boundless optimism and an intense drive to win.

"You look at a state our size and the facilities we have?" Caveness says. "That's his competitiveness. Even when we played golf, he wanted to beat you. He's got that competitive in him."

Broyles' tenure hasn't been without controversy, of course.

Football hasn't maintained the standard Broyles set. Houston Nutt is the sixth coach to try to get there. Three were fired. Ken Hatfield left before getting the boot. Joe Kines returned to defensive coordinator after serving as interim head coach.

The state was divided in recent years by Broyles' crusade to pull some

Donald W. Reynolds Razorback Stadium is just o:
many state-of-the-art athletic facilities along
Razorback Road on the Arkansas campus.

football games away from Little Rock, back to the Fayetteville campus. His firing of basketball coach Nolan Richardson in 2002 led to a federal civil rights lawsuit (it was dismissed, but has been appealed).

Broyles has been a lightning rod on those and other issues, but he and others say his decisions have been made with pure motives: "I believe people who have watched me through the years know that every decision I make . . . [is] based on what's best for the University of Arkansas and what's best for the athletic department," he says.

Through the years, Broyles has survived, and the Arkansas athletic department has thrived. He is far and away the longest-serving athletic director at an NCAA Division I school. Longtime observers say his impact cannot be underestimated.

That impact has gone beyond athletics. Broyles has often said his chief job was to promote the entire university. His efforts have been instrumental in securing funding for various academic projects.

"People might think this is an overstatement," says Clemson athletic director Terry Don Phillips, a former Arkansas player and associate athletic director, "but I just don't think the University of Arkansas would be what it is today without Frank Broyles.

"I truly believe this," Phillips continues. "He brought to the state of Arkansas a great pride and a great sense of dignity. . . . He built a football program they could really be very proud of. I think it transcends even what Senator Fulbright meant and what President Clinton meant to the state.

"He brought a sense of pride and dignity to the state that no other leader brought."

Broyles retired after the 1976 season, a few weeks before his fifty-second birthday. He was acting in part on the advice of former Army coach Earl "Red" Blaik. At a coaches convention, a young Broyles heard the legend suggest coaches should retire at age fifty. The message: "You'll have a better life."

"Of course," Broyles says with a smile, "people didn't live as long then as they do today."

Broyles, with then-Governor Bill Clinton in 1991, may have brought more pride and dignity to Arkansas than any other figure.

Joe Ferguson was one of the Hogs' best quarterbacks, even though he played on disappointing teams in the early 1970s.

Broyles had considered retiring earlier. After the loss to Texas in the Big Shootout of 1969, Arkansas' football fortunes went into gradual decline. Despite stars such as Ferguson and Dickey Morton, the Hogs hadn't approached the excellence of the 1960s.

There were highlights, of course: Ferguson passed the Longhorns silly in a 31–7 win in 1971 in Little Rock and, three years later, the Hogs upset fifth-ranked Southern California 22–7 in Fayetteville (the Trojans didn't lose again, and went on to claim a share of the national championship). In 1975, Scott Bull's pass to "the immortal Teddy Barnes" jump-started a rout of then-number-two Texas A&M, and sent the Hogs to the SWC title and the Cotton Bowl, where they routed Georgia.

Broyles considered retiring then but, with the nucleus of the 1975 team departing, he stayed in part to ensure a solid recruiting season. His career ended with a 29–12 loss to Texas, which dropped the Razorbacks to 5-5-1 in 1976.

Broyles didn't really retire, he just traded in one Hog hat for another. In 1969, Arkansas' board of trustees had given Broyles full tenure as a professor and promised him the athletic director's job when it opened. As football coach, he, in essence, had a lifetime contract. For three years, he doubled as coach and athletic director.

When Broyles hung up the whistle,

he considered getting into private business. He weighed an offer or two from corporations, but chose to remain at Arkansas. He did take a part-time gig with ABC television, which offered him a chance to provide color commentary for its college football broadcasts and kept him at Arkansas. For nine seasons, Broyles teamed with legendary play-by-play man Keith Jackson on Saturdays.

"That kept me busier than I would have been just being the athletic director," Broyles says. "And it kept me close to the game. I might have gone crazy if

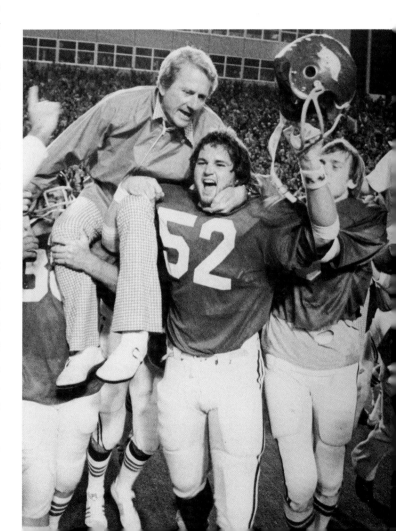

Hogs carry their happy head coach off the field after beating Texas A&M in 1975. Broyles considered retiring after ending the season with a win in the Cotton Bowl, but decided to coach one more year.

I'd just retired to be the athletic director. If I hadn't done that, I believe I would have left athletics."

Broyles saw it as a win-win situation. He would be occupied and could stay somewhat involved with college football. Arkansas would be spotlighted at least once a broadcast, when Jackson mentioned the Razorbacks' score that afternoon or opponent that night. And Broyles would not be at those Arkansas games—something he recognized as a good thing, since once a coach, always a coach.

The job kept Broyles away from Fayetteville on football weekends, but it didn't prevent him from reaching toward his goal of creating an all-sports program. To do so, he needed to raise money. When he became athletic director in 1973, Arkansas had perhaps $100,000 in reserve. The entire athletic department budget was less than $1 million. Football was the school's only revenue sport, and its facilities had fallen well behind several Southwest Conference rivals. Most other sports awarded few or no scholarships; many were coached by members of the physical education department.

Broyles and longtime right-hand man Wilson Matthews embarked on a priority-seating program. They studied South Carolina, which, at the time, was perhaps the only school with such a program (though it's long since become the standard), then presented a similar version to 300 top boosters, who had been longtime holders of large blocks of tickets.

Since the 1950s, banks and other businesses had been buying as many as 100 tickets (sometimes more)—"through the years, they had needed to be sold," Broyles says—and distributing them in whatever fashion they chose. Broyles and Matthews created a priority-seating plan, which tied the right to buy season tickets to contributions to the athletic program. To sell it, they first met at Little Rock's Pleasant Valley Country Club with a handful of influential boosters, including Little Rock investment banker Jackson T. "Jack" Stephens (a longtime ally who later served as the chairman of Augusta National Golf Club; Broyles became a member of the exclusive club through Stephens) and Ed Penick, who was president of Worthen Bank.

Broyles presented the plan, which he said would generate necessary funds to raise the rest of the athletic program up to the level attained by football. In other words, Broyles wanted an athletic department the football team could be proud of. After securing the support of the smaller group, he gathered the larger group and presented the plan once again.

"It's sad when every high school baseball player in the state, who would like to be a Razorback, has to go out of state," Broyles told the boosters. "Or track. Or tennis. Or golf. They're all leaving the state."

Essentially, Broyles asked the boosters to give back the vast majority of their tickets. The plan typically limited donors to four tickets in premium sections, but allowed them to "have all they wanted in the end zones." Only two objected, but Broyles persisted.

"The minute I got home, I called both of them and won them over," Broyles says.

The funds from the priority-seating program were funneled into the Razorback Foundation, the private fund-raising arm of the athletic department. The money raised allowed Arkansas' athletic programs to be completely financed through private funds, without state subsidization.

The initial funding allowed Arkansas to upgrade its football facilities. The North End Zone Complex was erected adjacent to Razorback Stadium's north end zone (it was later renamed the

Broyles Complex; after renovation in the 1990s, it was renamed the Broyles Athletic Center).

From there, Broyles turned his attention to the other sports. In 1974, he hired Eddie Sutton, a promising young coach at Creighton University. Broyles pledged to renovate Barnhill Arena and Sutton promised he would turn basketball into a winner, and a moneymaker.

Soon enough, Sutton was correct. Helped along greatly by the recruiting of the famed Triplets, Sidney Moncrief, Ron Brewer, and Marvin Delph (all from Arkansas high schools), Sutton went undefeated in the SWC in his third season and reached the Final Four in his fourth. The next year, without Brewer and Delph, Arkansas fell one game short of a return.

As Sutton developed a powerhouse, Arkansas quickly added priority seating to its basketball ticket program. His success was built on by Nolan Richardson, who took Arkansas to three Final

Razorback Stadium has undergone dramatic changes since the 1960s.

Fours and won the national championship in 1994. The basketball Razorbacks moved into twenty-thousand-seat Bud Walton Arena in 1994.

In 1977, Broyles promoted John McDonnell, a young Irishman, from cross-country coach to oversee the entire men's track-and-field program. Twenty-eight years later, Arkansas is to NCAA track and field what UCLA once was to basketball, with this difference: Arkansas's dynasty has continued far longer. Through spring 2005, McDonnell's teams had earned forty national championships.

There's more. The baseball Razorbacks have been to the College World Series five times. Golf and tennis and . . . the list goes on.

Arkansas' athletic department budget has grown to almost $40 million. Arkansas has more than ten thousand donors, who annually give anywhere "from a few dollars to not much," Broyles says. Annually, it adds up to millions of dollars. Unquestionably, Broyles has been the catalyst for the grassroots donor base, crisscrossing the state repeatedly for Razorback Club functions such as fish fries or golf tournaments.

Lindsey described a typical scenario: "He's down in some small town in east Arkansas, and the temperature is one hundred four degrees. Coach has driven four or five hours to get there. And he's standing at a tee with every foursome that comes through, shaking hands and talking about the Razorbacks and helping whatever cause they're working on."

"It's a phenomenal story of the fans, the supporters, and I think unquestionably, it's tied to the goodwill from all the years of coach Broyles standing on the tee boxes and going to those fish fries," Lindsey says. "Unbelievable. Nobody knows the hours, nobody can guess the work. Nobody has a clue today what all has gone into those forty-something years of totally dedicating his life."

There are reasons Broyles is called a visionary. His most important decision caused a ripple throughout college athletics. In the late 1980s, he discerned troubling trends in the Southwest Conference. Attendance was dropping around the league (though not at Arkansas). Income was declining. He believed the league was dying.

"It looked liked the Southwest Conference was gonna be dramatically changed, or ended," Broyles says. So, even though Arkansas had been a charter member of the league, which had formed in 1915, he began preparing for a move. In 1988, he went to Birmingham, Alabama, to play golf with then-Southeastern Conference commissioner Harvey Schiller and then Tennessee athletic director Doug Dickey (a former assistant coach under Broyles).

Broyles used the outing to inform Schiller and Dickey that Arkansas would like to join if and when the league expanded. And when, in 1990, the SEC voted to add two teams, Arkansas quickly jumped (South Carolina was also extended and accepted an invitation to join).

"He could see the SWC falling apart," says former tailback Bill Burnett. "He was, in that sense, a visionary. He had the good sense to make a move before it fell down around our ears."

The Hogs started a chain reaction in the major-college landscape. The Big East added football members. Penn State joined the Big Ten. Eventually, the Atlantic Coast Conference expanded. In 1995, the SWC folded; Texas, Texas A&M, Texas Tech, and Baylor joined the Big Eight, which became the Big 12. Houston, Rice, SMU, and TCU were left out of the mix.

"It's sad that all that history has been abandoned, but we had to look to the future," Broyles said when the formation of the new league was announced.

Although some wistfully ponder what might have been if Arkansas had moved with its former rivals to the Big 12—geographically, membership in the league would seem to make great sense—no one, not even Broyles, was certain where the pieces of the SWC would end up. Or if Arkansas, which as the only non-Texas school had often felt like the league's stepchild, would be included.

"I didn't know whether we would be included in anything that Texas or Texas A&M decided to do on their own," he says.

The move was tough on Arkansas' football program. The SWC had always been a matter of beating Texas. Other schools rose and declined, but there were almost always several so-called gimme wins on Arkansas' schedule, most notably the smaller, private schools. With the exception of Vanderbilt, that can't be said of the SEC, which is otherwise comprised of large state universities.

Most years, top to bottom, the nation's best college football is played in the SEC.

"There's no question about that," says Arkansas receivers coach James Shibest, who set receiving records for Lou Holtz and Ken Hatfield in the mid-1980s. "Back at that time, there was probably four or five teams you could line up against in [the SWC], not play outstanding, and still have a good chance to win. You don't have that advantage in this league. You've got to play well every week."

Making things more difficult, Arkansas, in terms of talent, went into the SEC for the 1992 season during a transitional period. And the Hogs' facilities didn't measure up to their new opponents' digs. It took a while to catch up.

Few would quibble over the positive financial impact of Arkansas' SEC membership. Arkansas' budget was just shy of $11 million in 1991, its last year in the SWC. Since 1992, Arkansas has received more than $70 million in the league's equally distributed payouts. The school received more than $9 million as its share in 2004, and the revenue should continue to increase.

"It's a conference with money, a conference with fans," Broyles says. "And when you join 'em, you are involved with some of the best sports in America—in all sports, I should say."

"I don't think there's any question he knew what was gonna happen," says Phillips. "He foresaw what was gonna happen to the Southwest Conference. Given how fast things were beginning

to move and the financial challenges that were gonna be out there, you needed to get with the strongs to get stronger."

Getting stronger has been Broyles' constant mission. It hasn't all been rosy, of course. Broyles' decisions haven't always been popular, or easily made. Critics have noted his penchant for remaining vitally involved in football. Former coaches say he never really stopped coaching. Meddling, they called it.

"Coach has maintained an active interest in football and the technical aspects of it all his life," says Hatfield diplomatically. "That's just him being him."

Broyles admits he has made sugges-

Broyles announces Lou Holtz's so-called resignation at a press conference in 1983. Houston Nutt is the sixth head coach in the twenty-nine years since Broyles retired from coaching.

tions from time to time. Those at the other end have sometimes called them orders. Danny Ford, who coached the Hogs from 1993–1997, said Broyles instructed him in 1997 to hire an offensive coordinator who would install a pass-oriented offense. Ford had wanted to use a run-based scheme, and had a candidate who fit that profile in mind. Instead, Ford hired Kay Stephenson, a veteran NFL assistant, and went with the passing offense.

When the Hogs went 4-7 for the second straight season, Ford was fired.

"I don't like the way he interferes," says Ford, who adds he doesn't have hard feelings toward Broyles. "He should be the athletic director and not try to be the football coach. But that's his personality, and that's what he does."

"He has his opinions," says Phillips, who was dispatched by Broyles to snatch Crowe before he could depart for Clemson with Hatfield in 1990, and was on staff when Broyles fired Crowe one game into the 1992 season, after a 10–3 loss to The Citadel. "He was a very successful coach. And he really doesn't brush that aside. He'll express his opinion. I suppose it has created some problems with some other coaches.

"But, for the most part, coach Broyles doesn't want to get involved like that. He wants to provide the resources necessary to put a coach in position to

be successful, and then leave 'em alone. That's what his preference is."

Broyles' firing of Nolan Richardson in March 2002 became a contentious issue that extended into federal court. When Broyles hired Richardson in 1985, he became the first black head coach in a major sport in the Southwest Conference—or, for that matter, at a major Southern university. When fired, he was the highest-paid coach on campus, unlike at most schools, where the football coach is paid more.

Broyles has said repeatedly he didn't hire Richardson because he was black, but because he believed he was the best man for the job after Eddie Sutton's departure for Kentucky. And although Broyles did not recruit black athletes for the football program until the late 1960s, that hadn't been his decision.

In 1957, his only year at Missouri, he signed that program's first two black players. Upon arrival at Arkansas, it was communicated informally to Broyles that the program was to remain segregated.

"Missouri was ready for it, and it worked out great," Broyles says. "Arkansas wasn't ready at the time. When the Southwest Conference was ready, we joined 'em."

SMU's Jerry Levias broke the SWC's color barrier in 1966. In 1969 Jon Richardson (no relation to Nolan), a running back from Little Rock's Horace Mann High School, became the

Razorbacks' first black scholarship football player.

Perhaps nothing in Broyles' career as an athletic director created more controversy than his push in 1999 and 2000 to move football games from Little Rock to Fayetteville. For the first time in memory, Arkansas fans were split into factions.

On one side was history and tradition. On the other, economics. There was an undercurrent: a rivalry between Little Rock, the state capital and traditional power base, and rapidly growing northwest Arkansas, an emerging economic force.

For more than fifty years, the Hogs had split their games between War Memorial Stadium and Razorback Stadium. John Barnhill, Broyles' mentor,

had pushed for the Little Rock stadium's construction, then scheduled at least three home games (and sometimes four) there most seasons, knowing the central location would allow fans to more easily attend. In fact, more games had been played in Little Rock than Fayetteville.

No one disputed that the split schedule had played an integral role in building the Hogs into a statewide passion. Through the years, many players said they looked forward more to games at War Memorial, though others said they weren't enamored of the travel to get there. Its tight bowl configuration earned a reputation as a cauldron of noise. When he was Kentucky's coach, Hal Mumme was once asked to describe the volume and fear factor at The

War Memorial Stadium has gained a reputation for loud crowds, which provides a significant home-field advantage. Its location in Little Rock makes it more convenient for fans from east and south Arkansas.

Swamp, as Florida's 88,548-seat stadium is affectionately known. Instead, he pointed toward Little Rock, saying War Memorial was the loudest SEC stadium his team had played in and provided a significant homefield advantage.

Houston Nutt's arrival did nothing to dispel that perception. Nutt, who grew up a couple of miles away from War Memorial, managed to stay out of the controversy, even as his teams won their first seventeen games in Little Rock. But Broyles believed the renovation and expansion of Razorback Stadium was essential if the Hogs were to consistently compete in the SEC.

The point was certainly valid. Razorback Stadium, a steel structure that looked like a really large high-school stadium, was in desperate need of an upgrade. Once completed, it would be necessary to play more games there to pay off $30 million in bonds sold to finance the expansion. Moreover, the revenue disparity between games in Fayetteville and Little Rock would be pronounced. Razorback Stadium would seat seventy-two thousand, almost eighteen thousand more than War Memorial Stadium, and would gross about $3 million per game, $2 million more than War Memorial. For financial reasons, Broyles and backers of moving the games said, it would be necessary to play more true home games.

Little Rock investment banker Warren Stephens, son of Jack Stephens,

countered with a proposal to renovate and expand War Memorial to 64,500, with luxury boxes. The proposal included various other incentives to lessen the potential financial disparity. Stephens also pledged something else: If games were pulled from Little Rock, he would discontinue his family's considerable financial support for the program (almost $150,000 in annual donations, and more than $1 million in additional annual support the company had helped raise).

Numbers from both sides were projected, and questioned. One side would note Little Rock had traditionally sold out a larger (fifty-three-thousand-seat) stadium more often than Fayetteville (fifty thousand). Why would that change?

Forget logic, though. Often, the arguments were more acrimonious. Fans took sides, and held them. For months, the topic buzzed on radio talk shows and on Internet message boards. Politicians, including the governor, got into the act. A group called Don't Hog the Hogs was formed. Other fans agreed with Broyles that the games should move. Still others wanted compromise.

It was a heated debate, to say the least. It generated more letters to the editor than another pretty important matter that had just concluded: the impeachment of a native son, President Bill Clinton. "People out of state joke about our obsession with the Razorbacks, but it's true," *Arkansas Democrat-Gazette* associate editor Meredith Oakley told the Associated Press.

The letter writers were certainly emotional. Some fans called for Broyles to resign. Others called for those fans to stop whining and to start traveling to Fayetteville. Fans' loyalty to the program was questioned; the program's loyalty to fans was questioned. And so on.

"If you can't drive to Fayetteville on a new interstate highway, you aren't a Razorback fan." This from a resident of Parkin, in east Arkansas (and perhaps four hours away from Fayetteville over those interstate highways).

Another eastern Arkansan had a different take. A resident of Moro wrote, "Did you ever wonder who the guy was who changed the Coke formula? Now we know: Frank Broyles."

A resident of White Hall, just southeast of Little Rock, suggested: "Tradition has overruled logic. In the face of all intelligence, fiscal responsibility, reason and the real interest of what is best for the Fayetteville campus, the deal will be done. . . . Fans who said, 'I love 'em Hawgs, but I ain't gonna drive all the way to Fay't'ville to see 'em play a home game,' will again boast of their loyalty."

Everyone had an opinion, but only a few mattered. In January 2000, a statewide television audience watched as the board of trustees listened to pro-

posals from Stephens and Chuck Neinas, a consultant hired by Broyles to study the issue and who recommended moving all the games to Fayetteville. Broyles pitched in with an impassioned pep talk worthy of a halftime locker room.

A few days later, Wally Hall, a Little Rock native and the *Arkansas Democrat-Gazette*'s longtime sports editor and columnist, weighed in:

> The issue for those who don't want the games moved has been simple: History and tradition have made us part of the program. . . .
>
> The issue has been only one thing—loyalty. The Razorbacks were Arkansas' team. They belonged to everyone. Richer or poorer.
>
> John Barnhill created it, and Frank Broyles nurtured it into a dynasty from the Delta to the mountains. Games in War Memorial Stadium were a statewide family reunion.
>
> Until Thursday.

Three weeks later, the board of trustees arrived at a compromise. In a 9–1 vote, it pulled one game back to Fayetteville. Through 2015, at least two games will be played in Little Rock each year. At least one must be a conference game.

When it was over, Broyles told reporters he had been through the most painful period of his career. "All heck

has broken loose, and I'd give anything if it hadn't happened. It has hurt me. I've spent at least four hours every day for eight months, trying to find a solution to make everyone happy."

Five years and counting, the debate has cooled, but remains "a very emotional thing," says Lindsey, who voted in favor of the compromise. "That's an issue that nobody can win on."

The completion of Reynolds Razorback Stadium in 2001—it was renamed because of a $20 million gift from the Donald W. Reynolds Foundation—soothed some of the lingering bitterness. Everyone agreed the new and improved stadium was a showplace.

Its seventy-two-thousand seats include 132 luxury boxes and almost nine thousand club seats. A 30-foot-by-107-foot video screen, dubbed the Pig Screen TV, sits atop the Broyles Athletic Center in the north end zone. A newly enclosed south end greatly increases the intimidation factor for visiting teams. The stadium rivals any other college football venue.

Essentially, it is the Taj MaHog.

Its impact is far more than aesthetic. Arkansas has averaged more than sixty-six thousand fans in Fayetteville; revenue from home games has jumped by approximately $10 million per year. Much of the revenue comes from the luxury boxes and from premium club seats; plans for expansion include perhaps than more fifty more luxury boxes.

"I'm very pleased with the breakdown we have now," Broyles says, "even though it's still controversial and some people think I should have kept the same number of games in both places."

Though it's several years away, another debate looms. Whether Little Rock will remain a part-time home of the Hogs once the current agreement expires is uncertain. But Gary Smith, a Little Rock businessman and chairman of the War Memorial Stadium Commission, told the *Democrat-Gazette* in late 2004 many people had come to terms with the initial change.

"To this day, as you talk to people, they may wish it was a different outcome, but I think over time people have gained a better understanding of coach Broyles' perspective and how football and basketball are the backbone of the budget for the entire program," Smith said. "I think that coach Broyles is committed to the fans throughout the state, but some of these decisions are business decisions and they have to be made that way.

"That's what coach Broyles is paid to do."

It's ironic that many Arkansans know Broyles only as athletic director. His legacy as football coach remains unsurpassed. And what might his administrative legacy be?

"History will tell that," Broyles says.

Not for a while, maybe. Broyles, who turned eighty in December 2004, isn't sure when he'll retire.

Broyles says there's still plenty left for him to accomplish at Arkansas. In June 2003, he was awarded a five-year contract extension; it rolls over automatically every year. Broyles jokingly suggests he might remain until he's ninety, or ninety-two.

Broyles is shooting to match or beat Amos Alonzo Stagg, who coached until he was ninety-eight (he died at 103).

"It's my understanding," Broyles says, "that Amos Alonzo Stagg was the only person that's ever been working at a Division I school at age ninety. I hope Frank Broyles can be number two.

"That's a joke, and all. But I wouldn't mind it happening, obviously."

No one who knows Broyles is likely to bet against him. He has battled various health issues over the years, including prostate cancer and an irregular heartbeat. He lost his wife, Barbara, in October 2004 after a long battle with Alzheimer's; the couple had been married fifty-nine years and had six children and nineteen grandchildren.

Frank missed about a month from work while at his wife's bedside; in months previous, he had done much of his work from home. Barbara's battle with the disease is one of the reasons he's not ready to slow down. In his research into Alzheimer's, he has come to believe in mental and physical activity as a preventive prescription.

Thus, Broyles continues to walk two or three miles five days per week.

He hits several hundred golf balls most afternoons, and shoots near his age (sometimes better) on the course. Shortly after Barbara's death, Broyles checked into the hospital because of an irregular heart beat. Even there, he kept in contact by telephone with the athletic department. After marking out a six-hundred-yard course around the hospital's third floor, he walked three miles per day, while pulling along a heart monitor and an intravenous drip stand.

If that seemed unusual, an accompanying decision to stretch caused a brief panic. Broyles found a carpeted section of a corridor, laid down, and began stretching. Suddenly, several nurses came running.

"They'd been told a patient had fainted," Broyles said. But that wasn't it, of course: "I just couldn't sit still."

Broyles' energy level, others say, is like that of a man half his age.

"He energizes all of us," Nutt says. "I don't look at him as an eighty-year-old. I see him as a much younger person. He's very passionate, enthusiastic about coming to work every day. He just simply energizes us."

And Broyles continues to energize Arkansas—the state and the university.

"I know coach has his idiosyncrasies and all that," Phillips says. "I know not everybody is enamored with him. But I believe that university has been very well served by coach Broyles being there all these years, and I believe it continues to be well served by him."

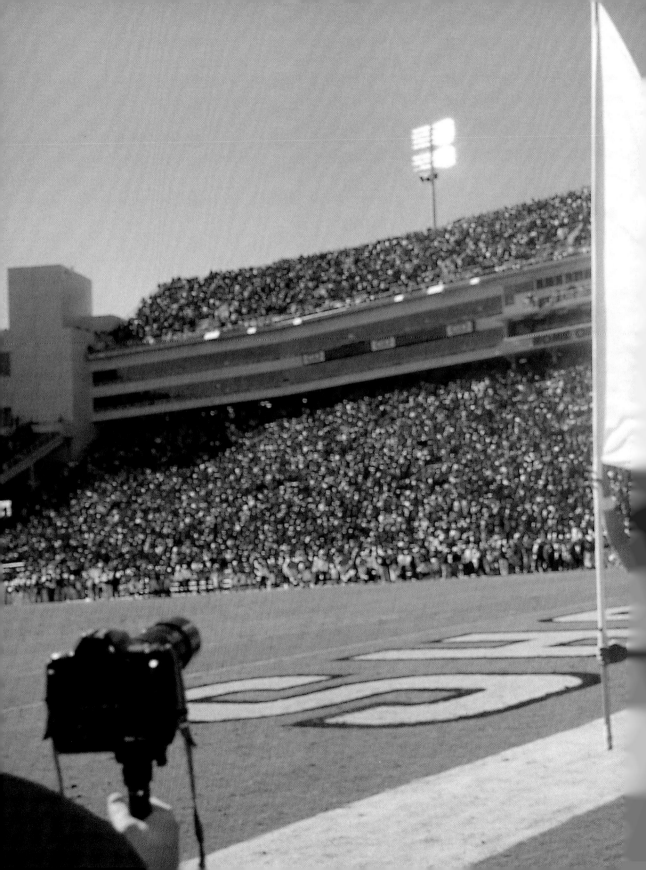

11

Adopted Heroes

R ONNIE CAVENESS re-
members wondering what he'd
gotten himself into. "They're
pretty serious about their football
here," he thought the first time
he visited Fayetteville. But soon
enough, the kid from Houston
was immersed in a new culture.
He had become a Razorback,

Arkansas fans' passion—and
the game-day pageantry—
prove alluring to many
out-of-state recruits.

Lance Alworth.

grafted onto the family. And his addition, like that of so many other newcomers, was essential.

The state of Arkansas doesn't regularly produce enough talent to sustain the football program. The Razorbacks' success over the years has been fueled by the steady flow of talent from other states, mostly nearby neighbors. Caveness, for example, developed into an All-American linebacker. He was a key component of the Hogs' drive for a national championship in 1964.

There have been so many others—out-of-state kids who arrived unsure, perhaps, what all the hog-calling was about, but who quickly learned. When they slipped on the uniform, they were adopted sons. "Once you're a Hog, you're always a Hog," says former quarterback Quinn Grovey. Here are just a few of the best.

LANCE ALWORTH

LETTERED: 1959–61
POSITION: HALFBACK
HOMETOWN: BROOKHAVEN,
MISSISSIPPI

He changed the game on the field, and off. When Frank Broyles lured Lance Alworth from Brookhaven, Mississippi, he had a spectacular playmaker who could "change a game with one play," as Alworth's teammate Mickey Cissell put it. And perhaps as important, Alworth's

presence translated into instant credibility for Arkansas with other big-time recruits.

Known as "Bambi" for his graceful running style, Alworth starred at wide receiver for the San Diego Chargers of the old American Football League. He was inducted into the Pro Football Hall of Fame.

Before all that, he was quite simply as good an athlete as has ever played for the Razorbacks.

"When you saw him run, he was a gazelle," says Barry Switzer, who was an Arkansas player and coach during Alworth's tenure. "His leaping ability, his hands, his speed, the grace he possessed. Gosh, none of the rest of us were in a league with him.

"He was thirty years ahead of everybody as an athlete."

And as a result, often thirty yards behind everybody. Cissell remembers a catch against SMU.

"It was a perfect pass," Cissell says. "Alworth caught it right over the middle and in two steps, he was literally ten yards ahead of everybody. He was that gifted."

It was a year earlier against SMU that Alworth might have had a bigger impact. He rushed for 131 yards, but it was his spinning, twisting run for a two-point conversion that gave Arkansas a 15–14 win and a share of the Southwest Conference championship.

Alworth led the nation in punt returns in 1960 and 1961. As a senior in 1961, he was an All-American after leading the Hogs in rushing (516 yards) and receiving (18 catches, 320 yards).

"He looked like he was about thirteen, but he could do anything," says former assistant Merv Johnson. "He could have played a jillion positions. He could have played cornerback or safety. He probably could have played quarterback."

Instead, Alworth stuck to halfback. He might have been stifled a bit in Arkansas' offense, but the Razorbacks were a few years away from adopting a wide-open passing attack, in which Alworth would certainly have been a receiver. As it was, he was a force to be reckoned with.

"He was like Herschel Walker was to Georgia," says Ken Hatfield, who arrived on campus about the time Alworth left. "He kind of had that extra aura about him that made everybody else play better. And [the aura] made the other teams figure out, 'Number one, we'd better stop Lance Alworth, and then worry about the rest of them.'

"He just had that kind of big-play quality about him."

Alworth was drafted by the San Francisco 49ers, but instead signed with San Diego of the upstart AFL. He was the league's first superstar, and a perfect fit for the Chargers' high-octane passing

Alworth was a threat to score on every play.

attack. In eleven seasons, he had 542 catches, 10,266 yards, and 85 touchdowns. He averaged 18.9 yards per catch.

"The good Lord usually takes something away from an individual to keep him from being perfect," Denver Broncos coach Mac Speedie told the *Sporting News* in 1968, "but He goofed when He came to Alworth."

LOYD PHILLIPS

LETTERED: 1964–66

POSITION: **DEFENSIVE TACKLE**

HOMETOWN: **LONGVIEW, TEXAS**

When Loyd Phillips started looking for the football, it was best to get out of his way.

"He arrived at the point of contact in a bad mood," remembers Bill Gray, a former teammate.

The 6-3, 230-pound defensive tackle got there often enough to become a two-time All-American and Arkansas' second Outland Trophy winner. Phillips, who started as a sophomore on Arkansas' 1964 national championship team, was a major factor in the Razorbacks' undefeated seasons that year and in 1965; Arkansas was 29-3 in his three-year career.

Phillips has called himself "an adequate player." Former teammates and coaches chuckle at the modest description. There may have been more talented defensive linemen who played for the Razorbacks, but there were none more intense, or effective.

Frank Broyles said Phillips "didn't have any technique that I know of, except no blocker could handle him." Phillips earned a reputation for running down ball carriers from behind, and for letting nothing stand in his way.

"I'd never seen anybody like him," says Merv Johnson. "He was big for those days, but just so mobile and quick. He was just consumed with a burning desire to get to the football.

"He'd go screaming and yelling and knocking guys down to get to the football."

Johnson, who later moved on to an assistant's position at Oklahoma, dishes

Ball carriers didn't much like this view of Loyd Phillips.

higher praise: "He dominated games like Lee Roy Selmon did," referring to the former Oklahoma all-timer.

Phillips was an All-American in 1965, and had 17 tackles in the Hogs' loss to LSU in the Cotton Bowl, which ended a twenty-two-game winning streak and prevented a second national championship.

"We pretty much dominated everybody we played," Phillips said.

In 1966, Phillips won the Outland Trophy as the nation's best lineman (Bud Brooks, in 1954, was the other Razorback winner). Phillips' younger brother, Terry Don Phillips, played alongside him during that 1966 season. Opponents ran plays away from Loyd,

and at Terry Don, but that might not have been the best strategy.

"It was a mistake to run my way, because Loyd was such a great player in pursuit," Terry Don Phillips told the *Arkansas Democrat-Gazette.* "I don't believe I've ever been around anybody as intense as he was. There just wasn't any quit in him."

Loyd Phillips was a first-round draft pick by the Chicago Bears, but played just three seasons at defensive end—"probably the smallest defensive lineman in the NFL," he said—then retired because of a leg injury.

He's been a secondary school administrator in northwest Arkansas for more than thirty years.

Loyd Phillips' younger brother, Terry Don (no. 68), played for Arkansas from 1966 to 1969.

CHUCK DICUS

LETTERED: 1968–70
POSITION: **WIDE RECEIVER**
HOMETOWN: **GARLAND, TEXAS**

He might have gone to Oklahoma State, or mighty McMurry College. Those appeared to be the college choices for young Chuck Dicus. He hadn't drawn much interest as a running quarterback from Garland, Texas.

But after taking a late look at Dicus, Arkansas offered a scholarship.

"He accepted, thank goodness," said Frank Broyles.

Chuck Dicus.

Dicus became an All-American, the receiving end of one of the most successful passing connections in Arkansas history. From 1968 to 1970, Bill Montgomery threw for 4,590 yards and 29 touchdowns; Dicus accounted for 1,854 yards and 16 touchdowns, numbers that would later land him in the College Football Hall of Fame. It wasn't coincidental that Arkansas was 28-5 during the same stretch.

Dicus and Montgomery had been high-school rivals, at least from afar, in the Dallas area; Montgomery had starred at Carrollton's R. L. Turner High School. At Arkansas, they became roommates, friends, and partners.

"Chuck and Bill developed a partnership, and they were so close in their techniques and worked so hard together," Broyles said. "They could improvise immediately on the field to any adjustment the defense made."

Dicus was recruited with the un-derstanding he would not play quarterback. As a freshman, the six-foot, 170-pounder was tried briefly at defensive halfback before coaches noted his penchant for running precise routes.

"He was smooth and explosive, with quickness," says Merv Johnson. "The guy could run all day. Chuck really honed his skills."

Dicus soon became known for his sure hands. He finished his career with 118 catches. That mark and the 1,854 career yardage mark stood atop the school receiving charts until the 1990s.

"I don't ever remember him dropping a pass," Broyles said. "If he touched it, he caught it."

Dicus had big performances in some of Arkansas' biggest games. In the 1969 Sugar Bowl win over Georgia, Dicus had 12 catches for 169 yards, including a 27-yard touchdown pass. He was named the bowl's most valuable player.

Dicus scores against Texas in the Big Shootout of 1969. Dicus had 9 catches for 146 yards.

A year later in the Big Shootout, Dicus had 9 catches for 146 yards, including a 29-yard touchdown. Another would-be score, this one a 26-yarder, was called back by penalty.

Texas won, 15–14. However, during a 2004 reunion of the Big Shootout, Texas defensive back Mike Campbell approached Dicus and jokingly asked if he could hug him, "because I never got this close to him in the game," Campbell told the *Arkansas Democrat-Gazette.*

Weeks after the loss to Texas, Dicus had 6 catches for 171 yards, including a 47-yard touchdown, in a 27–22 Sugar Bowl loss to Ole Miss.

Dicus, who played two years for the San Diego Chargers and one year for the Pittsburgh Steelers, has been the president of the Razorback Foundation since 1990.

STEVE LITTLE

LETTERED: 1974–77

POSITION: KICKER/PUNTER

HOMETOWN: SHAWNEE MISSION, KANSAS

Just before halftime, the kicker came to Lou Holtz with a request. Trailing Texas 6–3, Arkansas had the football at midfield with the wind.

"Coach," said Steve Little, "I can kick it."

"There's no way," Holtz said, but he let Little kick that day in 1977. The resulting 67-yard field goal tied the game, and an NCAA record that still stands.

"He just pranced off the field," remembers Ron Calcagni, Arkansas' quarterback that day.

On the other sideline, Little's counterpart had a different demeanor. Texas' Russell Erxleben had set the initial record, hitting a 67-yarder two weeks earlier against Rice. And he was convinced Little, who had initially set the tee at the Arkansas 44, then moved it back to the 43, "stuck it in [his] face."

Little, a member of Arkansas' all-century team and an All-American in 1977, was part of a triangle of extraordinary kickers who played at the same time in the Southwest Conference. Little, Texas' Erxleben, and Texas A&M's Tony Franklin considered themselves part of an exclusive fraternity, and with good reason. All hit field goals of at least 60 yards; in 1976, Little hit a 61-yarder.

Little accounted for 7 of the 15

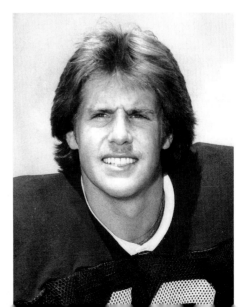

Steve Little.

longest field goals in Arkansas history. He twice hit 57-yarders.

"Any time we crossed the fifty-yard line, we were in Steve Little's range," former Arkansas assistant Ken Turner told the *Arkansas Democrat-Gazette.* "He had an unbelievable leg."

Although his career percentage was only 59.6 percent (53 of 89), that was partly because almost any time they did cross midfield, the Hogs could try a low-risk field goal. At the time, opponents were given possession at their 20 after missed field goals. In 1978, the rule was changed to return the ball to the original line of scrimmage.

Little routinely put kickoffs through the uprights. He averaged 44.4 yards per punt in 1976, 44.3 yards in 1977, and he wanted to do more.

"This guy could have played anywhere on the field," Calcagni says. "He could have played receiver or quarterback, but he had one gifted leg."

It was gifted enough that Broyles said he visited Little's home in Shawnee Mission, Kansas, more than any other player he recruited. When the coach learned Little wanted to wear number twelve, he put in a call to Arkansas legend Clyde "Smackover" Scott and asked if he would allow the only retired jersey in school history at the time to be temporarily reactivated. Scott's acquiescence was a factor as the Hogs acquired one of the best kickers in the history of college football.

Bud Wilkinson, the former Oklahoma coach who had moved on to the St. Louis Cardinals, took Little in the first round of the NFL draft.

Later paralyzed in a car wreck, Little died in September 1999.

BILLY RAY SMITH

LETTERED: 1979–82
POSITION: DEFENSIVE END
HOMETOWN: PLANO, TEXAS

He followed in his father's footsteps, but had no trouble filling them. Billy Ray Smith, Sr., had been a fine defensive lineman for the Razorbacks; he's a member of the school's all-century team. So is his son.

And few would argue Billy Ray Smith, Jr., had the more impressive college career.

Billy Ray Smith, Jr.

"Billy Ray disrupted more plays than anybody who ever wore a Razorback uniform," Frank Broyles once said. "He was so quick that he had the ability to destroy an opposing offense. The offense knew the snap count, but they couldn't get the jump on Billy Ray."

Smith, who was born in Fayetteville but grew up in Texas, was an All-American in 1981 and 1982. He finished as the runner-up for the Outland Trophy both years.

"Billy Ray," said former Arkansas coach Lou Holtz, "is the best football player I've been around."

Smith started every game of his Arkansas career. The mark of forty-eight is a school record. "Billy Ray stood out from the start," former assistant Jesse Branch told the *Arkansas Democrat-Gazette.*

Smith started as a 6-3, 210-pound nose guard, though he gradually bulked up to around 235 pounds. His career really took off when Holtz hired Don Lindsey away from Southern Cal as defensive coordinator. Lindsey moved Smith from nose tackle to standup end. He finished his career with 63 tackles for loss, another school record.

"He was so dominant, it was amazing to watch him on the corners coming off the edge," says David Bazzel, who played linebacker at the time. "Very few tackles could block him. He was so skilled at the moves and the quickness, it was really fun to watch him."

In 1981, Smith's recovery of a fumble on Texas' first possession set the stage for the Hogs' 42–11 rout of the number-one ranked Longhorns. He spent much of the day in the backfield, harassing Texas quarterback Rick McIvor.

Smith, who is a member of the College Football Hall of Fame, was a first-round draft pick by the San Diego Chargers; moved to linebacker, he played ten seasons with the Chargers.

Again, he followed in his father's footsteps. Billy Ray Smith, Sr., played for the Baltimore Colts, winning a Super Bowl. And Junior credited Senior, who died in 2001 at sixty-six, with helping develop his knack for making plays.

With a full head of steam, Smith was a fearsome sight.

"I had a nose for the football and I think my dad taught it to me," Smith told the *Arkansas Democrat-Gazette.* "We'd get together when I was a little boy, seven or eight years old, and he'd take all of the chairs out of the dining room and move the table and he'd run me through some things to work on. . . . He taught me to look for things in an offensive lineman's stance, to look for things in a quarterback's demeanor, his approach to the center.

"If you can get that down, you can have a pretty good idea where the ball's going to go."

Despite his father's heritage as a Razorback, Smith had a choice, Arkansas or Texas, until his father told him he could drive a new car to Fayetteville or walk to Austin.

GARY ANDERSON

LETTERED: 1979–82
POSITION: TAILBACK
HOMETOWN: COLUMBIA, MISSOURI

Gary Anderson's reasons for becoming a Razorback were simple enough.

"I was looking more at Oklahoma until I saw the Orange Bowl the year before," says Anderson, referring to Arkansas' 31–6 win over the Sooners in 1978. "That's when I really started looking at Arkansas."

He really stopped looking at faraway schools, including USC, when an airplane carrying the Evansville Aces' basketball team crashed. It didn't hurt that Anderson had spent part of his childhood living with grandparents in the south Arkansas town of Bearden.

The biggest reason he came to

Arkansas, Anderson says, was "the good situation as a running back. All the top backs were leaving."

And one came in. For four seasons, the speedy but small Anderson—he played at 6-1, 175 pounds—provided a big-play threat for Lou Holtz's teams. He finished as Arkansas' all-time leader in all-purpose yardage (4,535). He ranks second in punt returns, tenth in receiving, and eleventh in rushing.

For a recent comparison, think of USC's Reggie Bush. That's the *wow* factor Arkansas had in Anderson, or better. Once, quarterback Brad Taylor found himself on the wrong end of Holtz's wrath for an unusual reason.

"I wasn't carrying my fakes out [in practice]," Taylor remembers. "But the reason was, I was watching [Anderson]. This guy doesn't weigh one hundred sixty-five, but he's amazing. These guys can't touch him. . . . He may have weighed one hundred seventy-five

pounds, but I never saw anybody face him up. You either arm-tackled him or you dragged him down, maybe. But you just couldn't hit him. He was a dadgum wet noodle going through there."

Yet, teammates sometimes wondered why Anderson didn't touch the ball more often. Holtz's preference was to give the bulk of the carries to bigger, stronger backs.

"There's a guy who should have gotten the ball twenty-five times a game," says David Bazzel, a former teammate. "Gary was so explosive. He wasn't a big guy, but he could pop through a hole. And gliding was the best way to describe the way he could run."

Anderson understands the sentiment. Like any running back, he wanted the ball, but he figured he got it plenty of ways. Anderson ran for 1,999 yards in four seasons. Holtz would split him out wide, send him in motion, all sorts of things.

Gary Anderson bolts for the end zone against Texas Tech.

"Coach Holtz's theory was to give me just enough to keep me healthy," says Anderson. "He'd move me around quite a bit for handoffs. Every running back wants to get the ball twenty or twenty-five times a game. That's what you want. But his theory was to give it to me just enough to keep me going."

Anderson did in Texas twice, scoring the winning touchdown on a 28-yard scamper as a freshman in 1979, then two years later breaking the Longhorns' backs with a 19-yard reception just before halftime in what would become a 42–11 rout.

He was at his best during bowl games. In the 1980 Hall of Fame Bowl, a 34–15 win over Tulane, Anderson rushed for 156 yards on 11 carries, including a 46-yard touchdown run. The total did not include Anderson's 80-yard punt return.

Two years later, in his final game as a Hog, Anderson rushed for a career-high 161 yards and 2 touchdowns. Arkansas beat Florida 28–24 in the Bluebonnet Bowl.

Anderson played three years with the Tampa Bay Bandits of the United States Football League, then eight years in the NFL.

QUINN GROVEY

LETTERED: 1987–90
POSITION: QUARTERBACK
HOMETOWN: DUNCAN, OKLAHOMA

Barry Switzer likes to say he gave Quinn Grovey to Arkansas. Pointing out Sooner quarterbacks Jamelle Holieway, Eric Mitchel, and Charles Thompson, the Oklahoma coach suggested to the Oklahoma kid that maybe Fayetteville would be a fine destination.

It's a good story, but for one nagging detail. Grovey claims it's not true.

"Nothing like that ever came down," Grovey says.

Anderson's jitterbug tendencies gave would-be tacklers fits.

Grovey, who grew up a Sooner fan, certainly understood the logjam Oklahoma had at quarterback in the mid-1980s. And if Switzer did actually help his alma mater secure Grovey, the Razorbacks are duly thankful.

Grovey was the perfect practitioner of Ken Hatfield's flexbone, a tough, quick runner who could pass, too. The three-year starter led Arkansas to two straight Southwest Conference championships and, as a result, two straight Cotton Bowls—the only Arkansas quarterback to achieve that feat.

"I told coach Hatfield right before I committed, 'I'm not coming to win games,'" Grovey says. " 'I'm coming to win championships.'"

He did just that. Grovey was named to Arkansas' all-century team in 1994. Ten years later, an *Arkansas Democrat-Gazette* poll of media members and fans named Grovey the Razorbacks' all-time best quarterback.

"It's definitely an honor, there's no question about it," Grovey told the newspaper. "Any time you can be rated the best in a long line of great quarterbacks at a university like Arkansas, it's an honor."

Known as a runner, Grovey had 4,496 career passing yards and 29 touchdowns, but he ran the triple option to near perfection, rushing for 1,756 yards and 21 touchdowns.

"Quinn Grovey is like a greased pig," an Ole Miss defender said after a game. "We would have him down behind the line, then we'd look up and he'd gained six or seven."

He finished his career as the Hogs' career leader in total offense (6,242 yards), and still ranks second. In 1989, when Arkansas produced a then-record 4,926 total yards, he was at the helm.

Grovey's most memorable performance came as a junior in 1989, when he led the Razorbacks to a 45–39 win over powerful Houston. Arkansas piled up 647 yards that day, third best in school history; Grovey threw for 256 yards and rushed for 79 more. He tossed touchdown passes of 65 and 51 yards and ran for three more scores.

"It was probably the best game I've been a part of," says Grovey. "The most exciting, with a lot on the line."

Grovey lives in northwest Arkansas; he's been a staple on Arkansas' radio broadcasts as a sidelines reporter.

Named the Hogs' all-time best quarterback in a poll of media and fans in 2004, Quinn Grovey was a perfect fit for Ken Hatfield's flexbone attack.

12

Houston, We Have a Revival

T HEY WAITED and watched, expecting the inevitable. This couldn't be real. No way could anyone be like this. Not really. Soon enough, reality would set in. All this would fade away.

Houston Nutt had come in like an evangelist returning to his home church. In December

Houston Nutt leads the Hogs in singing the fight song after a win. The coach's enthusiasm enthralled Arkansas fans.

1997, Arkansas' new football coach met with his team for the first time. He shed his coat, tossing it onto a chair, and began pacing the floor, waving his arms, preaching the gospel of Arkansas football.

What a great opportunity this was for him. How much it meant to come home. How there were lots of Lions and Tigers and Bears, but only one Razorback.

To a skeptical, battle-weary bunch of Razorbacks, the message seemed . . . well . . .

"It was fake to a lot of us," says Russell Brown, an offensive lineman who had just completed his third season as a starter. "We walked out of that meeting saying, 'That won't last. He'll throw the pompoms down. That's not him.'"

Except, it was him. Nutt didn't throw down the pompoms. If anything, he shook them harder. He kept on preaching, until a revival was in full bloom. And eventually, even the most skeptical Razorbacks had been converted. After almost a decade spent wandering in college football's wilderness, few would have blamed Brown and his teammates and Arkansas fans for doubting the new coach's message.

But when Houston Nutt called, the Hogs followed.

"He brought the noise back," says Quinn Grovey, who served on the search committee that recommended Nutt's hire. "He lived and breathed the program. He was definitely the shot in the arm this program needed."

It's a strange irony that while Frank Broyles built an all-around sports program, football had faltered. After twenty-two straight seasons without a losing record, Arkansas went 3-8 in 1990, the year after Ken Hatfield's departure. That was just the beginning. The Razorbacks managed one winning record in the next seven seasons, their worst stretch since World War II.

An NCAA-mandated forfeit by Alabama in 1993 gave the Hogs a second winning season on paper. But in on-field wins and losses, Arkansas finished above .500 only in 1995 (8-5), when a seasoned group of seniors gutted their way to the SEC's West Division title.

By the time Nutt arrived, the program was mired in mediocrity, or worse.

"Boy, it was sad," says Marcus Elliott, a former standout offensive lineman under Lou Holtz and Ken Hatfield. "We struggled for a long while."

The decade had begun with a hasty hiring. Two years later came an even more hasty firing.

When Hatfield left for Clemson in January 1990, a few days after the Hogs' second straight Cotton Bowl loss, Broyles hurriedly hired Jack Crowe, Hatfield's offensive coordinator. Crowe was essentially pulled off Clemson's private plane just before it whisked Hatfield away.

The hire was unprecedented. Broyle's policy, passed down from John Barnhill, was to hire only established head coaches. The athletic director later admitted he shouldn't have deviated from his stance.

Crowe, as it turned out, wasn't ready to assume control of an entire program.

In 1990, dragged down by a suspect pass defense, the Hogs lost seven straight games, and by stunning scores. In the first four losses, to TCU, Texas Tech, Texas, and Houston, Arkansas gave up an average of 53.5 points. Only a season-ending win over SMU prevented the humiliation of a winless conference record.

The Hogs rebounded just a bit in 1991, their final season in the Southwest Conference. A 14–13 win over Texas—the last regularly scheduled game in the series—was the biggest highlight. But after starting 5-2, quarterback Jason Allen tore up a knee. Arkansas lost four of its last five games, including Georgia's 24–15 win over Arkansas in the Independence Bowl.

It didn't count as an SEC game, but it was a harbinger of things to come, and soon.

So, 1992 rolled around. As the Hogs headed into the SEC, there wasn't much enthusiasm. Just 35,828 fans attended the season opener against The Citadel in Fayetteville, meaning there were more than fourteen thousand empty seats. They watched a debacle.

The Citadel, an NCAA Division I-AA military college, upended Arkansas

LEFT
Jack Crowe succeeded Ken Hatfield as coach, but didn't succeed.

RIGHT
A win over Texas in 1991 was one of the few highlights of Jack Crowe's tenure.

10–3. Broyles called it "the low point of fifty years of Razorback football."

The Citadel hadn't even been on the original schedule. Miami, which had beaten Arkansas 31–3 in 1991, was supposed to get a rematch. Instead, the Hurricanes were dropped for a "softer" opponent. Never mind that The Citadel had beaten four of its last five Division I-A opponents. The Bulldogs collected a $250,000 paycheck and were supposed to come in and take a walloping, the better to prepare the Hogs for SEC play.

The next day, Broyles met with Crowe. Then, not long after Crowe conducted his standard Sunday news conference to rehash the game—and spoke of how the Hogs would go on, and his hopes for the rest of the season, and so on—the school made a startling announcement. Crowe and Broyles said in statements they had reached a mutual decision: Crowe had resigned. It was transparently obvious, though, the coach had been fired with five years left on a recently rolled-over contract.

"What was happening was a severe erosion of both fan support and team morale," Broyles told reporters. "We reached the decision that it was going to make it difficult to play our best. . . . It was going to be very difficult to salvage the season.

"We probably would have made the decision a few weeks later or at the end of the season anyway. I decided we

should change the focus immediately."

In later years, Broyles said the decision to hire an assistant rather than a proven head coach had been wrong, but he believes the decision to fire Crowe was correct.

"It was radical," he says. "I just thought it was the thing to do at the time. I thought hard and carefully about it, got support, and did it."

These days, Broyles describes Crowe as a friend. Interestingly enough, Crowe hasn't expressed bitterness toward Broyles. He has described Broyles as "compassionate." His dismissal, Crowe told the *Arkansas Democrat-Gazette* in 1994, was "just business the way Frank saw it. It wasn't personal."

Defensive coordinator Joe Kines was quickly named interim head coach. His first move was to gather the team and have them sing the fight song.

"We had to start somewhere," he said.

Like from square one.

The next week, Arkansas opened SEC play with a 45–7 win over South Carolina (which was also making its SEC debut). Two losses later, however, Kines called a friend, former Clemson coach Danny Ford, and asked him to come to Fayetteville as a consultant.

Ford had won ninety-six games and a national championship in eleven seasons at Clemson, but had been forced out in January 1990 amid an NCAA investigation in which he wasn't named.

As Hog fans well knew, Hatfield had replaced Ford at Clemson. And there was one other connection in the triangle of irony; Hatfield had hired Crowe away from Ford and Clemson.

There was a significant highlight that season. Todd Wright's 41-yard field goal with two seconds left gave the Hogs a 25–24 upset of number-four Tennessee in Knoxville. It was Wright's fourth field goal of the day.

Arkansas had trailed by 8 points in the waning moments, but Orlando Watters' 71-yard punt return with 2:28 left cut the deficit to 24–22; a two-point conversion attempt failed. After the Hogs recovered an onside kick, freshman quarterback Barry Lunney moved them into position for Wright's game-winner.

After two Tennessee timeouts, Wright knocked it through. Moments later, riding down a pressbox elevator, Broyles said, "We have risen from the dead!"

Well, not quite. Arkansas finished 3 7 1, and it wasn't much of a surprise when, three days after a season-ending win over LSU, Ford was named the Hogs' third head coach in three months. Well, one person was surprised. Ford says he simply came to Arkansas to help Kines, a longtime friend. He figured it was a way to get back into coaching. He insists he had no designs on the top job.

"People may believe this and they may not believe this," says Ford, who is retired and living in South Carolina. "It really doesn't bother me if they don't. But I went up there to try to help Joe Kines get that job. That's the only reason I came up there. They called and asked for help."

There didn't appear to be hard feelings. Kines stayed on for two seasons as Ford's defensive coordinator.

Ford had never set foot in Arkansas before he arrived. He knew plenty about the football program's rich tradition, though, which is why he was surprised and appalled to find, "they were way, way behind," Ford says. "They were behind in facilities, they were behind in athletes. [The program] had just slipped some. It wasn't there."

Entering the SEC was an eye-opener in both departments. Recruiting had become difficult with rumors of a rift between Hatfield and Broyles, and had declined even more during Crowe's brief tenure (though there were gems such as the luring of Fort Smith's Lunney).

Arkansas never had looked so slow as it did against Alabama in a 38–11 loss in 1992. The Crimson Tide was en route to a national championship. Arkansas appeared headed for a long drought.

And the SEC members' facilities? Newer, bigger, and better than anything Arkansas had seen—and competed against—in the Southwest Conference. "There was no great need to keep up with the Joneses," Ford says of the Hogs' status in the SWC, "because they were the Joneses."

When Arkansas joined the SEC, Razorback Stadium was the ninth-largest stadium; as other schools upgraded, it slipped to eleventh-largest, ahead of only Vanderbilt. For a time during Ford's tenure, as the Broyles

Center was renovated, Arkansas athletic trainers occupied a double-wide trailer; the coaches officed in a dormitory.

Broyles agrees with Ford's assessment.

"Our football program really didn't have the infrastructure to win," he says. "It wasn't all [the coaches'] fault. It was the fact that schools with considerably better facilities were getting the top athletes, more than we were getting.

"You can't outcoach many people. You can outwork a few, but you can't outcoach 'em. You've got to get some stars to play. And we didn't have the facilities to recruit competitive with the top teams in the SEC."

As Ford took control, the Hogs entered a gradual building period in both categories. Though he had coached Clemson to the national championship in 1981, Ford's laid-back, low-key style never really fired up the Arkansas fan base. Actually, the biggest problem was that the Hogs continued to lose, with one significant exception.

Ford, who had played for Bear Bryant at Alabama, was a practitioner of old-school, smash-mouth football, but Arkansas' talent deficit made winning that way difficult. Still, in Ford's third season, he brought back a veteran unit.

"We were getting some pretty good football players," Ford recalls. "We were finally growing up a bit."

The biggest question in 1995 was at

quarterback, where Ford had to choose between Lunney, a seasoned senior, and Robert Reed, a sophomore with tantalizing potential.

Lunney's Arkansas career had played out like a Greek tragedy. His signing in February 1992 had been hailed as a key to the program's future. When as a true freshman making his first start, Lunney helped lead Arkansas to the upset of Tennessee in 1992, some believed the savior had arrived.

Instead, Lunney presided over growing pains. Playing behind suspect offensive lines, he played inconsistently. And he was a target for fans' wrath. On talk shows and in coffee shops, the backup quarterback (any backup quarterback) was consistently more popular than Loon-y (correctly, it's "Luh-nee"), who suddenly could do no right.

Lunney's second career as a pitcher for the Arkansas baseball team, which precluded his participation in spring practice, had long irked Ford. In 1993 and 1994, Lunney had won quarterback competitions during August practices. But, in 1995, Reed got the nod in the season opener at SMU, ending Lunney's consecutive-start streak at twenty-eight.

SMU, which was still reeling from the NCAA-mandated death penalty, would lose ten games that season, but not the first one.

When Reed was ineffective in the first two series, as SMU bolted to a

10–0 lead, Lunney was inserted. Completing 14 of 22 passes for 168 yards and a touchdown, he was effective enough to move the Hogs into position for a win.

Trailing 17–14 in the fourth quarter, Arkansas drove 79 yards to the SMU 1 in 16 plays. With less than a minute remaining, Lunney took the snap and began his surge behind the line. Instead of a touchdown, one more chapter was added to his story.

The football slipped from his grasp and SMU recovered. And the Hogs had been beaten by a team that would lose its next ten games.

Lunney understood the immediate reaction. The inevitable question, he says, was, "If they can't beat SMU, how can they beat anybody else?"

The loss was a turning point. A day later, the quarterback quandary was answered when Reed quit the team.

A homegrown hero, Barry Lunney struggled along with the rest of the Razorbacks, until blossoming in 1995.

"In hindsight, it was a real crucial springboard for us," Lunney says. "There was a question within the team of who was supposed to be the quarterback. After [Reed left], everyone knew that it was me, that I was the quarterback. If that had not happened, I wouldn't have played with the confidence that I played with. I know that for sure.

"So when you look back, all those events—from Robert being named the starter, to me coming in, to me fumbling, to Robert quitting—all that stuff was a cornerstone in what the year became."

It became the Razorbacks' first taste of SEC success. They won eight of their next nine games to capture the SEC's Western Division crown.

The week after SMU, sophomore running back Madre Hill, who would go on to the best rushing season in Arkansas history (1,387 yards), scored 6 touchdowns in a 51–21 rout of South Carolina, but the bigger win came a week later in Tuscaloosa, Alabama.

The Crimson Tide led 19–13 in the final minutes, but Lunney led Arkansas on an improbable drive to win. His 3-yard pass to tiny J. J. Meadors tied it with six seconds left, and Todd Latourette's extra point gave Arkansas its most significant win to that point in SEC play.

"Throw it back to the Barry Lunney leadership," says Russell Brown,

who started that season as a freshman. "He was phenomenal."

Arkansas rolled on to an 8-2 record. Then, the Hogs lost their last three games.

"We just ran out of gas," Lunney says. "We overachieved, truthfully, for what the makeup of our team was. We played about as well as we could possibly play for about eight weeks in a row. We just played to our maximum abilities every time out. It just kind of went our way. And we just kind of ran out of juice.

"We didn't play at that level any longer."

Ford was unable to build on the success. That 1995 team was the only real bright spot in what grew into a decade of disappointment. Arkansas struggled to replace Lunney and other

With 1,387 yards in 1995, Madre Hill produced the best rushing season in school history, but suffered a serious knee injury in the SEC Championship game that year.

veteran leaders. It sure didn't help that Hill tore up a knee in the SEC championship game and missed the 1996 season.

Arkansas stumbled to 4-7, then did it again in 1997. After a 3-1 start that included another win at Alabama, the Razorbacks lost six of their final seven games. One day after a season-ending loss at LSU, Ford was fired.

"It was a long haul there," Ford says, "but give our kids credit. They hung in there. I was real pleased with their progress, even though we didn't win enough football games.

"At the end, we were able to compete."

Though it perhaps wasn't obvious, the Hogs were ready to do more than that.

Arkansas' candidates included Miami coach Butch Davis and Ole Miss coach Tommy Tuberville, both of whom had ties to Arkansas. Nutt, who had just completed his first year at Boise State, was an ex-Hog who would get a courtesy interview.

Except Nutt was *not* an ex-Hog. Not hardly. As the entire state would soon find out, he had never forgotten his Razorback roots.

Nutt had grown up nearly in the shadow of War Memorial Stadium. He had watched games from end-zone seats with his father, Houston Nutt, Sr., and three younger brothers: Dickey, Danny, and Dennis. He had served as ball boy

on the visitors' sidelines, until Broyles decided the state's premier high-school quarterback needed to be working the home sidelines.

After a heralded schoolboy career at Little Rock's Central High, Nutt chose Broyles and Arkansas over Bear Bryant and Alabama. He feared Bryant might soon retire (he lasted through 1982) and

ABOVE

Though Ford was unable to lead the program back to its former winning ways, he laid the foundation for later success with solid recruiting.

BELOW

A talented schoolboy star at Little Rock Central, Houston Nutt chose Arkansas over Alabama.

didn't believe Broyles would (he retired after Nutt's freshman season). More important, though, was the call of the Hogs.

Nutt started four games as a freshman after starter Ron Calcagni was injured, and also played basketball for Eddie Sutton. Lou Holtz's arrival brought the veer, an offense not suited to Nutt's drop-back passing skills. He lasted a year as a backup, and then transferred to Oklahoma State, where his father had played basketball for legendary coach Henry Iba.

"The bottom line was, a part of my heart was always in Arkansas," Nutt says.

Nutt played football and basketball at Oklahoma State, then moved into coaching. He coached two different stints at Oklahoma State and Arkansas before getting his first head-coaching job at Murray State in 1993. Except it wasn't that simple.

Nutt, then Arkansas' receivers coach, wasn't one of the five finalists for the Murray State job. Only after a candidate withdrew from consideration did he convince the athletic director he deserved an interview. Nutt blew away the search committee.

"He has an electric personality," Mike Strickland, Murray State's athletic director at the time, told the *Arkansas Democrat-Gazette*. "He crackles. . . . He completely mesmerized the committee."

From there, Nutt commenced rebuilding the Murray State program, on and off the field. Trying to combat student apathy, he climbed atop a fraternity house with a bullhorn. Stopping a party in its tracks, he challenged the kids to attend the next day's game. Murray State had been averaging less than two hundred students; the next day, more than three thousand showed up.

Nutt also taught his players to sing the school fight song. He'd had to dig up the words in a 1951 yearbook, since he couldn't find anyone who remembered them. After every win, Nutt and his Racers turned to the stands and sang, "Let's fight Murray, on to the goal . . ."

A few years later, the process was eerily similar. Arkansas' search committee of six former players started with about thirty names and conducted thirteen interviews. Several coaches declined to interview; others didn't seem all that interested in the task of rebuilding the long-faltering program. Among the coaches who turned away: Bob Stoops (a Florida assistant), Gary Crowton (Louisiana Tech's head coach), and Tommy Bowden (head coach at Tulane).

Nutt, forty, who had just finished his first (and last) season at Boise State, was interested. Very interested. Risking a backlash from Boise State fans, he came out and said so.

When Nutt arrived to interview, he changed the dynamics of the search. In an impromptu news conference held before the interview, he won a legion of grassroots supporters. Several times, the Boise State coach used the word *we* when referring to the Razorbacks.

"I've always had chills on my back every time I woke up since four or five years of age when I knew it was Saturday," Nutt told reporters. "I knew it was Saturday because on the screen of the TV was 'Go Hogs Go,' and I knew there was a football game in town, and there was only one game in town."

And there was one other thing: "I believe we can win a national championship," he said. "I believe we can win an SEC title."

All of it was music to fans' ears. Nutt supporters, most newly minted, began flooding radio airwaves and Internet message boards. Phone calls, faxes, and e-mails flooded the Arkansas athletic department (and newspapers and television stations, as well).

Arkansas fans wanted Nutt. So did the university.

In an interview that lasted more than four hours, Nutt showed game tapes and presented a written report, listing his goals and how he planned to achieve them. He told the search committee he would "work from sunrise to exhaustion" to bring Arkansas football back to prominence. He told them he was willing to work for free the first year.

He told them he wanted "to come back here so bad, and lead that team through that 'A.'"

"I think they felt that," Nutt says. "One of my strengths is getting in front of people."

"He brought back an Arkansas flavor," says Scott Bull, the former Arkansas quarterback who served on the committee. "I knew that was something we needed. . . . He also brought an enthusiasm that we just had to have. There had to be someone that could come in and be a spark plug to the program.

"And Houston Nutt was the most enthusiastic coach we had ever seen."

A week later, the committee voted to recommend Nutt be hired.

Before making the decision, Tuberville had been interviewed in New York. Later, Arkansas officials and Tuberville offered different versions of what occurred. Tuberville said he was offered the job, but turned it down. The Razorbacks insisted the job wasn't offered, that when it became apparent the committee was split over Nutt and Tuberville, the Ole Miss coach pulled out.

Back in Boise, Nutt's younger brother, Danny Nutt—like Houston, a former Central High and Arkansas quarterback, and then a Boise State assistant—saw a report on ESPN that Tuberville had accepted the job. A little later, in the wee hours of the morning, the phone rang.

It was Houston: "You ready to go home?"

"What? What are you talking about?" Danny asked.

"I got the job."

Danny began screaming. And the celebration continued the next day, when Houston was announced as the Razorbacks' twenty-ninth head football coach.

"Dreams do come true, and this has been my dream, to stand up here in front of you with a Razorback helmet," Nutt said.

Houston hopped onto a whirlwind. Besides recruiting and spring practice, his first offseason included more than eighty speaking engagements. Fish fries in the Delta. High-school athletic banquets in the Ozarks. He met with alumni at country clubs and farmers at coffee shops and kept going, and going, and going.

"I only have one speed," he told the *Sporting News.* "My parents taught me if I want something, I have to work for it. This job has been my dream since I was a ten-year-old ball boy at Razorback games."

Fans responded tangibly. By the time the season started, season-ticket sales were up by more than six thousand from the previous year.

"He has energized every possible football fan in this state with optimism about the Razorbacks," Broyles told the *Democrat-Gazette.* "That's the first thing a coach has to do. It's been twenty years since we've had that."

It was at about that point a light came on in Broyles' mind.

A few years earlier, Arkansas had actually *reduced* Razorback Stadium's size by almost twenty-seven hundred, removing bleacher seating in the south end zone and replacing it with a flower bed—smart-alecks suggested the area, which looked somewhat like a memorial, might have been where the football program was buried.

Now, though, Broyles could see the impetus to expand. Two months before Nutt coached his first game, Broyles went public with a proposal to add more than twenty thousand seats, and to renovate the aging steel structure.

One important thing remained, of course. Would Nutt's charisma translate

One of Houston Nutt's first acts as Arkansas' head coach was calling the Hogs. He made clear his love for the program and its traditions, and promised the Razorbacks would win.

into wins? By the time SEC media days had rolled around, senior wide receiver Anthony Lucas was convinced. He likened Nutt to the Energizer Bunny. Others still weren't sure. Not yet.

Brown remembers an August afternoon when he wondered—again—if Nutt and his staff had what it took to produce winners. Ford had been of the old school. Give him ninety-five-degree heat for two-a-days, and he'd wish for 105. Nutt was different.

On the only real hot afternoon of the Razorbacks' preseason camp, the players pulled on full pads, ready to get to work. "We think we're fixing to go to battle, you know?" Brown remembers.

Instead, Nutt whistled the team up, and sent the Hogs to the swimming pool at the nearby HPER (Health, Physical Education, and Recreation) building.

The move baffled the veteran Hogs. "You've got to realize the way we'd been brought up [under Ford]," Brown says. "We appreciated it. But when we got back to the locker room, I remember we were sitting around saying, 'We lost a day of work. This may come back to hurt us fast. This isn't good. This isn't being serious.'"

Looking back though, "it was a breath of fresh air," Brown says.

If the players were uncertain of Nutt, so were many of the fans. At least, they weren't confident in the program. Everywhere Nutt had gone during that offseason barnstorming tour, he had

been asked a variation of the same plea: "Can you please just beat SMU?"

As much as anything else, the questions illustrated how far into disrepair the program had tumbled, and how far into despair the fans had fallen. The Hogs had lost three straight years to the lowly Mustangs, who hadn't beaten anybody else very often.

Arkansas could definitely beat SMU. After opening the Nutt era with an easy win over Louisiana-Lafayette, the Hogs whipped SMU 44–17. Even though Arkansas didn't put away the pesky Mustangs until the third quarter, it was apparent something was different from the game's very first play, when Lucas took a short pass and raced 87 yards for a touchdown.

"Next, they wondered if we could beat Alabama," Nutt recalls.

And they did—42–6, in fact.

"That's when we believed," Nutt says. "That's when I felt like it was fi-

Wide receiver Anthony Lucas' catches helped the Hogs get off to an 8-0 start in 1998. Lucas bought into Nutt's vision early.

nally my team, after that Alabama game. I really felt like the players had bought in, we had chemistry, there's an attitude here."

Suddenly, anyone who hadn't been on the bandwagon was grabbing ahold, scrambling for a seat. These Hogs just might be pretty good, after all.

Ford might not have won consistently, but he had laid a considerable foundation. The nucleus of Nutt's first squad was a talented, mature group of juniors and seniors. Nineteen returning starters had been through tough times. They were hungry and self-motivated.

"You had a group that was the closest thing to a fraternity or a brotherhood there was," says Brown, who's now an investment banker in Tulsa, Oklahoma. "It was really a close group of guys. We believed in ourselves."

"I thought it was gonna be the first time we might be on an even plane with everybody, and not be trying to catch up," Ford remembers. "It was finally the time we were gonna get some dividends."

Nutt understood what he had inherited, as well.

"I knew we had something special. But we just needed to realize that," Nutt says. "And then we got on this roll and just started believing. It just became contagious. It was just a perfect fit, because they were just so beat up mentally and emotionally.

"Things hadn't gone right for 'em.

The ball would bounce the wrong way, a tipped ball would go into the opponent's hands, things like that. But our attitude just changed overnight."

The wins kept coming. And after each one, Nutt and his Hogs gathered, turned toward the stands, and sang the fight song:

Hit that line! Hit that line! Keep on
  going.
Move that ball right down the field!
Give a cheer. Rah! Rah!
Never fear. Rah! Rah!
Arkansas will never yield!
On your toes, Razorbacks, to the finish,
Carry on with all your might
For it's A-A-A, R-K-A-N, S-A-S for
  Arkansas,
Fight! Fight! Fi-i-i-ght!

Finally, the Razorbacks arrived in Knoxville, Tennessee, for a showdown that no one would have predicted before the season.

Tenth-ranked Arkansas might have been the most surprising 8-0 team in recent memory. Despite their newly earned ranking, not many gave the Razorbacks much of a chance against top-ranked Tennessee. The conventional wisdom was: It's been a nice ride, but it's about to end. And the perfect season did indeed end, but not in the fashion anyone expected. The Hogs jumped to a 21–3 first-half lead over Tennessee, and appeared poised to spring a gigantic upset.

The Southeastern Conference championship? A Bowl Championship Series berth? A- hold your collective breath, Hog Nation—national championship? All appeared attainable for the first fifty-eight minutes that night in Neyland Stadium.

And then, trying to run out the clock, quarterback Clint Stoerner got tangled with senior guard Brandon Burlsworth. Stoerner stumbled. Fumbled. And the rest was unhappy history.

Tennessee recovered the football. And, given new life with the kind of charmed break that defines championship seasons, the Volunteers cashed in the winning touchdown. And went on to win the national title.

Nutt wasn't sure where the Hogs might be headed. As he walked slowly toward the locker room, it was his turn to wonder about his team. Were the Razorbacks really the gritty, hungry, selfless bunch they had appeared to be? Or would a loss like this reveal a flawed foundation, cracked character? He knew he was about to find out.

Inside, it was like a morgue. After telling the Hogs he was proud of them, Nutt opened the doors to the media, and reporters swarmed into the room, surrounding the players.

"There was Clint Stoerner, he was taking the full blame," Nutt remembers. "Then Brandon Burlsworth steps over in front of a camera and says, 'No, it wasn't his fault. I stepped on his foot.'

And then Benji Mahan, the deep snapper who hasn't had a bad snap in his career, had snapped one over a guy's head. And he says, 'No, it was my fault.'

"No one was gonna blame anyone else. It was just total team.

"It was really good."

Still, a hangover lingered into the next week, although hangover might not be the best term. Arkansas, which had moved up to number nine in the rankings despite the Tennessee loss, should have won at Mississippi State despite a lackluster performance, except that placekicker Todd Latourette had been left at home by Nutt after he was arrested on suspicion of driving while intoxicated two days earlier. The case was later dismissed.

Though the Hogs didn't play well, falling behind 16–0, they were ahead 21–19 late. But Mississippi State's Brian Hazelwood kicked five field goals, including the game winner with seven seconds left.

Twice in the second half, Arkansas' offense reached field-goal range. Both times, Nutt chose not to attempt a field goal with a freshman walk-on. Once, the Hogs turned the ball over on downs. The other time, they punted.

The loss knocked Arkansas out of the SEC championship game (though they shared the SEC West title), but the Hogs got well with a 41–14 win over LSU. And Broyles' intense lobbying of SEC commissioner Roy Kramer re-

sulted in a trip to the Citrus Bowl, which gets first choice after the SEC's BCS teams have been selected.

There, defending national champion Michigan pulled away late to win 45–31. Still, looking back, the Razorbacks realized how close they were to playing for a national title. Ford, who watched much of the season from his ranch, whittled it down to the fumble.

"If it hadn't been that one play, they probably could have gone undefeated," he says. "They sure did an excellent job of coaching."

"Coach Nutt sold us on the fact that we could do it, and we did," Stoerner said.

Arkansas football was back. And the state was alive with passion.

"Morale in the state of Arkansas leaped," Broyles told reporters before the Citrus Bowl. "People are happier in their jobs, in the grocery stores, even at church on Sunday. It's remarkable the turnaround Houston has engineered in such a short time."

The revival continued. In 1999, the Hogs were meteoric. They avenged the loss to Tennessee, this time winning when the Vols were ranked number three (Stoerner got sweet redemption, throwing the winning touchdown pass to Lucas with less than four minutes left, then kneeling to run out the clock). They also lost three straight in a forgettable October stretch.

Still, 7-4 was good enough to earn a Cotton Bowl berth opposite old rival Texas. A 27–6 victory sent fans into Hog Heaven, and sent Stoerner and Lucas, among others, out with cemented status as heroes who helped lead the program back to winning.

From there, a new generation of Razorback heroes emerged, including the lanky Matt Jones, who came in as a quarterback but defied description en route to becoming a Razorback legend. And the Hogs produced plenty of highlights, if not that elusive SEC championship.

In 2002, Jones' last-second heroics gave Arkansas a 21–20 win over LSU in Little Rock. Jones threw passes of 50 and 31 yards to achieve the Miracle on Markham, as it quickly became known, and send Arkansas to Atlanta as the SEC West champion. A year later, Jones and

◄ FACING PAGE
Clint Stoerner tripped over offensive lineman Brandon Burlsworth's feet and lost the football. Moments later, the Hogs lost their perfect season.

Justin Scott's jubilation was matched by more than fifty-five thousand fans after a dramatic touchdown pass beat LSU in the Miracle on Markham in 2002.

the Hogs upset Texas in Austin, winning 38–28 in a game that wasn't that close. Jones scored touchdowns running (102 yards) and passing (139 yards).

Jones wasn't the only celebrated Hog. Cedric Cobbs, a running back from Little Rock's J. A. Fair High School, finished his career as Arkansas' third-leading rusher, with 3,018 yards. His 1,320-yard 2003 campaign ranks second all-time, to Hill's 1,387 in 1995. Shawn Andrews was a two-time All-American at offensive tackle; Kenoy Kennedy and Ken Hamlin were dominating from the safety position.

Arkansas also gained recognition for an uncanny tendency to play more than sixty minutes. A lot more. The Hogs have played in the three longest games in NCAA history.

Twice, they've gone to seven overtimes. In 2001, Arkansas beat Ole Miss 58–56. In 2003, the Hogs outlasted Kentucky 71–63, a score more befitting the schools' basketball rivalry. Tennessee outlasted Arkansas 41–38 in six overtimes in 2002.

In comparison to those epics, a double-overtime win at Alabama (2003) and a single-overtime win at Mississippi State (2000) were routine walks in the park.

"If you want to win, sometimes you're going to be tested to see how much you want to win and that's what the seven-overtime game does," Arkansas receiver George Wilson told the *Arkansas Democrat-Gazette* after the 2003 win over Kentucky. "At least that's what it has done to us, a battle of the will, survival of the fittest, see who's in the best physical shape, see who's in the best mental shape."

There have been disappointments, of course.

Arkansas has been back to the Cotton Bowl (a 10–3 loss to Oklahoma to end the 2001 season). However, the Hogs have also traveled to the Las Vegas and Music City Bowls, losing both, and the Independence Bowl (a win over Missouri).

The next step, moving to the elite Bowl Championship Series level, has been a difficult one to make.

Although the Miracle on Markham over LSU propelled Arkansas to the SEC West title in 2002, Georgia demolished the Hogs 30–3 in the SEC championship game.

Then there was 2004. Jones, a senior, was the only returning offensive starter; Arkansas suffered its first losing season under Nutt. One play, as it turned out, was the difference in keeping the Hogs home for the holidays, snapping a six-season bowl streak that had matched the longest in school history.

In September, the Hogs trailed Texas 22–20 in the closing minutes, but had possession deep in Longhorns' territory. They were well within field-goal range of their second straight upset of the hated rivals (and fourth straight win in the series). But as Jones scrambled for more yardage, a Longhorn poked the football loose.

Texas pounced on it, and escaped with victory.

Just suppose Jones doesn't fumble. Even if no intangible results (increased confidence, for instance) are considered, Arkansas goes 6-5, heads to a lower-tier bowl, and everyone is mollified—look what Arkansas did with one returning offensive starter!

Such is football, of course.

The 5-6 finish led inevitably to grumbling about whether the program's progress had stalled. Such talk comes with the territory when expectations have been raised.

Nutt's tenure, which is now longer than any other Arkansas coach since Broyles, has done at least one thing. In the 1990s, getting to a bowl game became rare. In the new era, it has become a given. And other programs have noticed: After the 2003 and 2004 seasons, Nebraska and LSU, respectively, inquired into Nutt's availability.

After tasting success again, Arkansas' fans want more.

"We have an expectation now," says David Bazzel, the former Hogs linebacker who's now a Little Rock radio personality. "The fans believe we should be winning championships."

Nutt and others believe the Hogs will soon deliver. It has become apparent Arkansas has recruited the speedy players necessary to compete in the SEC, but depth has been an issue. Recruiting was also hindered for several years by the effects of an NCAA investigation that began just before the 2000 Cotton Bowl.

A booster was found to have overpaid several athletes by an average of

Like linebacker Caleb Miller reaching for a loose football, the Razorbacks continue to fight and claw toward elite status.

$215 during the mid-1990s for work at his Dallas trucking firm. The investigation, which stretched for thirty-nine months, resulted in the reduction of ten scholarships over a five-year period, and an intangible might have been more damaging.

As the investigation dragged on, Nutt and his staff found themselves fighting negative recruiting by other schools, who whispered phrases such as, "Arkansas is going on probation, you won't play on television, no bowl game."

"It was always out there, the NCAA hadn't decided yet," Nutt says. "You'd go into a [recruit's] living room and you're fighting bullets. It was all those negatives. But that's behind us."

Nutt believes Arkansas has a solid foundation on which to build an elite program. The Hogs' facilities (finally) rival any program, anywhere. With the specter of the NCAA no longer an issue, recruiting has picked back up. Nutt says the Hogs are ready to take the next step. Others agree.

"I think our football program will improve significantly in the next five years," Broyles says. "I think Houston would be the first to say that with the new facilities, the new weight room, the things that are going for him, he's an optimist just like I am—we think we'll be more competitive in football than we've been since nineteen-eighty-nine."

Nutt agrees. But he'd like to go even further. He remains true to his goal of bringing another national championship to the Ozarks. And many believe Nutt is the man to do it.

"I have no doubt they're going to get the ring someday," says Marcus Elliott, the former offensive lineman. "The big ring, I mean. I think they can win the national championship. I really do."

Nutt does nothing to discourage such talk. He remains as optimistic and energetic as the day he was hired. He continues to call the Hogs upward.

"We're in the toughest league in America, but I just think we can do it," Nutt says. "You've got a chance to really get a top-twenty program and compete for BCS bowls.

"And then every so often, the ball bounces your way—and here we go!"

HOGS!

Nutt believes Arkansas is on track for greatness, and he wants to lead the Hogs there.

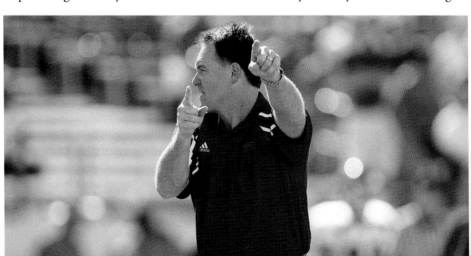